1 August 1994

Mr. Silas,

Management is never more put to the test than in a crisis. The decisions are immediate and so are the results.

Gary W. Sitrick

IT CAN'T HAPPEN HERE:
All Hazards Crisis Management Planning

IT CAN'T HAPPEN HERE:

All Hazards Crisis Management Planning

by GEARY W. SIKICH

PennWell Books
PennWell Publishing Company
Tulsa, Oklahoma

DISCLAIMER

The information contained in this book will be used to establish a baseline, and provide a guideline for the development of emergency management/preparedness plans, appendices, and implementing procedures. The user should determine to what extent it is practicable and advisable to follow them. This decision will often involve considerations not discussed in these documents.

The author assumes no liability for injury, loss, or damage of any kind resulting directly or indirectly from the use of the information contained in this book and other related materials.

Copyright© 1993 by
PennWell Publishing Company
1421 South Sheridan/P.O. Box 2160
Tulsa, Oklahoma 74101

Sikich, Geary W.
    It can't happen here: all hazards crisis management planning/by Geary W. Sikich.
      p.   cm.
    Includes bibliographical references and index.
    ISBN 0-87814-402-1
    1. Crisis management. I. Title.
HD49.S56 1993
658.4—dc20   93–30866
                                                CIP

Printed in the United States of America

1 2 3 4 5 97 96 95 94 93

DEDICATION

This book is dedicated to those who are helping steer their companies on a path of continuous improvement, risk/vulnerability reductions, and effective resource management. It is also dedicated to those who follow in their footsteps. Hopefully the path will be less bumpy, but no less fulfilling.

ACKNOWLEDGMENTS

Books such as this are inevitably the result of research, analysis, frustration, and trial and error. Countless inputs during many engagements represent a wide spectrum of public and private sector entities, each with its own peculiar needs and requirements. There are many people whose effort, both direct and indirect, have gone into this book and many will unfortunately remain nameless. Those who can, and should be, acknowledged include H.C. Clayton, D.L. Doyle, C.R. Plug, E.N. Saccoccia, J.A. Unnerstall, G.G. Vassallo, and R.S. Wilkerson. Each has contributed research, concepts, ideas, thoughts, evaluations, and refinements, although the responsibility for the use and applications of those remains solely with the author.

Special thanks to my associate, Stacey L. Simmons, without whose efforts this manuscript would not exist.

Last, thanks to my family, Karen, Aaron, and Drake, who have provided continuous support for my efforts in good times and bad.

Contents

Chapter 5 Demonstrating Proficiency: Establishing and Maintaining Performance Standards 191

Chapter 6 Communicating in a Crisis: The Management of Public Information 232

List of Acronyms and Recognized Abbreviations

AIChE . . . . . American Institute of Chemical Engineers

ASSE . . . . . . American Society of Safety Engineers

ATSDR . . . . . Agency for Toxic Substances and Disease Registry

CAER . . . . . . Community Awareness and Emergency Response

CERCLA . . . . Comprehensive Environmental Response Compensation and Liability Act of 1981 (PL 96-510)

CFR . . . . Code of Federal Regulations

CMT . . . . . . Crisis Management Team

CWA . . . . . . Clean Water Act

DOT . . . . . . Department of Transportation

EBS . . . . Emergency Broadcast System

EDC . . . . Emergency Damage Control

EM . . . . Emergency Manager

EMS . . . . Emergency Medical Service

EMO . . . . . . Emergency Management Organization

EMP . . . . Emergency Management Plan

EMRO . . . . . Emergency Management/ Response Organization

ERO . . . . Emergency Response Organization

EOC . . . . Emergency Operations Center

EPA . . . . Environmental Protection Agency

EPIP . . . . Emergency Plan Implementing Procedure

EPZ . . . . Emergency Planning Zone

FIC . . . . Field Incident Commander

HAZMAT . . . Hazardous Materials

HAZOP . . . . Hazard and Operability Study

ICS . . . . Incident Command System

ISD . . . . Incident Support Director

LEPC . . . . . . Local Emergency Planning Committee

NCP . . . . National Contingency Plan

NRC . . . . National Response Center

OCC . . . . On Scene Command Center

OEM . . . . . . Onshift Emergency Manager

OSC . . . . On Scene Incident Commander (Federal designation)

OSHA . . . . . . Occupational Safety and Health Administration

RCRA . . . . . Resource Conservation and Recovery Act

RQs . . . . Reportable Qunatities

SARA . . . . . . Superfund Amendments and Reauthorization Act of 1986 (PL 99-499)

SERC . . . . . . State Emergency Response Commission

SPCC . . . . . . Spill Prevention Control and Countermeasures

Preface

This book describes an approach to emergency management planning. The techniques and methodology described herein have been applied to a variety of industrial and commercial settings. This material is designed to serve as a planning guide which will help management and response personnel identify the steps and establish priorities for responding to an incident regardless of the triggering event. While the emphasis has been placed on the industrial setting, the material contains considerable information that would be applicable to other settings any place in the world.

Along with providing critical insight for developing an emergency management strategy, this book discusses factors which can contribute to the success or failure of the operation. By reading the book, you should be able to establish planning priorities and identify limitations that can be categorized and addressed in the Emergency Management Plan.

This book is not intended to be a step-by-step guide for every conceivable emergency situation. Rather, the intent is to provide information which will enable you to evaluate hazards, identify alternatives, and prepare plans reflecting your organization's capabilities to respond.

Experience gained over a number of years in a variety of business, government, industry, and military settings provided the basis for developing an *all hazards* approach to emergency management planning. Additionally, the growing number and complexity of government (all levels) regulations addressing emergency planning requirements provided an impetus for developing an approach to planning that can be easily adopted to regulatory requirements, while providing consistency in terms of implementation during an incident.

The approach to emergency management planning described herein applies to all levels of management. It has been successfully implemented in the petroleum, chemical, industrial, gas, agrichemical, health care, domestic and foreign military services, and within various elements of government.

The table of contents is organized in such a way as to serve as a subject index and provides easy access to the information contained in the book.

1

It's Not "What If," It's "When": Overview of Emergency Management Planning

CHAPTER HIGHLIGHTS

In this introductory chapter we will begin our investigation into the development and ongoing maintenance of an emergency management program. I have prepared a discussion of key issues designed to assist you through the development process.

This chapter focuses on an overview of the core concepts presented in the remaining chapters. It includes a discussion of:

- Basic program elements

- Evaluation (Pre- and Post-) processes

- Establishment of objectives

The chapter concludes with a brief discussion on establishing the planning team.

INTRODUCTION

Your phone rings on 4:00 AM Friday.

A simple phone call and all your weekend plans are canceled.

5:15 AM—Another phone call.

Your weekend has just been redefined by an event that occurred somewhere in your plant.

The phone rings again. You now have a full scale crisis on your hands.

An incident you knew nothing about an hour before will become a quick study for you and your staff.

Another phone call; you can't believe the amount of emotion, confusion, and misinformation generated by one incident.

Our focus is on crises. Three Mile Island, Pennsylvania; Bhopal, India; Chernobyl, Soviet Union; Phillips Petroleum, Texas; Exxon Valdez, Prince William Sound, Alaska; and a growing number of other incidents and locations. Suddenly, they became a crisis.

Accidents don't make appointments. They can occur anytime and under the most unfavorable circumstances.

You might ask yourself, "What is an accident?" For our purposes, the following definition will be used: an accident can be defined as any unplanned event or the occurrence of a sequence of events that has a specific undesirable consequence.

Today, individuals responsible for the management of businesses and public agencies must deal effectively with increasingly complex laws and issues or face the consequences. Hazardous waste, occupational safety, and air and water pollution are but a few examples. The reasons for focusing on such problems may result from a firm's commitment to protect its workers and the general public; compliance with federal, state and local regulations; or to protect the firm from possible liabilities and litigation. The consequences for not focusing on these issues can be disastrous.

Potentially hazardous material spills, transportation accidents, accidental releases from a manufacturing facility, spills into waterways, evacuations of homeowners due to an air release, and other events are crises that can alter one's otherwise peaceful life.

The above sampling indicates the need for a viable emergency management program—an *all hazards* program. Failure to have a workable emergency management program is akin to playing Russian roulette with an automatic pistol: you don't have the luxury of pulling the trigger on an empty chamber.

You may think that it's too difficult and time-consuming to develop a cohesive emergency management program. However, when broken down into its basic elements, a program consists of only four parts. These are:

- Compliance

- Preparedness

- Training and retraining

- Information management

Although no two programs will be exactly alike, these are the critical aspects of any program. We will discuss each of these aspects briefly. However, before we delve into the four aspects, let's look at some basic objectives. Ask yourself, "Why do we need a program with an all hazards approach?"

Simply, the purpose in establishing a standard format for emergency management plans allows you to provide for:

- Effective coordination of activities among the organizations having a response role

- Early warning and clear instructions to the general public in the affected area if an incident occurs

- Continued assessment of actual or potential consequences both on-site and off-site

The structure of the all hazards Emergency Management Plan and supporting materials should be flexible enough to serve in any facility, yet provide consistency from location to location. The framework should, of necessity, be the same throughout your company, with site-specific details varying from location to location. Regulations aside, this planning approach makes it possible to fit a generic plan to a wide variety of operations.

Before we begin our discussion on the four basic elements, a brief discussion of the common weaknesses in emergency management planning may prove helpful. As you read the discussion on the four basic elements, keep these weaknesses in mind. You may also want to assess your current plans as to their relationship to these weaknesses.

Briefly, the most common weaknesses in emergency management planning are:

No systematic collection of planning information. This includes such aspects as hazard analysis, organizational information, regulatory guidance, company policy and procedures, and location specific data.

No systematic dissemination of planning information. You've assembled a wealth of information (or lack of) and have not shared it with the affected population—those whose responsibility it is to implement the plan!

Failure to identify and establish an incident command structure. This is a common pitfall, as many planners try to fit their organization into a standard incident command system not designed around their particular needs.

No or minimal coordination with affected entities. Poor communications with the community, neighboring industries, and identified support entities (fire, police, hospitals, and so forth) can lead to confusion and chaos during an emergency. A simple issue such as who is the primary contact for off-site agencies during an emergency can cause major disruption.

Lack of or poorly defined organizational responsibilities. And there is a failure to provide clear, concise procedures defining people's functions, duties, and tasks upon assuming their emergency organization position. This weakness can lead to finger pointing—"It's not my responsibility!"—"I thought it was yours!"

Once developed, the program is not maintained or is poorly maintained at best. Your program was developed to meet a regulatory requirement. Heck, you never intended to test it. Why should you? You're not planning on having any accidents! There is no provision for continued evaluation and periodic update of the material. Frequently, changed material, such as telephone numbers, are buried in various paragraphs throughout the plan.

The material you developed is not user-friendly. Your plan contains information—lots of it. Unfortunately, the user has to be a brain surgeon to figure out his/her role in its implementation. You did not provide simple, easy-to-use supplemental materials that can be used as a quick reference guide during an emergency. Worse yet, you didn't train anyone on the plan and his/her role in its implementation.

You didn't disseminate the plan to the proper authorities. Failure to include appropriate parties on the distribution list most often leads to their failure to respond in the manner you had hoped for.

COMPLIANCE

How do you reduce the vulnerability posed by potential emergencies? You need a system that will advise you of the initiatives to be addressed. This will allow you to act responsibly to fulfill the purpose and intent of existing legislation. It can also provide a framework for anticipating future legislation.

There are three major initial steps a company must take even before it develops an effective compliance program. They are:

1. Conduct a hazard analysis of all operations

2. Organize operations in order to involve all levels of management

3. Assign ownership of the program and grant the responsible party the authority to effectively implement the program.

Before an effective system for compliance can be developed, you must know what laws and regulations pertain to your operation. It is essential to have accurate and detailed knowledge of the applicable laws and regulations. A comprehensive hazards analysis can help accomplish this task.

The hazard analysis survey should include:

- General administrative information

- Management awareness and control programs

- Identification of high hazard areas

- Hazardous materials handling practices

- Recordkeeping/regulatory compliance

- Site characterization

The hazard analysis should include the following information:

1. ***Personnel Interviews*** will consist of a questionnaire regarding the knowledge of the extent of site hazards, general information on-site emergency preparedness, identification of hazardous materials, hazardous materials handling, collection and storage, recordkeeping, and training.

2. **Overview of Written Plans and Procedures** would consist of a comparison of any written plans and procedures for hazard determination in accordance with applicable federal, state and local laws, ordinances, and mandates.

3. **Site Familiarization** would consist of a tour of the facility to accomplish the following:

- Identify major material storage locations at the site

- Identify potential areas of vulnerability

- Become familiar with the general layout and neighboring facilities/ entities.

After the hazard analysis is conducted, you will be able to identify areas in need of attention, establish a list of compliance commitments, and document current efforts.

Once the survey program has been developed and implemented, it must be evaluated and kept up-to-date. This can be accomplished by reviewing actual responses and by conducting a detailed audit of each department.

The survey program is the initial step toward reducing vulnerability. Next, you must organize the operation. The management chain is critical to this process. You must ensure that all levels of management become part of the program.

This can be achieved in several ways:

- Make a manager directly responsible to top management. The formal assignment of a senior manager to the position of crisis management programs director, or some other appropriate title, can accomplish this. Additionally, you will want to establish within the individual's job description some measurement standard to evaluate performance. This goes both ways. Upper management has to take responsibility for developing measurable and attainable goals for the program director to achieve.

- Set aside specific time for reports on emergency preparedness issues. This can be accomplished by preparing an agenda for staff meetings that includes a discussion of emergency preparedness and safety as a mandatory item. You have to give it more than lip service, though. Also, you must make the discussion substantive. You should provide more than the dull and tiring statistics on OSHA reportable accidents. For example, include all levels of personnel in the presentation process. This can be very effective and it gets the message out to all personnel that your company is serious about emergency preparedness.

- Make emergency planning issues part of the strategic planning process. In one aspect, the regulations such as the Oil Pollution Act, OSHA 1910.120, and others are defining strategic implications for companies. Additionally, for publicly held companies, the Securities and Exchange Commission (SEC) requires a discussion of potential liabilities in the management analysis and discussion section of annual reports. Another perspective on this issue really begets changing the "corporate culture" by making emergency preparedness a part of the way you do business.

- Communicate compliance through all levels of the organization through company policy and procedures. This can be accomplished through formal adoption of policy at the highest levels of the company. Generally, this will require the approval of the board of directors. It is essential, however, that companies become more aware of their responsibilities in these areas—and this is one way to build the awareness.

This discussion is limited by the space available to a brief highlight of some approaches that can be undertaken. Each company will find its situation and circumstances to be unique to its corporate culture. Therefore, an in-depth analysis of your company's operating environment should be undertaken before developing a program or attempting to address the above items.

After organizing the operation, the next step is to develop and implement an emergency preparedness evaluation program. The purpose of developing the evaluation program is to institute a standard means for performing a comprehensive assessment of the overall adequacy and effectiveness of the emergency preparedness program.

A primary goal of this program is to determine whether the organization is complying with applicable laws and regulations. Secondary goals may be to determine if the organization's own policies and procedures are being followed. The assessment should find whether or not there is reasonable assurance that appropriate measures are being taken to comply with the laws and regulations. Any deficiencies preventing a positive finding must be reported.

The assessment program should be designed to facilitate an integrated look at emergency preparedness. By the very nature of this primary goal—to evaluate the overall effectiveness and adequacy of the emergency management program—the assessment should be directed into areas for which explicit regulatory requirements may not currently exist. The assessment should, however, be directed toward evaluating the total emergency management program in terms of capabilities, performance, and identification of major inadequacies, not toward the identification of noncompliance.

The assessment must be designed to assess the ability of the organization to mitigate an emergency and to comply with applicable laws and regulations. The findings, in relation to the organization's ability to meet the criteria for compliance, should be based upon the audit of nine Essential Elements of Analysis (EEA). The nine Essential Elements of Analysis were developed by Logical Management Systems, Corp. and have been applied as a basis for assessing emergency preparedness.

The following definitions and examples illustrate the structure of a typical audit data base. The terms were developed by Logical Management Systems, Corp. over the course of conducting assessments and audits of emergency preparedness for a variety of clients representing a cross section of industry.

The table of contents for a limited operational review of emergency preparedness is shown in Table 1–1. Any detailed review would include an in-depth investigation of these areas. See Chapter 3 for in-depth information on the contents of the emergency management plan.

ESSENTIAL ELEMENT OF ANALYSIS (EEA)

An Essential Element of Analysis (EEA) is a structure that encompasses a major aspect of the emergency planning and preparedness process. For example, "Administration" is a major area of analysis; that is, it is not dependent on another structure to define its own structure. Definitions of the nine EEA follow in the next section.

MEASURES OF EFFECTIVENESS (MOE)

A Measure of Effectiveness (MOE) depends on the Essential Element of Analysis for structure. Measures of Effectiveness form subgroups of information relating to specific areas encompassed by the Essential Element of Analysis.

For example, within the Administration EEA, a Measure of Effectiveness might be the "Assignment of Responsibility." Measures of Effectiveness are not stand-alone structures; however, when grouped they form an Essential Element of Analysis.

MEASURES OF PERFORMANCE (MOP)

A Measure of Performance (MOP) is a data structure. Measures of Performance answer a specific question and are grouped to form Measures of Effectiveness.

Measures of Performance are measurable and observable; that is, they provide a quantitative basis for evaluation of a specific area. For example, a Measure of Performance might be, "Is there an individual at the site formally assigned/appointed as the emergency planning coordinator (by job description, job title or memorandum)?"

THE NINE ESSENTIAL ELEMENTS OF ANALYSIS

ADMINISTRATION

Administration deals with the administrative aspects of the emergency response program. Program structure, assignment of responsibilities, authority, and documentation are analyzed.

EMERGENCY MANAGEMENT/RESPONSE ORGANIZATION

The Emergency Management/Response Organization (EEA) deals with the composition of the Emergency Management/Response Organization. Plant systems operations, augmentation of the Emergency Management/Response Organization, and organizational structure are analyzed. The Emergency Management/Response Organization (EMRO) is composed of two elements. These are the Emergency Management Organization and the Emergency Response Organization.

Each element provides specific benefits. Each is composed of a cross section of personnel representing expertise in a variety of fields. The Emergency Management Organization is focused on support for response and mitigation activities, management of nonaffected operations, interface with external organizations (regulators, upper management, neighboring facilities, etc.) general continuity, and resumption of normal business operations. The Emergency Response Organization's primary focus is on response and mitigation of the incident. Each element provides support for the other. When combined, they form a flexible team that can focus on the expanded purview of emergency management and response activities.

EMERGENCY RESPONSE TRAINING AND RETRAINING

Emergency Training and Retraining deals with the training and retraining of the Emergency Management/Response Organization. Formally developed lesson plans, program implementation, and evaluation of the training are analyzed.

EMERGENCY RESPONSE FACILITIES AND EQUIPMENT

Emergency Response Facilities and Equipment deals with the facilities and equipment that the Emergency Management/Response Organization uses during emergency operations. Facility plans, layout and equipment type, availability, and operability are analyzed.

EMERGENCY PLAN IMPLEMENTING PROCEDURES

Emergency Plan Implementing Procedures (EPIPs) deal with the procedures for defining the functions, duties, and tasks of personnel assigned to the Emergency Management/Response Organization. The EPIPs can be categorized using the standard industry breakdown described earlier: administrative, emergency classification, emergency management/response organization, emergency operations, and reentry and recovery.

COORDINATION WITH OFF-SITE AGENCIES

Coordination with Off-site Agencies deals with the procedures for defining the functions, authorities, and relationships with off-site Emergency Response Organizations.

DRILLS AND EXERCISES

Drills and Exercises deal with the procedures for operating the drill and exercise program. Two of the Measures of Effectiveness under this element might be, "Establishment of a drills and exercise program" and "Observation of walk-through, drills and exercises."

COMMUNICATIONS AND PUBLIC INFORMATION

Communications deals with the setup, operation, information exchange, and coordination of the communications systems used during emergency operations.

HAZARD EVALUATION

Hazards Evaluation deals with the analysis of procedures for determining the susceptibility or vulnerability of a geographical area to hazardous materials release. Areas of analysis include, hazardous materials, chemical process, physical operations, equipment design and plant location, and layout evaluations.

Table 1-1
Limited Operational Review of Emergency Preparedness

EEA: 1.0 ADMINISTRATION OF THE EMERGENCY MANAGEMENT PLAN
  MOE: 1.1 Assignment of Responsibility
  MOE: 1.2 Authority
  MOE: 1.3 Selection and Qualification
  MOE: 1.4 Coordination
  MOE: 1.5 Emergency Management Plan

EEA: 2.0 EMERGENCY MANAGEMENT/RESPONSE ORGANIZATION
  MOE: 2.1 On-site Organization
  MOE: 2.2 Augmentation of the Emergency Management/Response Organization
  MOE: 2.3 Organizational Structure
  MOE: 2.4 Resources

EEA: 3.0 EMERGENCY PREPAREDNESS TRAINING AND RETRAINING PROGRAMS
  MOE: 3.1 Administration of the Emergency Preparedness Training and Retraining Program
  MOE: 3.2 Program Implementation

EEA: 4.0 EMERGENCY RESPONSE FACILITIES AND EQUIPMENT
  MOE: 4.1 Emergency Response Facilities and Staging Areas
  MOE: 4.2 Assessment Facilities
  MOE: 4.3 Protective Facilities
  MOE: 4.4 Emergency Equipment

EEA: 5.0 EMERGENCY PLAN IMPLEMENTING PROCEDURES
  MOE: 5.1 General Content and Format
  MOE: 5.2 Emergency Alarm and Abnormal Operating Procedures
  MOE: 5.3 Implementing Instructions
  MOE: 5.4 Implementing Procedures
  MOE: 5.5 Supplementary Procedures

EEA: 6.0 COORDINATION WITH OFF-SITE AGENCIES AND MUTUAL AID
  MOE: 6.1 Off-site Agencies
  MOE: 6.2 General Public
  MOE: 6.3 News Media
  MOE: 6.4 Mutual Aid Organizations

EEA: 7.0 DRILLS AND EXERCISES
  MOE: 7.1 Program Established
  MOE: 7.2 Program Implementation
  MOE: 7.3 Observation of Walk-throughs, Drills and Exercises

EEA: 8.0 COMMUNICATIONS AND PUBLIC INFORMATION
  MOE: 8.1 Coordination
  MOE: 8.2 Information Exchange
  MOE: 8.3 Information Dissemination
  MOE: 8.4 Information Sources and Data Base Sharing
  MOE: 8.5 Notification Procedures
  MOE: 8.6 Clearinghouse Functions

EEA: 9.0 HAZARD EVALUATION ANALYSIS
    MOE: 9.1 Hazards Identification
    MOE: 9.2 Hazards Analysis
    MOE: 9.3 Vulnerability Analysis
    MOE: 9.4 Probabilistic Risk Analysis

EEA: 10.0 PREPARATION FOR EVALUATION/AUDIT
    MOE: 10.1 Personnel
    MOE: 10.2 Equipment
    MOE: 10.3 Inventory
    MOE: 10.4 Operations

EVALUATION PLANNING GUIDELINES

Evaluation planning/guidelines can help set goals for the emergency management program. These goals should provide benchmarks that will reflect the progress being made and ensure that the program is headed in the right direction.

In planning the pre- and postevaluation of the emergency management program, three things need to be identified. These are:

1. What goals did the emergency management program set?

2. What goals does the evaluation have?

3. What actions will be taken to resolve identified deficiencies?

In planning for each of these issues, you should include a review of the nine Essential Elements of Analysis (EEA) cited earlier. By looking at the answers to the evaluation questions for each EEA, one would end up with an overall view of the emergency management program. The results will help to consistently improve the emergency management program.

An evaluation guide will provide a useful reference on how to assess each EEA. By means of questions, appraisal criteria, follow-up actions and specific steps to perform, the evaluation process can be accomplished with minimum disruption to the daily activities of the staff and plant.

Evaluation guides provide the following specific advantages:

1. Extensive complete checklists based on regulatory guidance, state and local guidance, and company policies

2. Reduced preparation time

3. Availability of key personnel at predetermined times

4. Uniformity in assessing similar installations

5. A record of compliance efforts

6. Enhance the assessment and review of the emergency management program

7. Respond to inquiries by sorting the emergency management program requirements into categories, such as:

   a. Regulation (federal, state, and local)

   b. Job description

   c. Training requirements

   d. Policy/procedure

   e. Specified individuals

8. Formulate schedules for commitment tracking and compliance initiatives

The evaluation will provide information on the status of the emergency management program. The results, determined against standards and criteria established by legislative authorities, will reflect the ability to deal with an emergency situation. The need to establish and maintain accurate and orderly files and records is essential to the emergency management program. In order to facilitate regulatory requirements, a record of compliance initiatives must be retained. These records serve to document the accomplishments, requirements, commitments, and reports relating to various regulatory requirements.

The identification of commitments in the areas of regulatory compliance, emergency preparedness, training, and other EEA, are vital to assemble and maintain the documentation necessary for the emergency management program. The establishment of a defined information management system structure, as we will discuss later, will ensure that documentation will be available when needed.

The evaluation will provide a summary of the strengths (capabilities) and weaknesses (shortfalls) underlying the planning effort. The areas not currently meeting the evaluation standards should receive primary consideration when preparing the management response to the evaluation report. The management response report should present a plan for ensuring that the identified items are remedied. The plan should include a schedule and specific commitment dates for each identified capability shortfall.

The ultimate benefits to be gained from the audit program are adequate emergency management planning, and preparedness for the employees and the general public.

Now that we have briefly discussed the aspects of compliance, we can turn our attention to the second element of the emergency management program: preparedness.

PREPAREDNESS

Preparedness used in the broadest context means any and all measures taken to prevent, prepare for, respond, mitigate, and recover from an emergency, crisis, incident, and/or accident. It's with this perspective that we begin to break down the aspect of preparedness. We will briefly discuss four critical aspects as they apply to the emergency management planning effort. Figure 1–1 provides a visual reference of the cyclical nature of overall preparedness.

Our discussion will highlight:

- Preparation and Prevention

- Detection and Incident Classification

- Response and Mitigation

- Reentry and Recovery

This brief overview will provide the basis for further dialogue in Chapter 3.

PREPARATION AND PREVENTION

Preparation and prevention includes any set of activities that prevents an emergency, reduces the chance of an emergency happening, or reduces the damaging effects of an emergency.

Prevention includes, but is not limited to, development and implementation of emergency management plans; development and implementation of EPIPs; and development and implementation of emergency management/response training.

Emergency Management
Critical Aspects

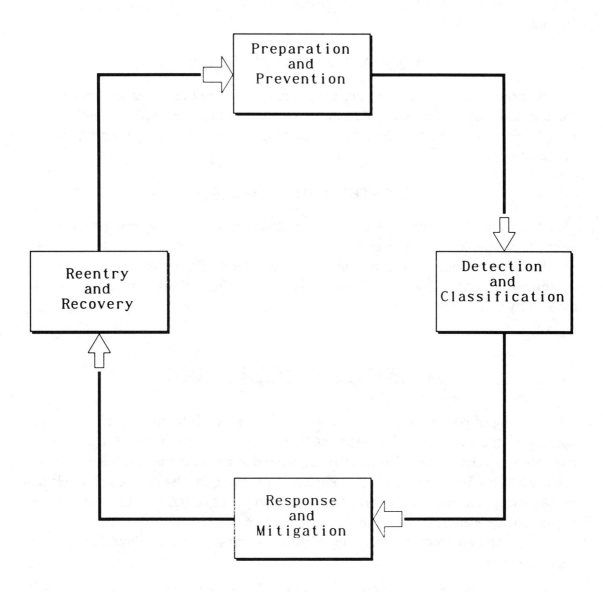

Figure 1–1: Critical Aspects of Emergency Management

DETECTION AND INCIDENT CLASSIFICATION

Detection and incident classification are those actions taken to identify, assess, and classify the severity of an incident.

Detection includes, but is not limited to, activation of Emergency Warning Systems; activation of EPIPs; and activation of the Emergency Management/Response Organization (EMRO).

RESPONSE AND MITIGATION

Response and mitigation actions save lives, prevent further damage, and reduce the effects of an emergency. Mitigation activities include, but are not limited to, EMRO operations; Affiliated EMROs' operations; and emergency response facilities operations.

REENTRY AND RECOVERY

Reentry and recovery actions are undertaken to create a normal or an even safer situation following an emergency.

Recovery includes, but is not limited to, activation of the reentry and recovery organization; coordination with affiliated recovery organizations; and activation of the reentry and recovery plan.

TRAINING AND RETRAINING

Training of personnel is the third component of the all hazards approach. The training of the Emergency Management/Response Organization (EMRO) is one of the critical success factors that must be addressed if an adequate response is to be achieved. The development of the compliance program, involvement of all levels of management, and establishing preparedness is only part of the overall process. To ensure an adequate response, a trained organization is required.

A systems approach to preparing effective training programs should consist of four elements:

1. *TASK ANALYSIS:* When designing an integrated training program, first determine the skills, knowledge, and procedures required for satisfactory performance of each task.

2. *LESSON DEVELOPMENT:* Learning objectives are defined from the skills, knowledge and procedures developed during task analysis. Instructional plans are then prepared to support the learning objectives.

3. *INSTRUCTION:* Lessons are systematically presented using appropriate instructional methods. Instruction may include lecture, self-paced or group-paced mediated instruction, simulation, and team training.

4. *EVALUATION:* Performance standards and evaluation criteria are developed from the learning objectives. Each trainee's performance is evaluated during the course and during field performance testing.

In addition to the formal training program, which we will discuss in more detail later in this book, a program of proficiency demonstration is also needed. We can accomplish this by building a program that supplements the training provided with drills and exercises. The drill and exercise program can vary in degree of complexity. We'll also discuss drills and exercises later in Chapter 5.

INFORMATION MANAGEMENT

Establishing and maintaining an ongoing dynamic emergency preparedness program is essential. The planning process doesn't end just because you finished the plan, are in compliance, have involved management, and have trained the staff. In order to facilitate planning requirements, a record of all initiatives should be retained. These records serve to document the accomplishments, requirements, commitments, and reports relating to various program requirements. The identification of commitments in the areas of compliance, emergency preparedness, and training is vital. The establishment of a defined information management system structure will ensure that documentation will be available when needed.

But information management is also critical during an incident. It is essential to have active systems to provide information on materials, personnel, capabilities, and processes. It is extremely important to have a system (and adequate backup systems) in place that serves to identify, catalog, set priorities, and track issues and commitments relating to emergency management and response activities.

The use of computer data bases that can be created to track the type, quantity, health hazards, location of storage, and other essential information is one method that can be employed to ensure that commitments are tracked and requirements are documented.

The information management system should provide a dynamic framework for the establishment of the necessary files required to accurately document various initiatives. This also serves as a starting point from which a detailed file system structure can be established to ensure the accurate recording of vital information.

A computerized commitment tracking and information management system can be designed to monitor the status of emergency management and response activities. A computerized system provides a user friendly structure that allows an individual the ability to track commitments, perform data entry, and perform routine data base maintenance. Additionally, the commitment tracking system provides a "tickler" that allows for the prompt scheduling and completion of commitments. The commitment tracking system allows for verification that the appropriate personnel and elements adhere to commitments. It also allows for the evaluation of commitments against new requirements, expanded regulations, changes to old requirements, and addition/deletion of the scope of emergency management/response initiatives.

EMERGENCY MANAGEMENT PROGRAM: OBJECTIVES

Now that we have established a basis for our all hazards emergency management program, we need to set some objectives. Our objectives should be measurable and observable. That is, we should be able to quantify them against the Essential Elements of Analysis (EEA) discussed earlier. We should tie them to our compliance initiatives and make management at all levels responsible for assimilating them into our corporate culture. You should also realize that the objectives set forth in your program will have the subelements or enabling objectives which support the major objectives.

The objective of the emergency management program should at a minimum be directed toward:

- Effective coordination of emergency activities among the organizations having a response role

- Early warning and clear instructions to the general public in the affected area in the event of an emergency

18

- Continued assessment of actual or potential consequences both on-site and off-site

- Effective and timely implementation of emergency measures

- Continued maintenance of an adequate state of emergency preparedness

The Emergency Management Plan, an essential part of the overall Emergency Management Program, describes the management/response program, including the nature of emergency response activities, and available emergency management/ response resources and facilities. In the next chapter we will detail the elements of the plan and its supporting documentation.

Experience shows that plans are not used if they are prepared by only one person or one agency. Emergency preparedness requires a coordinated response and cooperation among the response agencies. Working together to develop and maintain an emergency management program provides an opportunity for interaction between responders and management.

The first step of the planning process (Fig. 1–2) should be the identification of the management and response organizations. The selection of representatives from each organization follows as the second step. In selecting the planning team, several considerations are important:

- The members of the planning committee must have the ability, resources, and commitment to get the job done.

- The planning group must possess, or have ready access to, a variety of expertise relating to the resources and potential emergency hazards identified in the plan.

- The planning group should be experienced in the planning process or have access to experts who are.

- There must be agreement on the central focus of the plan and the planners must be able to work as a unified team.

- The planning team must be representative of all elements comprising the EMRO.

- The size of the planning team should be manageable.

- There should be a means of soliciting ideas from members of the

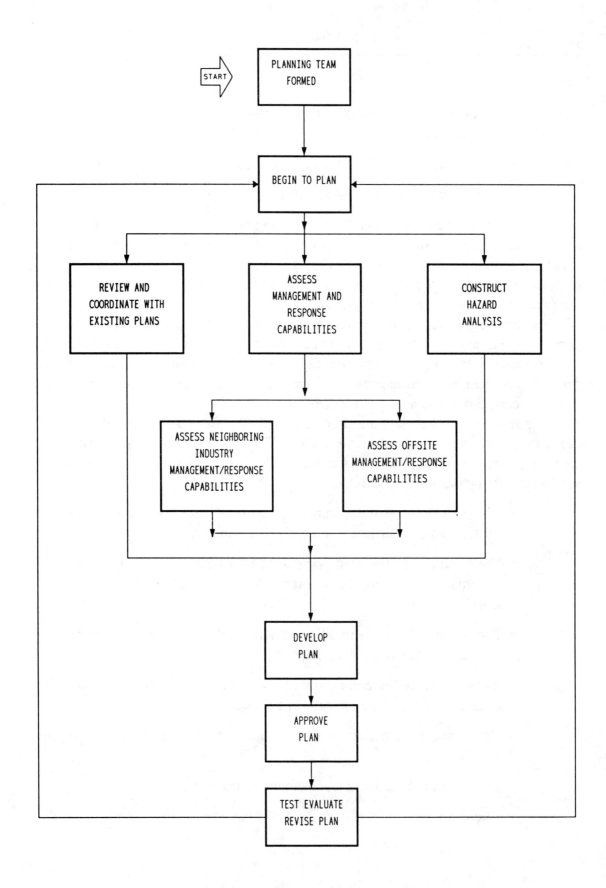

Figure 1–2: Overview of the planning process

response organizations regarding their specific sections of the Emergency Management Plan and the EPIPs.

- The planning team should have a central work area. The work area should be properly equipped and staffed with the appropriate support and administrative personnel.

The responsibility for minimizing the effects of an accident rests with the management team. It is important that management devote the necessary resources to prepare, implement, and audit an effective emergency management program.

SUMMARY

In this introductory section we have suggested an approach to establishing an emergency management program. This approach is based on four initiatives: compliance, preparedness, training/retraining, and information management.

Our approach also seeks to establish a basis for standardizing the steps of the planning process, encouraging management participation, and introducing a framework for evaluation. The evaluation framework consists of nine Essential Elements of Analysis (EEA) supported by various Measures of Effectiveness (MOE) and Measures of Performance (MOP).

We have set the basis for selecting a planning team and beginning the process of developing an emergency management program. The following sections of this book are designed to take you through the development process. A framework for an Emergency Management Plan is provided. You should apply this framework to your specific situation with due diligence. New regulations, local initiatives, and company policy and procedures may dictate a different format. However, by applying the principles presented herein, you can develop a program that will meet your specific needs, while ensuring compliance, establishing preparedness, focusing on developing human resources (training), and providing for an information management system to ensure the program's vitality over an extended period.

In subsequent chapters we will examine, in detail, the steps for preparing your Emergency Management Plan and its constituent parts.

2

Hazard Analysis Assessment:
Establishing the Essential
Elements

CHAPTER HIGHLIGHTS

In this chapter we review an approach to the development of an *all hazards* hazards analysis. Our focus is not on the detailed step-by-step approach for each aspect of the analysis, but rather to expand the analysis to include areas not normally associated with the process safety or hazard operability type of analysis.

This methodology, in conjunction with the hazard operability and process safety management approach, has been used to provide our clients in the petrochemical, industrial, gas, steel, health care, municipality, and government sectors with a basis for developing their emergency management programs. It is important to note the effectiveness of this approach in helping to identify potential hazards not covered by a hazard operability or process safety management assessment. Please note, however, this approach *does not* supplant the process safety management or hazard operability assessment programs/approach. Rather, it serves to supplement and add to these assessment tools.

INTRODUCTION

Critical to the development of any emergency preparedness program, and particularly the all hazards program presented herein, is an extensive analysis of the hazards that may contribute to an emergency. A valid hazard analysis is an essential aspect for the development of your emergency management program. In this chapter we will discuss in some detail the elements constituting the hazard analysis. By its very nature the hazard analysis can be an extremely detailed process. And, as many other volumes have been devoted to this particular subject, my focus will be to highlight the essential steps. I will not concentrate on a detailed discussion on the operational hazard analysis (such as process safety management). I will, however, attempt to direct you into areas that, while apparent, are often overlooked in the process of developing the emergency management program.

The purpose of this chapter is to make generally available the hazard evaluation methodology we have used to establish a basis for the emergency management program. I will also show how this data can be associated with process hazard analysis to provide the basis for an all hazards emergency management program.

While the hazard evaluation process described herein is in sufficient detail, you can select the most appropriate approach to conducting your analysis. It is strongly suggested that you research current literature and expertise to ensure that the most up-to-date information is available for you to use. The literature review should include an analysis of applicable regulatory guidance, engineering standards, and other applicable resource material for your own particular industry.

In Chapter 1, we presented a framework for establishing an emergency management plan. Nine Essential Elements of Analysis (EEA) were presented and briefly discussed. One of these, the hazard analysis, forms the basis upon which we move forward to develop the program. Hazard analysis by its very nature is a dynamic process. Once the initial analysis is complete, it should be reviewed and your hazard assessment document revised accordingly. This is an active process of continuous improvement. You should use the information gained in this step to reduce your vulnerability by attempting to eliminate potential incident triggers. As an example, you find that your company stores excessive quantities of chlorine. You may be able to eliminate the hazard by switching to a less hazardous material or reduce the hazard by carrying less material in inventory.

HAZARD ANALYSIS GOALS

A primary goal of any hazard analysis should be to reduce vulnerability. Additionally, the hazard analysis should serve as a basis for development of the emergency management program and identify potential worst-case scenarios. The hazard analysis described herein is a form of safety review, and should be considered for integration into the hazard and operability study process or process safety management program. You should also consider evaluating data from these programs for incorporation into your hazard analysis report.

As such, you should take note of potential impacts to:

- Safety and loss prevention issues

- Process/operational system design

- Process operations

- Health, environment, and safety

- Public and private property

- Business interruption and resumption

- Sources of information

HAZARD ANALYSIS TEAM SELECTION

A critical factor concerning the quality of the hazard analysis is the credentials of the personnel performing the analysis. Personnel selection should take into consideration experience and expertise in emergency management and response planning, operations, and technical skills. It is also helpful to get people who can work well in a team. Weakness in one of these areas can be made up for by strength in the others. The number of team members depends on the scope and complexity of the project. An ideal size is between three and five people.

The following list, however, may be used as a guide when selecting a team:

- Environmental representative

- Process or chemical representative

- Operations representative

- Maintenance representative

- Safety representative

- Management representative

- Public affairs representative

- Legal affairs representative

- Human resources representative

One team member should be appointed (by management) as team leader. Selection of the right individual will prove to be extremely important to the success of the hazard analysis. The leader's most critical task is to keep the team's attention focused on the steps identified herein while preventing sidetracking and the tendency to solve problems outright.

While outright problem-solving by team members may prove to be a beneficial result of the hazard analysis, it should not become a deterrent to the team's ability to complete the initial hazard analysis. The team leader, therefore, should identify issues for detailed investigation but not become so heavily involved in the problem-solving process that he/she fails to complete the overall task at hand.

The team leader's additional jobs will include acquiring analysis data, materials, organizing review sessions, encouraging input from team members, discouraging negativism, and maintaining the team's perspective. Selection of a team leader accordingly places more emphasis on managerial and interpersonal skills than on technical competence.

Someone should be assigned the duties of documentation. These duties include keeping all analysis records, filing status reports if required, maintaining a current list of recommendations, and organizing the final report. It is crucial to keep accurate, legible, and intelligible records of all aspects of hazard analysis.

It is essential that every step in the hazard analysis be documented. This ensures that nothing is overlooked and that work is not replicated. Additionally, accurate records allow team members to refresh their memories with the logic that led them to issue any recommendation.

A recommended format for the Hazard Analysis Assessment is provided below.

- General site information

- Assignment of responsibility/emergency planning

- Identification of hazardous materials

- Extremely hazardous substance list

- Release state of material (i.e., gas, liquid)

- Release pathways

- Release history

- Hazard analysis

    Hazop methodology

    Hazard categories

    Prioritized hazard list

    Summary of processes, storage, transfer locations, and so on

- Highly toxic materials handled

- Other major risks

- Other hazards (external to location/company)

- Surface and ground waters (including public/private water supply impacts)

- Wildlife and national resource damage assessment

- Worst-case scenarios

- Prevention programs

- Waste stream analysis

- Summary

Figure 2–1 serves to illustrate some considerations within the broad-based perspective of hazard analysis. Some of the items cited will obviously not apply to your particular situation. You should, however, consider these from the perspective of impact on your company, not merely your specific location.

TYPICAL HAZARDS AND ISSUES FACED BY COMPANIES

Manufacturing Process Hazards

Process Failures
- Explosions
- Fires
- Materials Spills/Releases

Utility Supply Disruption
- Electric
- Water

Feedstock Supply Disruption
- Due to Accidents
- Due to Market Forces

Chronic Environmental Contamination

Transportation Hazards

Accidents
- Explosions
- Fires
- Materials Spills/Releases

Disruptions
- System
- Political/Economic

Product Related Hazards
- Product Contamination
- Product Liability
- Product Defect
- Market Loss

Employee Related Hazards
- Labor Strife
- Operator Error
- Employee Sabotage
- Hostage/Violent Acts
- Contractor Actions
- Litigation
- Employee Drug Use
- Maintenance Oversight

Societal Hazards
- Political Instability/ Civil Disorder
- International Conflicts
- Hostage/Terrorist Acts
- Executive Kidnapping
- Consumer Protests/Boycotts
- Product Tampering

Governmental Regulations
- Manufacturing Process
- Product-Related
- Work-Place (Health/Safety)
- Environmental

Financial Hazards
- Hostile Takeover/Leveraged Buyout
- Stock Market/Price Collapse
- Embezzlement
- Executive Misconduct/Fraud

Natural Disasters
- Floods
- Hurricanes
- Tornadoes
- Earthquakes

Miscellaneous Hazards
- Executive Succession
- Computer Failure/Virus

External Hazards
- Neighboring Sites

Figure 2–1: Typical Hazards and Issues Faced by Companies

THE HAZARDS ANALYSIS PROCESS

The hazards analysis is a necessary step in development of the emergency management program. The all hazards approach depends on a clear understanding of what hazards exist and what risk they pose for the location.

The hazards analysis described in this section is a three-step decision-making process to identify potential hazards facing the facility. All three steps should be followed, although the level of detail will vary from site to site. The hazards analysis is designed to consider all potential hazards. It also identifies which hazards are of high priority and should be addressed in specific Emergency Plan Implementing Procedures (EPIPs) developed to support the emergency management program. Depending upon the size and nature of operations at the facility, the hazards analysis may be complex or relatively easy. Access to necessary experts can be helpful.

As highlighted in Chapter 1, the hazard analysis should at a minimum include:

- General Information (Site History)

- Management awareness and control programs

- Identification of hazardous materials

- Hazardous materials handling, collection, and storage

- Recordkeeping/regulatory compliance

- Site characterization

The three steps for the hazard analysis should generally be to conduct:

Personnel Interviews: The personnel interviews should consist of a questionnaire regarding the knowledge of the extent of site hazards, general information on-site emergency preparedness, identification of hazardous materials, hazardous materials handling, collection and storage, recordkeeping, and training.

Overview of Written Program: The overview would consist of a comparison of any written program materials for hazard determination in accordance with, but not limited to, Occupational Safety and Health Administration (OSHA) guidance 29 CFR 1910.1200 (d). Also, the following sections of the Superfund Amendments and Reauthorization Act (SARA) must be examined: Section 302, Facility Notification; 304, Emergency Release Notification; 311, Hazardous Chemical Reporting Tier I; 312,

Hazardous Chemical Reporting Tier II; and 313, Toxic Chemical Release Notification, as applicable. Also examine RCRA permits; TSCA notifications; DOT; and other applicable regulations.

Site Familiarization: The site familiarization would consist of a tour of the facility to accomplish the following:

- Identification of major material storage locations at the site

- Identification of potential areas of vulnerability

- Familiarization with the general site layout

The site familiarization typically provides specific information on situations that have the potential for causing injury to life, or damage to property and the environment due to a hazardous material spill or release. In addition to those items cited here, a detailed assessment and acquisition of data on the following should be accomplished:

- Chemical identities

- The location of process, treatment, or storage areas for hazardous materials

- The type and design of chemical container or vessel

- The quantity of material that could be involved in an airborne release

- The nature of the hazard most likely to accompany hazardous materials spills or releases (e.g., airborne toxic vapors or mists; also other hazards such as fire, explosion, large quantities stored or processed, and handling conditions)

The site familiarization should also identify neighboring facilities, areas in the community that may be affected or exposed, and individuals in the community who may be subject to injury or death from specific hazardous materials. Also identified are facilities, property, or environment that may be susceptible to damage should a release occur.

This expanded analysis of external hazards provides information on:

- The extent of emergency planning zones (that is, an estimate of the area that may be affected in a significant way because of a spill or release of a known quantity of a specific chemical under defined conditions)

- The population, in terms of numbers, density, and types of individuals (such as, facility employees, neighborhood residents, people in hospitals, schools, nursing homes, prisons, and day care centers) that could be within the emergency planning zone

- Private or public property (such as, critical facilities, homes, schools, hospitals, businesses, offices) that may be damaged. This includes essential support systems (such as, water, food, power, communication, medical), transportation facilities, and corridors

- The environment that may be affected and the impact of a release on sensitive natural areas and endangered species

To have an accurate view of the potential problems, you will need to address all of the steps in hazards analysis outlined above. Each of the three steps should be followed even if extensive information is not available for each site. The process anticipates that local judgment will be necessary.

This survey will enable you to identify areas in need of attention, establish a list of compliance commitments that have to be met, and document current efforts. Once the hazard analysis has been developed and implemented, it must be evaluated and kept up-to-date. This can be accomplished by reviewing actual responses and by conducting a detailed assessment of each affected entity.

PRIORITIZATION OF HAZARDS

You will want to prioritize the highest concentration of risk at your facility and rank order each area. Next, you will want to do an analysis of the hazard categories/priority list. A simple breakdown may consist of location/unit, pressure, temperature, throughput, and hazard category.

The prioritization can be accomplished simply by dividing each risk category into "high," moderate," and "low," and basing an overall rating (hazard category) on the number of highs, moderates, and lows. A sample definition of each breakout area is provided below:

	Pressure
Low	= less than 50 psi
Moderate	= 50–200 psi
High	= greater than 200 psi

30

Temperature

Low	= less than 300° degrees Fahrenheit
Moderate	= 300–500°F
High	= greater than 500°F

Throughput Capacity

Low	= less than 15,000 b/d
Moderate	= 15–40,000 b/d
High	= greater than 40,000 b/d

Hazard Category

Low	= heavy oil, no light ends, fewer toxics
Moderate	= medium oil, some light ends, some toxics
High	= light oils, light ends, more toxics

Planning personnel who apply the steps presented in this section can obtain a great deal of knowledge and insight into the specific threats facing their facility. You should use this knowledge directly in an attempt to plan for all possible scenarios. Time and available resources are critical to ensuring a comprehensive plan will be developed. For all intents and purposes, the entire set of incident scenarios, and considered during the hazard analysis in aggregate, will become the basis of the planning effort.

Those who do not have the resources available to plan for every possible contingency, or who have other threats competing for attention, may wish to prioritize their planning efforts by focusing on the most important situations. This can be accomplished by screening worst-case scenarios to identify those that have a reasonable likelihood of occurrence in the future, and/or which may have significant consequences in the absence of an organized, rapid, and effective response effort.

FINAL REPORTS

A final report should be written for the hazard analysis. This report acts as a formal conveyance of recommendations to management. It also provides a historical record for planning efforts. Such a record will be invaluable if a future analysis is conducted at the facility. The hazard analysis should be incorporated into the emergency management program as an appendix to the Emergency Management Plan. It should be highlighted in an executive summary to the Emergency Management Plan.

Now that we have set the basis for our planning effort by identifying the hazards and defining our planning criteria, we can move to the next phase: planning development. In the next chapter, we will discuss plan development and the supporting materials that supplement the plan.

3

Emergency Management Planning: The *All Hazards* Planning Process

CHAPTER HIGHLIGHTS

Environmental, occupational safety, and health concerns continue to be an important issue. Management must make effective use of information in the planning process. Management must be effective in the implementation of its emergency management plan. Environmental, occupational, and health risks can be handled. The following sections of this chapter will explore in detail the development of the Emergency Management Plan and its supporting components—the appendices and Emergency Plan Implementing Procedures (EPIPs).

Additionally, we will outline an organizational structure that can be applied to the Emergency Management Plan. This structure strives to blend the traditional Incident Command System (ICS) structure with the organizational structure and hierarchy common to business and the industrial setting. The attempt here is not to replace the role of the traditional ICS organization, but to enhance the basic structure in order to better support the response effort.

EMERGENCY MANAGEMENT PROGRAM: COMPONENTS FOR AN EFFECTIVE CAPABILITY

Most organizations plan for business contingencies. Yet few plan for the potentially devastating effects of natural or man-made disasters. Incidents can occur at any time and under the most unfavorable conditions. Every organization has an obligation to protect its assets and interests. In the area of emergency preparedness, federal and state legislation extends this obligation beyond a company's site boundaries or a community's local jurisdiction.

Consider the dilemma of the typical industrial facility. Since 1975 the 2,061 federal and state compliance regulations have grown to more than 60,000; that does not even count local regulations and ordinances. This regulatory mountain will continue to grow as new acts are passed and old regulations are reauthorized.

While not all of these regulations address emergency preparedness, management must address emergency planning from several perspectives.

Examples of these are:

- Safety of employees, local populace, others

- Compliance requirements (Federal, state, and sometimes local regulations)

- Company policy and procedures

- Measures of standard of care

A typical facility may have to comply minimally with:

- Occupational Safety and Health Administration (OSHA) 29 CFR 1910.38, Emergency Planning and Fire Prevention

- OSHA 29 CFR 1910.120, Hazardous Waste Operations and Emergency Response

- OSHA 29 CFR 1910.119, Process Safety Management of Highly Hazardous Chemicals

- OSHA 29 CFR 1910.155–165, Fire Protection

- OSHA 29 CFR 1910.36, Egress (Evacuation)

- OSHA 29 CFR 1910.156, Fire Brigade

- EPA 40 CFR 300, Superfund Amendments and Reauthorization Act Title III

- 40 CFR 112, Oil Pollution Prevention, Nontransportation-Related Onshore Facilities

- Hazardous Materials Uniform Transportation Safety Act

- Oil Pollution Act of 1990

- Clean Air Act

- Department of Transportation 49 CFR Part 194, Response Plans for Onshore Oil Pipelines

OSHA 29 CFR 1910.120 provides an example of the complexity of the laws. The regulation requires that covered entities have an emergency plan covering the following elements:

- Preemergency planning and coordination with outside parties

- Personnel roles, lines of authority, training, and communication

- Emergency recognition and prevention

- Safe distances and places of refuge

- Site security and control

- Evacuation routes and procedures

- Decontamination

- Emergency medical treatment and first aid

- Emergency alerting and response procedures

- Critique of response and follow-up

- Personal protective equipment (PPE) and emergency equipment

OSHA 1910.120 further states in its section on training:

(iii) Training.

(A) Training for emergency response employees shall be completed before they are called upon to perform in real emergencies.

Such training shall include the elements of the emergency response plan, standard operating procedures the employer has established for the job, the personal protective equipment to be worn, and procedures for handling emergency incidents.

Another example of a growing trend in regulatory guidance is the Oil Pollution Act of 1990. As a result of this act, the Coast Guard, Department of Transportation, and Environmental Protection Agency have all promulgated regulations requiring compliance with emergency planning initiatives.

Just within the Department of Transportation regulations, 49 CFR 194 contains the following requirements for spill plans:

Section 1: Information Summary

Section 2: Notification Procedures

Section 3: Spill Detection and On-Scene Spill Mitigation Procedures

Section 4: Response Activities

Section 5: List of Contacts

Section 6: Training Procedures

Section 7: Drill Procedures

Section 8: Response Plan Review and Update Procedures

Section 9: Response Zone Appendices

The development of a comprehensive approach to these issues is an undertaking. The alternative, however, may be worse: the development and maintenance of several emergency plans that focus on meeting various regulatory compliance initiatives. Imagine this situation. You are the facility manager of a multiunit plant. You have spill plans, as required under the various agencies governing oil pollution. You have stated-mandated plans. You have a Hazardous Waste Emergency Operations Plan (HAZWOPER) as mandated under OSHA 1910.120. And you have a variety of other plans as mandated by various and sundry regulations and policies.

An incident occurs at one end of the facility. Your response personnel assess the situation, and unbeknownst to you, initiate the oil spill response plan. You, on the other hand, based on advice from your management team, initiate your chemical safety contingency plan.

You attempt to communicate with your response personnel, who are busily implementing a plan that does not integrate with your plan. They begin calling for assistance. Unfortunately, the telephone numbers in their plan do not correlate with the telephone numbers in your plan. You begin calling for assistance and both of you begin a required notification sequence—to the same agencies, or in some cases, different agencies. The result is confusion and the impression that you have lost control over the situation. Regulatory agencies begin to demand information—your plan doesn't contain the forms they require. You begin a frantic search for the appropriate forms, leading to more confusion, lost time, and a worsening situation. Agencies are indicating that they will take over the response if you don't get control of the situation. Sound familiar?

What is needed is a solid basis for compliance, as well as a program that incorporates not only regulatory compliance issues but a well-thought-out framework for management and response integration.

An approach to developing an emergency management program built upon compliance, preparedness, training, and information management should focus on the following:

- Emergency Management Plan and appendices

- Emergency Management/Response Organization (EMRO), a type of Enhanced Incident Command System

- Emergency Plan Implementing Procedures (EPIPs)

- Proficiency demonstration (training, drills, and exercises)

- Commitment tracking

The *all hazards* approach presented in the remainder of this chapter consists of developing documentation and supporting materials to support a plan; appendices; and implementing procedures that serve as the basis for responding to any situation, regardless of the triggering mechanism.

Our first step will be to define the elements of the Emergency Management Plan, the core element for the all hazards approach. The goal of developing an all hazards plan will be to establish a higher degree of preparedness to deal with incidents, company policy and procedure requirements, as well as statutory planning requirements levied by federal, state, and local governments.

The Emergency Management Plan, an element of the program, should take an all hazards approach. The plan should describe the management/response program, including the nature of emergency management/response activities and available emergency management/response resources and facilities.

PREPLANNING AND MANAGEMENT COMMITMENT

The responsibility for minimizing the effects of an on-site incident rests with the facility management/response team. This team consists of response personnel and management personnel. Management must devote the necessary resources to prepare, implement, and audit an effective emergency management program.

By segmenting the planning process and analyzing each segment, the planning team will be able to determine where it should invest the majority of its effort in order to maximize resource allocations. A first step in the planning process is to conduct a hazards analysis. The hazards analysis, as presented in Chapter 2, should be a detailed review of all the potential hazards present on-site, processes, safety aspects, and off-site hazards that could have an impact on operations.

The hazards analysis should be periodically reviewed and updated in order to fully evaluate all potential hazards, type of emergency response required, and applicable laws and regulations to be addressed. It is best to model the analysis against set standards as described in Chapter 2. This will provide a profile of weaknesses, opportunities, threats, and strengths which underlie the planning process. The following sequence of steps provides a simplified breakdown of the planning process:

1. *Analyze Tasks:* Determine the planning basis; select a viable time horizon; study past experience; list assumptions; determine key variables; conduct evaluation.

2. *Develop Objectives:* Build scenarios for each variable; develop a strategy for each scenario.

3. *Review with Experts:* Analyze each strategy.

4. *Make Final Decisions:* Develop optimum response strategies.

5. *Question Key Decision Makers:* Determine questions that need to be answered to demonstrate the level of understanding of the plan.

Once this preliminary analysis has been accomplished, the formal planning process can begin. The planning process is dynamic; by its very nature it provides flexibility. This will allow management to be able to respond to anomalies that impact the program.

One key aspect of the planning process that is sometimes overlooked is the need to have personnel who are knowledgeable with the implementation of the emergency management plan. It is essential to train managers and key decision makers in order for them to fully benefit from the planning process. It makes little or no sense to build an emergency management plan if the people who are responsible for implementation are not trained to use it. The objectives of the program—effective coordination of activities, early warning, accident assessment, timely implementation of emergency measures, and a high state of readiness—can be achieved through careful planning.

ELEMENTS OF THE EMERGENCY MANAGEMENT PROGRAM

The Model Emergency Management Plan discussed below features four major elements:

1. Preliminary information in the form of a preamble consists of the following:

Preface

Controlled Distribution List

Concurrence Sheet

Record of Changes

Authority

Promulgation

Executive Summary

Table of Contents

Instructions on Plan Use

2. A core plan consisting of 10 key sections

Section 1: Administration

Section 2: Organization

Section 3: Concept of Operations

Section 4: Communications

Section 5: Emergency Classification

Section 6: Emergency Facilities and Equipment

Section 7: Public Information

Section 8: Postincident Operations

Section 9: Maintaining Emergency Preparedness

Section 10: Evaluation

3. Appendices containing supporting materials

The appendices to the Emergency Management Plan include, but are not limited to:

Letters of Agreement

Hazard analysis

Equipment lists

Other supporting material subject to frequent change

4. Emergency Plan Implementing Procedures (EPIPS)

EPIPs are organized in the following categories:

Administrative

Emergency classification

Emergency Management/Response Organization (EMRO)

Emergency operations

Reentry and recovery

The 10 key plan sections present the basic concepts of the emergency management strategy. This approach allows full conceptual development of prevention/preparation, detection/classification, mitigation/response, and reentry/recovery in a flexible format.

The appendices contain reference material in support of the key sections. The information in the appendices consists of material generally subject to frequent change. This information is location-specific and may consist of telephone lists, equipment resource listings, maps, or other such information.

The EPIPs, designed for specific functions, duties, and tasks, contain detailed instructions for emergency preparedness and response. The EPIPs assign firm responsibilities to personnel and provide step-by-step instructions augmented by checklists and flowcharts where appropriate. Information in EPIPs is the most dynamic and specialized, requiring regular review and revision. A detailed discussion of the EPIPs is presented later.

Let's now turn our attention to the contents of the Emergency Management Plan. To start, we need to look at the front portion of the plan. For this section you will want to develop the following material. Please note that some of the material may seem to be optional or superfluous. However, these sections serve as a guide to the plan, appendices and EPIPs, and can be quite useful as controlled distribution for personnel who do not require the entire plan (appendices and EPIPs included).

PREAMBLE

The preamble serves as an introduction to the Emergency Management Plan. The Preamble contains a record of changes, authority for the plan, concurrence, and general administrative information. The executive summary serves as a quick reference guide to the plan. It contains a brief description of the site and area analysis, overview of the hazards analysis, key sections of the plan and supporting materials (appendices and EPIPs). A brief summary of the key areas in the preamble follows.

Preface: The preface is a functional guide to locate various parts of the plan, appendices, and the controlled distribution list.

Controlled Distribution List: The controlled distribution list provides a list of controlled copies of the plan, distribution, and location.

Concurrence Sheet: Each official with an emergency role signifies concurrence and date on the concurrence sheet.

Record of Changes: The record of changes identifies all changes to the plan.

Authority: The authority section lists the legal basis for the plan.

Promulgation: The letter of promulgation gives the plan official status. It is signed by the facility manager and superintendent of safety and industrial hygiene.

Appendices: Appendices supplement the Emergency Management Plan with specific information. Specific titles are shown in the table of contents. Appendices to the Emergency Management Plan contain information subject to frequent change.

Emergency Plan Implementing Procedures (EPIPs): EPIPs supplement the Emergency Management Plan. An appendix to the plan should be provided as a reference document, listing all the EPIPs. EPIPs are step-by-step, task-oriented sequences of activities, supported by checklists and flowcharts.

Instructions on Plan Use: The instructions section of the preamble should contain information on the purpose of the plan, its use, and the plan's interrelationship with its appendices and the EPIPs. Information on the distribution, control, and updating of the emergency plan should be provided in a separate paragraph. A listing of the key personnel and agencies that receive the plan should be provided. Also, this introductory material should explain the plan's use and organization.

Copies of the Emergency Management Plan, appendices, and EPIPs should be distributed by the emergency planning coordinator to those individuals and organizations concerned with emergency preparedness planning for the facility. These documents should be packaged in an emergency management planning manual. Each emergency management planning manual should be assigned a control number. Revisions to these documents can be issued in accordance with the site procedural requirements for controlled documents to ensure that the holders of these documents possesses up-to-date emergency management planning manuals.

RECORD OF AMENDMENTS

This section of the preamble describes the record of amendments to the original Emergency Management Plan. Examples of the information contained here would be the date of issue, the facility manager's signature, and the record of changes form.

A list of the documents and legal instruments which establish authority for the plan (federal, state, and local) should be detailed in an appendix cross-referencing the regulations to specific parts of the plan, and listed as a reference in this section of the Preamble. For example:

- Comprehensive Environmental Response, Compensation, and Liability Act (CERCLA), Section 105

- OSHA 29 CFR 1910.36, Means of Egress (Evacuation)

- OSHA 29 CFR 1910.38, Employee Emergency Plans and Fire Prevention Plans

- OSHA 29 CFR 1910.119, Process Safety Management of Highly Hazardous Chemicals

- OSHA 29 CFR 1910.120, Hazardous Waste Operations and Emergency Response

- OSHA 29 CFR 1910.156, Fire Brigades

- OSHA 29 CFR 1910.165, Employee Alarm Systems

- OSHA 29 CFR 1910.1200, Hazard Communication

- EPA 40 CFR 112, Oil Pollution Prevention

- EPA 40 CFR 261, Identification and Listing of Hazardous Wastes

- EPA 40 CFR 300, Title III of the Superfund Amendments and Reauthorization Act of 1986

- State acts

- Local ordinances

EXECUTIVE SUMMARY

The executive summary highlights the key points of the Emergency Management Plan, appendices, and EPIPs. The executive summary will be helpful as it allows a reader to grasp the essence of your plan and supporting materials in a format that is not as detailed as the actual plan. It also can serve as a quick reference guide and a controlled distribution to external entities. The executive summary should be a concise and easy-to-read document.

TABLE OF CONTENTS

The table of contents provides an outline of the material by key section heading and subheading. It should list all the appendices and EPIPs. Appendix A provides a sample table of contents and list of EPIPs.

NONDISCLOSURE STATEMENT

It is important that you protect proprietary or confidential information in a nondisclosure statement. This is difficult to do. The Community Right-to-Know Law, Freedom of Information Act, and local initiatives make it cumbersome. However, you have a right to protect your plan from disclosure by unauthorized sources. A typical nondisclosure statement is seen in Fig. 3–1.

SECTION 1: ADMINISTRATION

Section 1, Administration, discusses the purpose and objectives of the Emergency Management Plan, and includes planning factors, a mission statement, and site description for the location. The site description includes geographic considerations, including latitude and longitude data, chemicals used in process, potential hazards, and possible release pathways. This section further describes the purpose, objectives, incident information summary, planning factors, general site information and potential hazards. It serves as the basis for the remainder of the plan. Closely related to Section 1 of the plan is Appendix H, Hazard Analysis.

Some of the information contained in this section includes the incident information summary. Initial information can be critical. A summary of the information, you are prepared to provide to external entities should be under this heading. This information can be highlighted in this subsection of the plan; it may include, but need not be limited to:

- Date and time

- Name of the facility and person, including title, placing the call

- Name of person receiving the call

- Name and telephone number of on-scene contact

- Location

- Nearby populations

Proprietary Information

Confidential

NONDISCLOSURE STATEMENT

This Emergency Management Plan includes proprietary information and trade secret data that shall not be disclosed outside the parties involved and shall not be duplicated, used, or disclosed in whole or in part for any purpose other than to evaluate this Emergency Management Plan. If, however, an agreement is concluded in writing, allowing external parties to manipulate this data, the parties shall have the right to duplicate, use, or disclose the data to the extent provided in the resulting agreement. This restriction does limit the parties right to use information contained in this document if it is obtained from another source without restriction. The material subject to this restriction is contained in all pages of the Emergency Management Plan whether marked as "Proprietary Information" or not.

Proprietary Information

Confidential

Figure 3–1

- Incident description

- Time of release (if any)

- Possible health effects and medical emergency information

- Number of dead/injured and where dead/injured are being taken

- Name of material released, if known:

    Manifest/shipping invoice/billing label

    Shipper/manufacturer identification

    Container type

    Railcar/truck four-digit DOT identification numbers

    Placard/label information

- Characteristics of the material, only if readily detectable

- Present status of material

- Total amount of material that may be released

- Other hazardous materials in area

- Amount of material released so far and the duration of release

- Whether significant amounts of material appear to be entering the atmosphere, nearby water, storm drains, or soil

- Direction, height, color, and odor of any vapor clouds or plumes

- Weather conditions (wind direction and speed)

- Local terrain conditions

- Personnel at the scene

A formal incident report form should be developed in accordance with regulatory requirements and included in an appendix to the plan and in specific EPIPs that address emergency notification and communication.

A designated individual of the appropriate management level should have the overall responsibility for the emergency preparedness program at the facility. Specific responsibility and authority for emergency management planning should be assigned to a section on the emergency planning effort.

Annually, or as required, emergency planning personnel should review the Emergency Management Plan, appendices, EPIPs, and any associated materials (for example, training, drill, and exercise programs). Updates of these documents should be undertaken accordingly.

In addition to maintaining the Emergency Management Plan and associated materials, emergency planning personnel should also be responsible for coordinating training, drills, exercises, the planning effort with support organizations, and evaluating emergency equipment needs.

A line and block chart should be used to illustrate the immediate and long-term interfaces between the facility Emergency Management/Response Organization (EMRO) and the organizations of the affected local, state, and federal agencies. The immediate interfaces with the site can be depicted as dashed lines. Long-term interfaces can be depicted by solid lines.

When developing the Emergency Management Plan, the following factors should be taken into consideration. These are:

1. Geography

Sensitive environmental areas

Water supplies

Population density

Particularly sensitive institutions

Climate

Mean temperature

Annual rainfall

Unusual weather conditions (seasonal)

2. Site characteristics

Particular characteristics of each facility and the transportation routes for which the plan is intended

On-site details

Neighboring population

Surrounding terrain

Known impediments

Other areas at risk

3. Other factors

Precise local conditions that make an Emergency Management Plan necessary

Hazards identification analysis information

Worst-case scenarios

A brief discussion of the relationship to other emergency plans should be prepared and inserted at the end of Section 1. It should highlight the title, location, and revision number of the related plans. A specific cross-reference to other plans for response to emergencies related to the site should be included in a separate appendix to the plan.

SECTION 2: ORGANIZATION

Section 2, Organization, discusses the normal operating contingent for the location as well as the EMRO. This section also discusses support from organizations off-site from the location, such as corporate groups, state and local agencies, federal groups, and private response organizations. Included with this section are organization charts which depict the Emergency Management Organization (EMO), Emergency Response Organization (ERO), and the overall EMRO formed when the two groups work together. Closely related to this section of the plan is Appendix R, Emergency Management/Response Organization Position Descriptions.

The normal operating organization at the facility provides the basic elements from which the EMRO is established. In developing the structure of the EMRO, particular attention should be paid to job descriptions, selection criteria, and the designation of primary and alternate position holders. The normal operating organization will provide a variety of skills and technical expertise to draw from. As such, some nonemergency positions should be designated to perform auxiliary functions when the EMRO is activated. These auxiliary positions should focus on normal operations that have to be performed under emergency conditions.

The EMRO should be composed of a cross section of personnel. The EMRO can be composed of personnel with specialties in operations, maintenance, engineering, environmental, management, material control, fire protection, security, and emergency planning. The core group of personnel for the EMRO should be drawn from the operating staff. The Enhanced Incident Command System (EICS) presented in the remainder of this chapter focuses on the responsibilities of the EMRO. When individual positions are described, it should be noted that the various functions can be compressed under different job titles depending on the size of the facility staff and capabilities on hand. You should, however, do a critical analysis to determine the potential need for additional staffing to ensure your capabilities to handle an emergency situation that would warrant the activation of the complete organization. Figure 3–2 provides a workpaper for use in gathering specific data on members of the EMRO.

A discussion of the position descriptions for a typical organization follow. The position descriptions are provided as examples and are not meant to indicate a rigid structure. Your unique circumstances will dictate the shape and functions of your EMRO.

ON-SHIFT EMERGENCY MANAGER

The position of on-shift emergency manager should be held by the senior ranking individual at the facility when the facility manager is not present. The on-shift emergency manager's function is to initiate expanded response activities and assist the field incident commander in carrying out the appropriate notifications.

The following are examples of some of the functions, duties, and tasks of all personnel who may assume the role of on-shift emergency manager.

- Assess the emergency condition.

- Determine and declare the appropriate emergency classification in coordination with the field incident commander and initiate all provisions of the Emergency Management Plan.

- Initiate notification of the EMRO.

- Ensure that notification of EMRO personnel has been completed, all personnel have reported to their assigned locations, and the EMRO is properly staffed.

EMERGENCY MANAGEMENT/RESPONSE ORGANIZATION (EMRO) DATA

EMRO MEMBER:	PHONE #s:
	OFFICE _____
	HOME _____
BASIC ASSIGNMENT:	EMERGENCY _____
	OTHER _____

ALTERNATE POSITION HOLDERS:	PHONE #s:
	OFFICE _____
	HOME _____
	EMERGENCY _____
	OTHER _____

RESPONSIBILITIES & ASSIGNMENTS:

KEY DATA:

REGULAR JOB TITLE –	IMMEDIATE SUPERVISOR –
DEPARTMENT –	NORMAL HOURS –

AREAS OF EXPERTISE –	ASSISTANTS AND SUBORDINATES –

HOME ADDRESS –	HOME PHONE –
SPOUSE'S NAME –	CHILDREN
YEARS WITH COMPANY –	PRIOR ASSIGNMENTS –
QUALIFICATIONS –	

REVISION DATE _____

Figure 3–2

- Ensure that communications with the field incident commander and incident support director are established and maintained.

- Coordinate response activities with the field incident commander.

- Coordinate all response activities until a transfer of authority with the emergency manager is accomplished, or the incident is terminated.

- Maintain a log, using an activities record sheet.

FIELD INCIDENT COMMANDER

The field incident commander is responsible for all activities *at the incident scene*. Generally this position is filled by the senior ranking fire fighter (fire chief) or equivalent. The field incident commander may come from an outside agency in some instances where the EMRO does not have the in-house capability.

The following are examples of functions, duties, and tasks of all personnel who may assume the role of field incident commander. The field incident commander will be responsible for the management of emergency response at the incident scene.

- Assess the incident.

- Classify the incident.

- Conduct initial briefing.

- Activate elements of the Emergency Management Plan.

- Brief, or designate a person to brief, personnel at the incident scene and staging area.

- Determine information needs and inform EMRO personnel, and non-EMRO personnel responsible for operations, maintenance, and so forth.

- Coordinate staff activity at the incident scene.

- Manage incident operations.

- Coordinate search and rescue activities.

- Coordinate requests for additional resources.

- Conduct periodic tactical and logistic briefings.

- Coordinate incident termination activities.

EMERGENCY MANAGER

The emergency manager position should be held by the facility manager. Designated alternates may include senior facility management. The emergency manager is responsible for overall activities at the facility during an incident. Close coordination with the on-shift emergency manager and field incident commander is essential to ensure continuity of operations.

Major function, duties, and tasks are listed below.

- Review the assessment of the emergency condition.

- Determine and declare the appropriate emergency classification, and initiate all provisions of the Emergency Management Plan.

- Verify notification of the EMRO as appropriate.

- Ensure that all personnel have reported to their assigned locations and that the EMRO is properly staffed.

- Establish communications with key on-site and off-site emergency personnel.

- Review and approve all public information and news media releases.

- Authorize the procurement of equipment, materials, and other resources, as necessary.

- Ensure 24-hour operations capability.

- Designate personnel to interface with federal, state, and local officials.

- Approve the protective action recommendations made to state and local officials.

- Coordinate all on-site and off-site emergency response activities.

- Inform external company resources of the need for additional resources beyond the capabilities of the EMRO.

- Provide situation updates to external corporate crisis management groups.

- Evaluate, coordinate, and control all company response activities, until the event is closed out or the facility recovery organization is formed.

- Authorize all reentries into evacuated on-site areas.

- Serve as a "qualified individual" as outlined in the Oil Pollution Act of 1990 guidelines.

OPERATIONS MANAGER

The operations manager positions should be filled by department managers from the affected and non-affected units or departments at the facility. Alternates may be assigned from departments with similar functions or from field supervisors from within the department. Careful analysis should be undertaken to be able to fill this position with an alternate. In some instances, the field supervisors will be too preoccupied with the incident to assume operations manager duties.

Major functions, duties, and tasks are shown below.

- Develop operations plan for the affected unit and unaffected units.

- Manage unaffected unit operations.

- Coordinate operations of the affected unit.

- Obtain briefings from the emergency manager.

- Brief assigned company personnel in accordance with the Emergency Management Plan.

- Determine needs and request additional resources.

- Assemble and coordinate personnel assigned to unaffected unit operations.

- Report information about special operational activities and occurrences to the emergency manager.

EMERGENCY DAMAGE CONTROL DIRECTOR

Emergency damage control is essential. It is important to facilitate activities at the scene in support of mitigation activities. It is also important for facilitating nonemergency activities performed under emergency conditions, such as normal maintenance operations. In selecting the emergency damage control director, one should consider the maintenance aspect of this position.

Major functions, duties, and tasks are listed below.

- Advise the incident support director and other personnel regarding the status of on-site emergency damage control activities.

- Coordinate emergency damage control activities through the incident support center.

- Advise maintenance personnel regarding any changes in facility conditions that may impact emergency damage control activities.

- Coordinate the requisition and ordering of emergency equipment and supplies through the logistics director.

- Supervise normal maintenance operations performed under emergency conditions.

LOGISTICS DIRECTOR

The logistics director provides support for all activities involving the supply of the EMRO. Individuals from purchasing and contract administration become useful candidates for this position.

Major functions, duties, and tasks are listed below.

- Coordinate, direct, and respond to requests from the EMRO for administrative and logistical assistance.

- Coordinate the recall and deployment of administrative support personnel in response to the incident.

- Ensure the general needs of all on-site emergency management/response personnel (including state, local, and federal personnel) are met as appropriate (for example, communications, equipment repair, food, sleeping facilities, or office supplies).

- Ensure timely completion of logistical assistance provided in support of emergency response and recovery efforts.

- Arrange transportation and temporary housing for on-site emergency management/response personnel, as needed.

- Assist in the acquisition of additional equipment and supplies, as required.

PUBLIC AFFAIRS DIRECTOR

The position of public affairs director and associated personnel are discussed in detail in the section dealing with crisis communications. The following descriptions highlight the public affairs director's functions.

- Formulate news releases concerning the incident.

- Ensure news releases are up-to-date and technically accurate.

- Assist the emergency manager or designated company spokesperson in news release briefings and presentations.

- Obtain approval for all news releases from the emergency manager.

- Coordinate news releases and rumor control activities with county, state, and local public information personnel, as appropriate.

- Arrange and coordinate press conferences or joint press conferences.

- Contact the jurisdictional agency in charge of the incident to coordinate public information activities.

- Establish a single news center, when possible.

- Receive all bona fide news media representatives courteously and help them in every way possible to gather the information they require, to the extent that such information is available from the company.

- As soon as it is safe and practicable to do so, grant to news media reporters and photographers supervised access to the scene of the incident.

- Refrain from interfering with the activities of newsmen and photographers operating outside company property.

- Arrange for monitoring press, radio, and TV coverage, and forward reports to the appropriate company officers.

SECURITY/COMMUNICATIONS COORDINATOR

Security can be critical during an incident. On-site protective actions (sheltering, evacuation), personnel assembly, and accountability may need to be carried out. Also critical is communications. The security/communications coordinator position combines these functions. He/she should be selected from the on-site staff if using a contract security organization, as contract personnel may not be required to remain at the facility during an incident. You should also consider the staffing implications for security during the negotiation process if using a contracted security company.

Major function, duties, and tasks are shown below.

- Coordinate and direct communications at the facility perimeter.

- Ensure that appropriate communications and record keeping procedures are being properly implemented.

- Request repair and additional communications equipment through the logistics director.

- Verify that security officers have been dispatched to emergency response facilities.

- Coordinate activities to ensure the security of the entire facility.

- Implement the facility security plan.

- Ensure that measures to establish security have been initiated at those activated emergency response facilities.

- Assist with assembly and accountability of personnel at the designated refinery assembly point(s).

- Ensure that all nonessential site personnel are evacuated, and unauthorized personnel cannot enter the site.

- Coordinate the movement and badging of all personnel entering the facility.

- Initiate personnel accountability procedures, and maintain accountability for those personnel working within the facility.

- Coordinate search and rescue operations with the field incident commander.

- Distribute numbered log/note books to EMRO members, as appropriate.

- Establish mail distribution system.

- Set up historical log to record daily events.

- Set up record keeping system for companies and agencies offering assistance.

- Maintain shift logs which document:

    Number of pieces and type of equipment deployed

    Number of contractor personnel employed

    Consultants employed

    Company personnel on-site

(This information is available from the appropriate EMRO member.)

- Prepare summary of daily events for emergency manager.

- Prepare weekly chronological report for emergency manager.

- Collect log/note books from EMRO members.

- Acquire and maintain list of radio call signs.

- Get necessary clearance from agency with jurisdiction over radio and telephone communication.

- Establish secure television transmission from incident site to emergency response facilities. Make arrangements for setup, if possible.

- Assign radio frequencies and call signs for the EMRO members.

- Issue communications equipment and maintain log.

- Set up telephone system for emergency response facilities.

- Test communications network for operation and security.

- Check system power source, tape recorders for conferences, and battery chargers.

ENVIRONMENTAL COORDINATOR

The position of environmental coordinator is apparent. Most, if not all, incidents involve some sort of environmental issue. A release to the environment (air, land, water) can be potentially devastating. The environmental coordinator should be selected from the facility staff and be trained on the use of computer/manual assessment methodologies.

Major functions, duties, and tasks are show below.

- Advise incident support director on environmental matters.

- Provide environmental support to the affected units.

- Identify the need for and coordinate any corporate or outside environmental assistance.

- Review news releases prior to their issuance to ensure technical accuracy.

- Ensure that emergency sampling and environmental survey procedures are being properly implemented, and that the resultant information is available to the emergency response facilities at the incident scene.

- Accumulate, tabulate, and evaluate data regarding incident conditions, such as meteorological data and monitoring readings, and environmental survey results.

- Arrange for environmental specialist to collect data and identify impact to water and air quality, commercial and subsistence fisheries, and human health.

- Determine when and where chemical dispersant should be used.

- Satisfy regulatory requirements for dispersant use, if applicable.

- Assess the impact of various response techniques on the environment.

- Contract with wildlife specialists for bird rescue and protection.

- Meet with federal Regional Response Team (RRT) and environmental agencies to learn their concerns about environmental impacts.

- Maintain a log of all actions and contacts.

- Determine which permits are required and prepare and submit applications. Seek waivers as appropriate.

- Prepare environmental guidelines for the field incident commander and contractors.

- Update list of environmental and commercial resources impacted and threatened by the release.

- Monitor environmental effects of cleanup operations on the environment.

- Inform public affairs manager and law advisers about status of cleanup operation and environmental impacts.

- Prepare technical report about spill history, impact, and cleanup operation.

- Investigate claims of pollution damage to private and government land.

- Identify areas for agency assistance and request agency support.

- Advise field incident commander of safety problems and risks to mobile command center and local communities.

- Provide technical support for dispersant decision process:

    Determine best dispersant for spill

    Estimate quantity of dispersant required

    Identify sources for dispersant

    Recommend contractors for dispersant application.

- Develop list of cooperatives with equipment that will be effective for spill response:

    Identify procedures for obtaining equipment from cooperatives

    Identify requirements for transporting equipment to the incident site

    Estimate time to deliver equipment

    Determine manpower needed for deployment and operation

- Obtain maps as needed by the field incident commander and EMRO.

- Prepare progress reports containing:

    Percent work completed

    Summary of response effectiveness

    Estimated time and level of effort needed for completion of response effort

    Problems encountered and recommendations for resolving them

- Provide support for recovery manager, cleanup contractor, spill monitor, and disposal contractor as appropriate.

- Ensure personnel are properly decontaminated, if necessary.

- Review and evaluate all on-site environmental data, including appropriate chemical analysis results.

SAFETY OFFICER

The safety officer should work hand-in-hand with the field incident commander and environmental coordinator to ensure the safety of all personnel involved in the response.

Major functions, duties, and tasks are shown below.

- Coordinate use of protective clothing, respiratory protection, and access control.

- Assess hazardous or unsafe situations and develop measures for assuring personnel safety.

STATUS BOARD PLOTTER

The status board plotter provides essential information to the EMRO during an emergency. A competent individual and alternates should be selected to fill this position.

Major functions, duties, and tasks are shown below.

- Establish and organize incident files.

- Establish duplication service and respond to requests.

- Retain and file duplicate copies of official forms and reports.

- Check the accuracy and completeness of records submitted for files.

- Correct errors or omissions by contacting appropriate company personnel.

- Provide duplicates of forms and reports to authorized requesters.

- Prepare incident documentation when requested.

- Maintain, retain, and store incident files for after incident use.

- Maintain the status boards in the assigned emergency response facility.

NEWS CENTER STAFF

The news center staff will be responsible for assisting in the development of news releases and coordinating activities of the press at the facility.
Major functions, duties, and tasks are shown below.

- Establish and organize news center files.

- Establish duplication service and respond to requests.

- Retain and file duplicate copies of official forms and reports.

- Accept and file news releases, reports, and forms submitted to news center by public affairs manager.

- Check the accuracy and completeness of news releases and reports submitted for files.

- Answer news media inquiries by reading the official news releases.

- Provide duplicates of forms and reports to authorized requesters.

- Prepare incident documentation when requested.

- Maintain, retain, and store incident files for after incident use.

RUMOR CONTROL AIDES

Rumor control aides can help the EMRO by allowing the members to focus on addressing the incident, rather than on quashing rumors. Generally, designated administrative support staff can fulfill this function. It is wise to have at least two primary holders designated.

Major functions, tasks, and duties are shown below.

- Establish and organize rumor control files.

- Establish duplication service and respond to requests.

- Retain and file duplicate copies of official forms and reports.

- Accept and file rumor control reports and forms.

- Check accuracy and completeness of reports submitted for files.

- Answer telephone inquiries by reading the official news releases.

- Provide duplicates of forms and reports to authorized requesters.

- Prepare incident documentation when requested.

- Maintain, retain, and store incident files for after incident use.

EMERGENCY RESPONSE FACILITY (ERF) ASSISTANT

As with rumor control and the status board plotter positions, the Emergency Response Facility (ERF) assistant can be drawn from the administrative/clerical staff. Support is a key function.

Major functions, duties, and tasks are shown below.

- Perform clerical and administrative duties such as distributing or posting information and copying documents.

- Respond to any requests from the Emergency Manager and other EMRO members.

- Maintain a log of all pertinent emergency response activities occurring in the assigned ERF, using a response and recovery activities log sheet.

- Interface with the assigned ERF communicators to obtain information related to the incident.

- Post information related to the incident on the sequence of events board.

INCIDENT SUPPORT DIRECTOR

The incident support director position is critical. He/she will serve as the primary interface with the emergency manager, EMRO staff, field incident personnel, and off-site response organizations. The person selected for this position should have sufficient seniority to fulfill this role.

Major functions, duties, and tasks are shown below.

- Review and evaluate all available environmental release data to assess the on-site and off-site consequences of any incident.

- Ensure that current and forecast meteorological data is obtained, and its effects upon any hazardous materials releases and any dose projections are determined.

- Ensure that appropriate records of environmental monitoring activities are maintained.

- Coordinate on-site personnel search and rescue operations if necessary.

- Coordinate the on-site environmental and/or hazardous materials assessment activities with those of the state and federal agencies.

- Advise the emergency manager and other EMRO personnel regarding the status of off-site emergency response activities.

- Maintain up-to-date knowledge of overall facility and incident conditions.

- Provide technical assistance to off-site response organizations stationed at or near the ERF.

- Provide a point of contact for assisting/cooperating agency representatives.

- Provide the emergency manager with environmental and hazardous materials data that will be used in formulating protective action recommendations to be submitted to the counties and state.

- Advise the emergency manager on matters involving environmental and hazardous materials safety.

- Send requests for support personnel, material, and equipment through the logistics director.

- Direct requests for engineering evaluations of special tools and equipment to the engineering manager.

- Provide the public affairs manager with accurate hazardous materials data for release to the public and the news media.

- Review corporate and company policy regarding environmental emergencies.

- Make recommendations to expedite response operations.

- Develop worst-case scenario and response strategy.

- Coordinate initial management activities for EMRO.

- Obtain support from affiliates, if any exist.

- Request assistance from nearby companies.

- Monitor response operation and provide support as required.

- Review worst-case scenario for changes created by:

  Response operation

  Environmental conditions

  Regulatory problems

  Legal problems

- Adjust staffing as required to allow continuation of normal company operations.

NEWS CENTER COORDINATOR

The news center coordinator will be responsible for running the news center and any press facilities established to facilitate the media.

Major functions, duties, and tasks are shown below.

- Direct and coordinate the activation of the news center.

- Ensure the security of the news center.

- Ensure that the news center is properly arranged.

- Ensure that telephones and communications equipment are properly placed.

- Notify the public affairs manager of news center activation.

- Assist the public affairs manager with coordination of the issuance of public information releases.

- Arrange for and coordinate news conferences.

- Supervise and direct those personnel assigned to the news center.

- Ensure that news media representatives receive a copy of any instructions to the news media.

- Assign appropriate news center aides to work stations.

- Provide rumor control with copies of the latest news releases as well as approved information from local and state officials.

COMPANY SPOKESPERSON

To ensure that your company speaks with one voice, thereby providing a consistent and controlled flow of information, the personnel authorized to speak to the media in an emergency should be restricted to one designated spokesperson. This individual (and backup spokespersons) will have been chosen in advance and trained to respond to the media. All other personnel at the site should respond to reporters' questions by referring them to the spokesperson.

The spokesperson serves as the primary source of information for your company at information briefings and at all press conferences.

Major functions, duties, and tasks are shown below.

- Coordinate scheduling of press conferences with the public affairs director and news center coordinator.

- Assist in the preparation of information to be presented and distributed (press releases, news releases, employee information summaries).

- Present the company's position within prescribed guidelines.

- Ensure that responses to inquiries requiring extended research are accomplished.

SYSTEMS TECHNICAL ASSISTANT

The systems technical assistant supports the spokesperson. Technical expertise is helpful in ensuring that a proper explanation is provided to the media and other off-site entities. The systems technical assistant helps the spokesperson to understand details of the emergency and assists the spokesperson during news conferences. He/she may also be available after news conferences to help the media understand facility systems and operations.

HAZARDOUS MATERIALS TECHNICAL ASSISTANT

The hazardous materials technical assistant also supports the spokesperson. Should hazardous materials be involved in the incident, a knowledge of the effects on personnel and the environment will be needed. This position should interface closely with the environmental coordinator. The hazardous materials technical assistant assists the spokesperson to understand details of the emergency as well as assisting the spokesperson during news conferences. The hazardous materials technical assistant may also be available after news conferences to help the media understand hazardous materials mitigation activities.

RECOVERY MANAGER

The recovery manager position may be assumed by the facility manager or from senior staff at corporate headquarters.

Major functions, duties, and tasks are shown below.

- Notify the appropriate agencies prior to terminating the event or initiating recovery operations.

- Determine and declare that a stable condition exists and that the facility is ready to begin reentry and recovery operations.

- Authorize funds and the utilization of manpower and equipment necessary to accomplish the recovery operation.

- Notify off-site authorities, in a timely manner, that a recovery operation will be initiated, and indicate any potential impact off-site.

- Designate personnel from the recovery organization to perform the following operations as necessary: posting of controlled areas; application of clearance tags; and decontamination and cleanup activities required to place the facility in an acceptable long-term safe condition.

- Assign personnel to perform further recovery operations, as necessary: performing detailed investigations of the causes of the incident and its consequences, both to the facility and to the environment; evaluating any work required to modify facility equipment; repairing and/or modifying operating systems and/or components; and developing test programs to confirm fitness for return to service of operating systems and/or components affected by the incident.

- Approve any information releases or protective action recommendations to off-site authorities.

EMERGENCY DAMAGE CONTROL (EDC) TEAM

Emergency Damage Control (EDC) Teams can be assembled from the technical staff at the facility or from within the company. Adequate training to meet regulatory requirements is essential to define the extent of the response from these personnel.

The team's major duty is to perform emergency damage control activities. These activities are normal maintenance activities performed under emergency conditions. EDC personnel are generally not involved in activities at the incident scene. All EDC operations are coordinated with the field incident commander to ensure the safety of EDC Teams.

ENGINEERING MANAGER

The engineering manager position should be filled by senior staff responsible for developing and operating all facility engineering systems. This position will interface closely with the Emergency Damage Control director, operations managers, and logistics director.

Major functions, duties, and tasks are show below.

- Coordinate, direct, and respond to requests from the EMRO for engineering, technical, and inspection assistance.

- Coordinate the recall and deployment of engineering support personnel to respond to the incident.

- Ensure timely completion of technical assistance provided in support of emergency response and recovery efforts.

- Supervise and coordinate the retrieval of engineering and technical drawings and documents for the EMRO.

- Ensure on-site records, management support, and record keeping efforts are being carried out.

- Assist the logistics director in the acquisition of additional equipment and supplies, as required.

CLAIMS REPRESENTATIVE

The claims representative position can be filled from staff positions involved in insurance, purchasing, and administration. Careful consideration should be given to addressing this position. It can be critical to ensuring that the needed funds are identified and appropriately disbursed to allow the facility to relocate essential operations and/or continue operations.

Major functions, duties, and tasks are shown below.

- Advise the emergency manager and/or recovery manager, and other personnel regarding the status of on-scene insurance claims activities.

- Coordinate insurance claims activities through the company insurance department.

- Request information regarding any changes in company policy and procedures that may impact claims activities.

- Coordinate the requisition and ordering of insurance claims supplies through the recovery organization.

- Coordinate with the accounting representative, as necessary.

- Coordinate with the law representative as necessary.

- Provide support to the company insurance claims representative and outside insurance claims personnel contracted by the company.

- Help law adviser prepare report on scope and size of potential claims against the company.

- Set up local claims office.

- Meet with affected citizens and communities and explain claims procedures.

- Set up record keeping system for direct claims (loss of income or property damage caused by emergency); indirect claims (loss of income by merchants and companies not directly impacted by emergency); and correspondence.

- Evaluate claims for approval.

- Negotiate claims settlement.

ACCOUNTING DIRECTOR

As with the claims director, the accounting director position is one of importance. The accounting director will facilitate the disbursement of funds to support groups assisting the response, and will audit their invoices for completeness.

Major functions, duties, and tasks are shown below.

- Advise the emergency manager and/or recovery manager and other personnel regarding the status of on-scene accounting activities.

- Coordinate accounting activities through the company accounting department.

- Request guidance and information regarding any changes in company policy and procedures that may impact accounting activities.

- Coordinate the requisition and ordering of accounting-related supplies through the logistics director.

- Coordinate with the company insurance claims representative, as necessary.

- Coordinate with the company law representative, as necessary.

- Provide support to the company accounting department representative and outside accounting personnel contracted by the company.

- Coordinate raw material and product schedule changes.

- Establish bank account and cash arrangements for the response operation. (The bank should be near the emergency site.)

- Prepare general ledger for tracking expenses.

- Work with emergency manager to ensure that contractors are aware of invoice and audit requirements.

- Set up inventory and warehouse control procedures.

- Develop separate books for emergency response, postincident operations, salvage, and transshipment of products.

- Provide cash advances for company employees, as requested.

- Set up record keeping system for contracts, work orders, purchase orders, invoices, and correspondence.

- Identify and request administrative support for field command post.

- Set up charge accounts with local vendors and merchants.

- Provide emergency manager with cost-to-date summary. (A line-item cost breakdown is required.)

- Process invoices and disburse payments.

- Conduct on-site audits to make sure that

    items charged are same as items received;

    contractor-provided labor and equipment is paid for; and

    consultant-provided services are purchased and paid for.

- Provide support for preparing contracts and purchase orders.

- Prepare cost summary for claims representative.

- Coordinate with affiliate counterpart (if applicable).

- Work with accounting manager to set up procedures to authorize and account for expenditures.

- Issue purchase order numbers with a not-to-exceed limit to authorized contractors, merchants, and vendors.

- Arrange for the contractor or carrier to prepare equipment manifest, bills of lading, and papers necessary for clearing customs.

- Determine lodging, food, and transportation requirements for cleanup contractors.

- Set up a purchase order with a hotel to provide meals and lodging for EMRO.

- Prepare contracts with time sheets for contractors and consultants.

- Coordinate field support services with emergency manager.

- Contract observation aircraft for Emergency Operations Center (EOC).

- Set up a field warehouse to store equipment and supplies needed for the response operation.

- Set up maintenance shop for response equipment.

- Receive, verify, and process invoices.

- Conduct inspections to make sure items received meet specifications for items ordered.

- For remote locations, make sure plenty of potable water is provided.

- Keep records of equipment purchased and issued to contractors.

- Recommend termination for contractors and consultants that are no longer needed.

HUMAN RESOURCES REPRESENTATIVE

The human resources representative will be helpful in providing information on personnel, as well as working with the public affairs director in addressing employee and family information issues.

Major functions, duties, and tasks are shown below.

- Establish humanitarian assistance program for company personnel and noncompany on-site personnel affected by the incident.

- Advise the emergency manager and/or recovery manager and other personnel regarding the status of on-scene humanitarian assistance activities.

- Coordinate humanitarian assistance activities through the company human resources department.

- Request guidance and information regarding any changes in company policy and procedures that may impact humanitarian assistance activities.

- Coordinate with the company accounting representative as necessary.

- Coordinate with the company insurance claims representative, as necessary.

- Coordinate with the company law representative, as necessary.

- Activate outside assistance (clergy, psychologists, counselors, etc.), as necessary.

- Provide support to the company human resources department representative and outside assistance (clergy, psychologists, etc.) contracted by the company.

MEDICAL REPRESENTATIVE

A medical representative can be helpful if contaminated personnel are sent to off-site facilities such as hospitals and clinics. The medical representative can help in identifying contamination and treatment issues. This position should be filled by a qualified individual with appropriate training.

Major functions, duties, and tasks are shown below.

- Advise the emergency manager and/or recovery manager and other personnel regarding the status of on-scene medical activities.

- Coordinate medical activities with hospitals and mutual aid organizations as necessary.

- Coordinate with on-scene insurance claims representative as necessary.

- Coordinate the requisition and ordering of medical supplies through the logistics director.

- Coordinate with the company accounting representative as necessary.

- Provide support to outside medical facilities used by the company.

- Provide support to outside medical personnel used by the company.

LAW ADVISER

A law adviser should be designated from the in-house staff or outside legal firm representing the company. Upon activation of any portion of the EMRO, the law adviser should be notified.

Major functions, duties, and tasks are shown below.

- Evaluate legal implications of emergency.

- Confer with other legal representatives, if appropriate.

- Inform emergency manager of potential problems that should be avoided by the EMRO.

- Assist public affairs manager to prepare press releases.

- Review contracts for services and labor.

- Conduct investigation to determine if a third party is responsible for the emergency.

- Maintain log of all contacts and recommendations.

- Monitor operations which have legal implications.

- Advise emergency manager of steps necessary to avoid legal problems.

- Review claims filed against company.

- File claims against other parties to recover costs.

EMERGENCY MANAGEMENT/RESPONSE SUPPORT ORGANIZATIONS

Various local, state, federal, and private emergency management/response organizations that provide personnel, equipment, and other support services are described in this subsection. When personnel from these various agencies/organizations are on company property, they are subject to the authority of the emergency manager, and for reasons of safety and security, they shall commence or cease their actions when so directed by the emergency manager.

Also described are the arrangements that have been made for requesting and effectively utilizing the described assistance and resources, and for accommodating federal, state, and local representatives at the Emergency Operations Center (EOC).

The key local emergency response organizations involved with emergencies at the site will be the county emergency response organizations. These organizations are responsible for implementing protective measures for citizens in their respective counties. Each organization is composed of numerous agencies which perform various duties in response to an emergency. The county should appoint an individual to be in charge of the emergency response organization and to direct the operations of the agencies. Letters of agreement with individual agencies, which delineate their support, should be included in a separate appendix, Letters of Agreement. Each county should have an emergency operations plan and manual of emergency procedures, which are predicated on the county's ability to respond, and which prescribe an emergency response based upon a declared emergency classification.

Listed below are examples of the agencies that need to participate in the emergency management plan.

Obtain an agreement with the county sheriff's departments to support the site emergency response with a commitment of officers and vehicles to assist in evacuation efforts, traffic control, and security. The sheriff's departments should also be responsible for county communications during an emergency condition at the site, including notification of those county officials who form the county emergency response organization. The sheriff's office in each county may provide the primary county Emergency Operations Center (EOC) for that county.

Local fire fighting support is provided to the site via a written agreement with the county volunteer fire department and letters of agreement with other fire fighting agencies. These organizations should be able to respond to the site within approximately 30 minutes with at least one fire truck.

The location of each fire department that has agreed to support the site should be stated in this section of the plan and referenced to specific EPIPs.

Written agreements with ambulance and emergency medical services should describe their support in providing backup assistance to the site to transport injured personnel to a local hospital. The ambulance service should be able to provide one ambulance with an Emergency Medical Technician (EMT) and a paramedic within 30 minutes.

A letter of agreement will be needed from the support hospitals to receive and treat injured personnel from the site who may have been contaminated with hazardous materials and require medical evaluation. The hospital facilities will need to be equipped to be able to treat at least five injured, contaminated persons simultaneously. Backup medical services, support, and definitive care should also be addressed, and a letter of agreement with the support organization and affiliated hospital will be needed. Injured personnel whose medical treatment is not complicated by contamination with hazardous materials may be sent to the local hospital or care facility.

As with the local agencies, all state support agencies that will respond during an emergency should be listed. Typically this will include a lead state agency and several support agencies: state emergency services agency, state department of health, and the state department of public safety.

The U.S. Environmental Protection Agency (EPA), Federal Emergency Management Agency (FEMA), and U.S. Department of Energy (DOE) will be the primary federal agencies responding to an emergency condition at the site.

Additional federal agencies such as the Federal Aviation Administration (FAA), Nuclear Regulatory Commission (NRC), Department of Commerce, Department of Transportation (DOT), and National Weather Service provide ancillary services and support to the primary agencies.

Management of the federal response, which is divided into technical and nontechnical aspects, requires the coordination of the three primary agencies with each other, with the company officials, with the state, and with local agencies. The EPA is responsible for the technical response, FEMA is responsible for the nontechnical response. The overall responsibility is shared by all three primary agencies.

The emergency coordinator or recovery manager should be able to call upon these agencies to support the site emergency response organization. Personnel within the emergency response organization should be assigned responsibilities for coordination of specific activities with the appropriate agency.

A description of the facilities for support of the federal emergency response efforts should be highlighted in this subsection of the plan. These may include listings of airports, motels, and the plant site facility.

The subsection on private support should list the private support organizations as well as public agencies. These organizations should be under contract or have a letter of agreement outlining their services included in the appendix containing the letters of agreement. These organizations may provide services or assistance that are useful to the company in training on-site and off-site emergency response personnel, or in supporting emergency response and reentry and recovery efforts. These services or assistance, which are readily available on a contractual basis, include, but are not limited to, the following: contract environmental services technicians; medical treatment services; hazardous material analysis and accident assessment; engineering analysis; and industry support resources.

Since most of these services and assistance are readily available, letters of agreement and descriptions of these services are not necessarily included in the plan.

SECTION 3: CONCEPT OF OPERATIONS

Section 3, Concept of Operations, describes the Enhanced Incident Command System (EICS), specific EMRO functions, organizational roles at various levels of response, and control elements. This section touches on the governing principles of direction and control during an incident. Included in this section is an overview of incident command philosophy, an introduction to the components of an EICS, and details of how the system is implemented at the specific location. The incident command system (ICS), originally developed as a result of large forest fires in Southern California in 1970, served as a basis for the development and application of the all hazards approach to emergency management/response planning. The ICS has been adapted to apply to the industrial setting, where the affected entities' management structure and response structure have seldom been integrated into a cohesive organization.

The industrial setting evokes a need to provide an EICS, addressing expanded emergency management/response functions and roles associated with industrial incidents. EICS is a flexible system designed to facilitate an integrated response to a variety of postulated incidents. EICS allows for a full range of activities, from planning to response, mitigation, and recovery activities. Figure 3–3 depicts the cycle of activities associated with emergency preparedness. Traditionally, the focus has been on the response activities portion of the figure.

This focus is changing. Management roles are being identified. Public demand for management accountability has increased. Personnel responsible for response are

Emergency Management
and Response
Critical Aspects

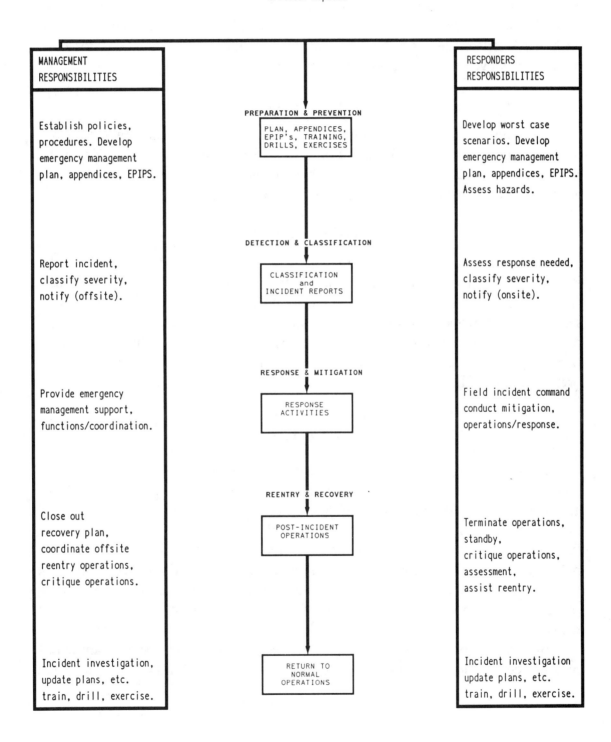

MANAGEMENT RESPONSIBILITIES		RESPONDERS RESPONSIBILITIES
Establish policies, procedures. Develop emergency management plan, appendices, EPIPS.	**PREPARATION & PREVENTION** PLAN, APPENDICES, EPIP's, TRAINING, DRILLS, EXERCISES	Develop worst case scenarios. Develop emergency management plan, appendices, EPIPS. Assess hazards.
Report incident, classify severity, notify (offsite).	**DETECTION & CLASSIFICATION** CLASSIFICATION and INCIDENT REPORTS	Assess response needed, classify severity, notify (onsite).
Provide emergency management support, functions/coordination.	**RESPONSE & MITIGATION** RESPONSE ACTIVITIES	Field incident command conduct mitigation, operations/response.
Close out recovery plan, coordinate offsite reentry operations, critique operations.	**REENTRY & RECOVERY** POST-INCIDENT OPERATIONS	Terminate operations, standby, critique operations, assessment, assist reentry.
Incident investigation, update plans, etc. train, drill, exercise.	RETURN TO NORMAL OPERATIONS	Incident investigation update plans, etc. train, drill, exercise.

Figure 3–3

demanding more management interface and support. Management is compelled to provide more support and play an integral role in the overall response to an incident. Figures 3–4 through 3–7 provide typical organization structures we have developed for clients in the industrial setting. It should be noted that not all of the positions listed on the organization chart may be filled. The functions for each position, however, need to be addressed by the EMRO.

CONCEPT OF OPERATIONS

The subsection concept of operations describes how the emergency response organization will operate in the event of an emergency. In it is a description of the site chain of command, reference to specific emergency response organization positions, and a discussion of the various augmentation organizations.

GOVERNING PRINCIPLES

Another subsection, governing principles, states the objectives and intent of the emergency response program. Any statements on company policy (site, corporate) and off-site policies should be documented here. The governing principles also serve to set the framework for organizational roles and responsibilities. A discussion of organizational control of the emergency response should be included. Separate paragraphs outlining the responsibilities of site, local, state, federal, and corporate organizations will be needed.

DIRECTION AND CONTROL
MINIMUM STAFFING

On-shift staffing and staff augmentation assignments are described in the subsection on direction and control minimum staffing. Details regarding specific duties and responsibilities should be detailed in the EPIPs.

At the onset of an emergency condition at the site, a system designed to ensure that minimum staffing of key positions is assured. This will enable the site personnel to begin shutdown procedures, assess the emergency condition, alert other site personnel, begin the emergency classification process, and determine if staff augmentation is needed. An additional benefit is the reduction of confusion that can result in an emergency.

In addition to the key emergency response personnel, other site organizations may be required to assist in the initial emergency response. These may include site

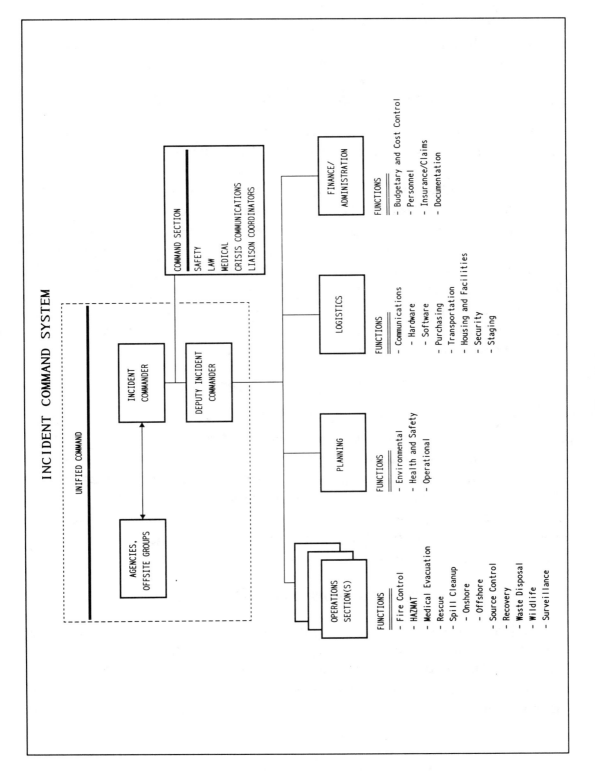

INCIDENT COMMAND SYSTEM

UNIFIED COMMAND

AGENCIES, OFFSITE GROUPS

INCIDENT COMMANDER

DEPUTY INCIDENT COMMANDER

COMMAND SECTION

SAFETY
LAW
MEDICAL
CRISIS COMMUNICATIONS
LIAISON COORDINATORS

OPERATIONS SECTION(S)

FUNCTIONS
- Fire Control
- HAZMAT
- Medical Evacuation
- Rescue
- Spill Cleanup
  - Onshore
  - Offshore
- Source Control
- Recovery
- Waste Disposal
- Wildlife
- Surveillance

PLANNING

FUNCTIONS
- Environmental
- Health and Safety
- Operational

LOGISTICS

FUNCTIONS
- Communications
  - Hardware
  - Software
- Purchasing
- Transportation
- Housing and Facilities
- Security
- Staging

FINANCE/ADMINISTRATION

FUNCTIONS
- Budgetary and Cost Control
- Personnel
- Insurance/Claims
- Documentation

Figure 3-4

operations, site fire brigade, site security, site administrative support, site engineering, and site chemistry.

RESOURCE MANAGEMENT
LONG-TERM AND EXTENDED OPERATIONS

Activation of the site Emergency Response Organization (ERO) generally will result in a response by essentially all personnel normally associated with the site, particularly management and key support personnel. Therefore, within several hours after the initiation of an emergency event, a decision by the emergency coordinator should be made to begin preparations for and to provide for a long-term, augmented emergency response. A subsection on resource management and extended operations describes the activities that should be considered when preparing for a long-term emergency response. This section should also describe the decision-making process for the formation of the recovery organization. Specific instructions for ensuring the continuity of resources, providing the emergency coordinator with authority to obtain the necessary assistance from outside agencies, should be defined in this subsection.

CORPORATE SUPPORT

The emergency coordinator should be designated in the corporate support subsection as the on-site individual responsible for requesting support from the corporate system. To assure that timely support from corporate resources is available to the site during an emergency, a Corporate Emergency Management Plan (CEMP) should be developed. This plan can be inserted into the site emergency plan as a separate appendix, and referenced in this subsection of the site plan. Specific corporate responsibilities (key positions) should be listed as in the subsection describing the key site positions.

SECTION 4: COMMUNICATIONS

Section 4 describes the normal communications and emergency communications systems and provides a summary of key communication elements and their operation. This section deals with communications systems of various types, including computer communications, fire/security systems, telephone systems, and on-site alarm systems.

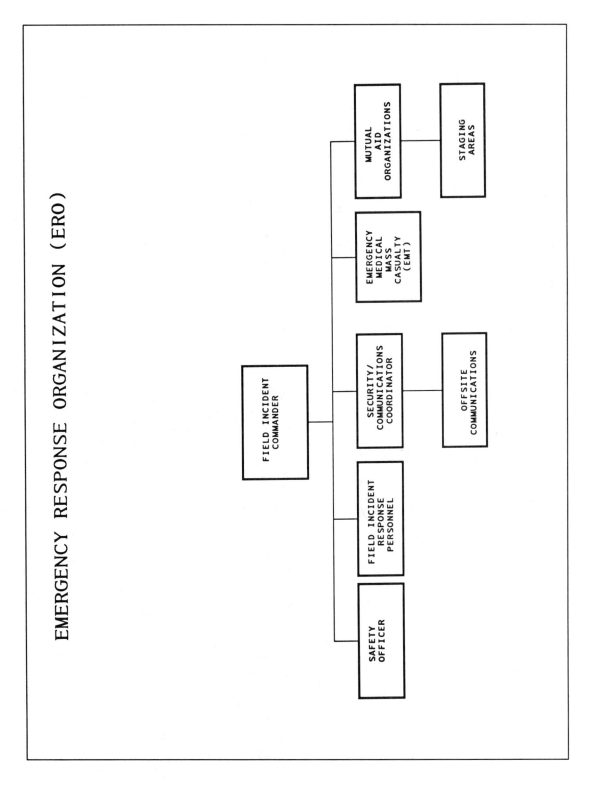

EMERGENCY RESPONSE ORGANIZATION (ERO)

Figure 3–5

EMERGENCY MANAGEMENT ORGANIZATION (EMO)

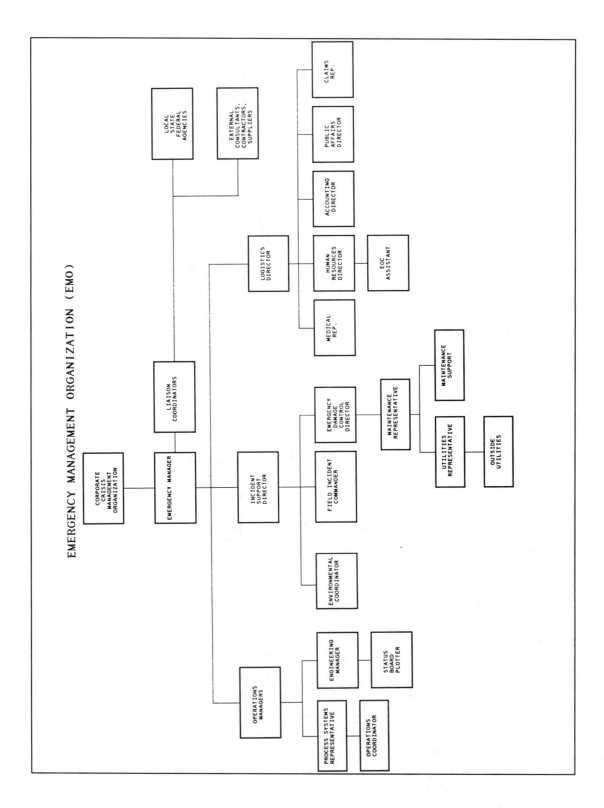

Figure 3-6

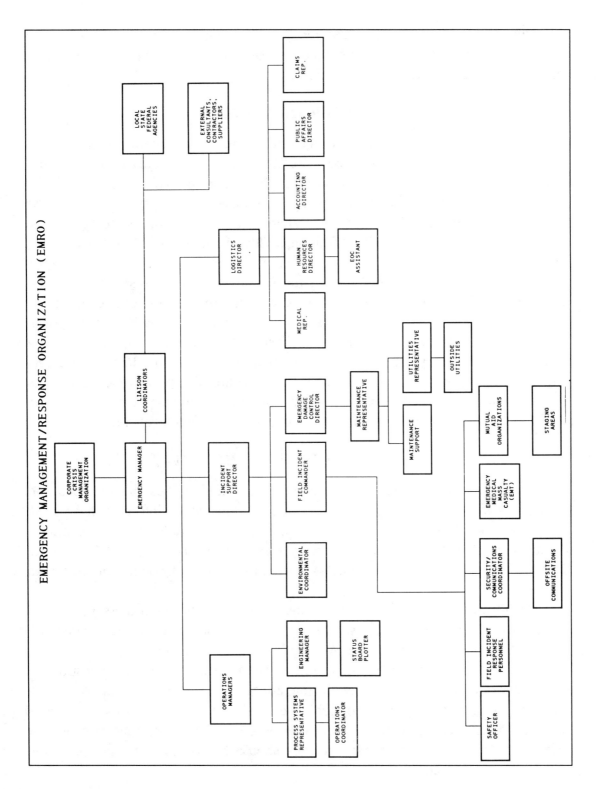

EMERGENCY MANAGEMENT/RESPONSE ORGANIZATION (EMRO)

Figure 3-7

This section also discusses emergency response notification procedures both on-site and off-site, and describes procedures for on-site reporting of injuries, environmental incidents, and radiation incidents.

COMMUNICATIONS LINKS

A comprehensive discussion of the communications system for intra-plant, plant-to-off-site, and off-site emergency communications systems should be addressed in the communications links subsection. Where possible, figures depicting the communications links should be used. Also important will be references to the specific EPIPs that detail emergency communications and record keeping. These will include system use, initial notification, follow-up notification, and continuous communications.

Communications responsibilities for the various emergency response organizations should also be detailed, using tables with information on emergency titles, location and name of organization, and a summary of the communications responsibilities. Separate subsections of this chapter should be allocated to descriptions of the plant page party system, the intra-plant telephone system, the intra-plant sound powered telephone system, the portable radio system, the public telephones, the two-way radio systems, the direct dial systems, the emergency evacuation alarm systems, and the uninterrupted lines to local, state, and federal agencies.

EMERGENCY RESPONSE NOTIFICATION

The emergency response notification subsection describes the methods and procedures by which site personnel will transmit emergency information to local, state, and federal authorities, and subsequently from such authorities to the public. Details required in the initial and follow-up messages and news release formats are described herein. Figure 3–8 delineates a typical sequence of notification during an incident.

Details on the content of the initial and follow-up notification messages should be outlined in separate paragraphs. However, EPIPs should address these communications functions in specific detail. A specific EPIP or instruction should detail the activation of the emergency response organization. This procedure or instruction should contain information such as office telephone number, home telephone number, and beeper number for the personnel assigned to the various emergency response organization positions. Information on the 24-hour telephone numbers for local, state, and federal response agencies should be listed in the plan and the communications procedures.

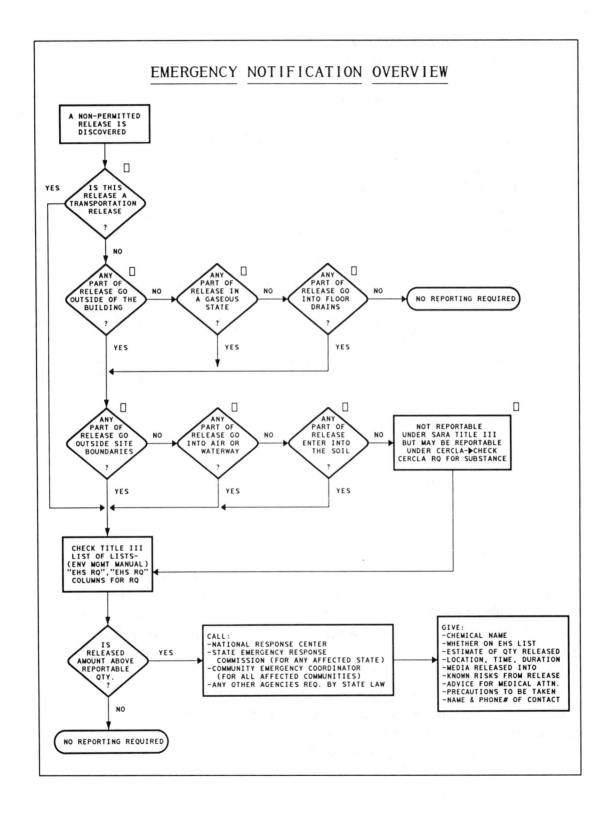

EMERGENCY NOTIFICATION OVERVIEW

A NON-PERMITTED RELEASE IS DISCOVERED

IS THIS RELEASE A TRANSPORTATION RELEASE ? — YES

NO

ANY PART OF RELEASE GO OUTSIDE OF THE BUILDING ? — NO → ANY PART OF RELEASE IN A GASEOUS STATE ? — NO → ANY PART OF RELEASE GO INTO FLOOR DRAINS ? — NO → NO REPORTING REQUIRED

YES / YES / YES

ANY PART OF RELEASE GO OUTSIDE SITE BOUNDARIES ? — NO → ANY PART OF RELEASE GO INTO AIR OR WATERWAY ? — NO → ANY PART OF RELEASE ENTER INTO THE SOIL ? — NO → NOT REPORTABLE UNDER SARA TITLE III BUT MAY BE REPORTABLE UNDER CERCLA▶CHECK CERCLA RQ FOR SUBSTANCE

YES / YES / YES

CHECK TITLE III LIST OF LISTS- (ENV MGMT MANUAL) "EHS RQ","EHS RQ" COLUMNS FOR RQ

IS RELEASED AMOUNT ABOVE REPORTABLE QTY. ? — YES →

CALL:
-NATIONAL RESPONSE CENTER
-STATE EMERGENCY RESPONSE COMMISSION (FOR ANY AFFECTED STATE)
-COMMUNITY EMERGENCY COORDINATOR (FOR ALL AFFECTED COMMUNITIES)
-ANY OTHER AGENCIES REQ. BY STATE LAW

GIVE:
-CHEMICAL NAME
-WHETHER ON EHS LIST
-ESTIMATE OF QTY RELEASED
-LOCATION, TIME, DURATION
-MEDIA RELEASED INTO
-KNOWN RISKS FROM RELEASE
-ADVICE FOR MEDICAL ATTN.
-PRECAUTIONS TO BE TAKEN
-NAME & PHONE# OF CONTACT

NO

NO REPORTING REQUIRED

Figure 3–8

Examples of the subsections are initial notification; verification of initial notification; notification at different emergency classifications; follow-up notifications; public warning; and methods for providing the public information regarding protective action recommendations and measures.

WARNING SYSTEMS AND EMERGENCY PUBLIC NOTIFICATION

The subsection on warning systems should describe the methods and systems that will be used to provide prompt notification and follow-up information to the public. Paragraphs on the following should be applied as appropriate. These are siren systems, tone alert radio systems, sound trucks, and the emergency broadcast system.

SECTION 5: EMERGENCY CLASSIFICATION

Section 5 describes the emergency classification system, accident assessment, and protective action decision-making processes.

The emergency classification system is important as it provides a framework for:

- Notification

- Determining severity of the incident

- Determining the appropriate response

- Determining protective action recommendations

- Assessing damage

- Ensuring the safety of employees and the public

The above list is not meant to be exhaustive; however it serves to illustrate the need for a system to classify emergency conditions. This section also discusses Emergency Planning Zones (EPZs), the areas of focus for planning purposes. For these planning zones, some discussion is given on incident assessment and protective action recommendations. Some guidelines are provided on notification, evacuation, and sheltering.

Section 5 includes a discussion of emergency actions by event classification, with the focus on emergency management, as opposed to emergency response. In this section the groundwork is laid for Enhanced Incident Command, wherein the emergency response organization is freed of unnecessary administrative burden and thus can effectively mitigate the crisis. Section 5 builds on Sections 2, 3, and 4 by defining the function of various EMRO elements, their interrelationships, and their communications tools.

An example of a typical classification system for emergency actions is shown in Table 3–1. Typical systems are based on operational, technical, and hazard analysis data.

The activities demanded by each type of event are described below. Figure 3–9 shows a flowchart of actions by event classification; Figure 3–10 shows the scope of each event.

Table 3-1
Emergency Classification Criteria
Internally Reportable Event

Criteria:	An incident has occurred; however, the incident does not require any notification of off-site or regulatory agencies.
Value:	This classification allows for the tracking of incidents at relatively low levels of severity and can serve to spot trends or areas in need of attention.

Unusual Event

Criteria:	An incident reportable to a regulatory or off-site agency has occurred. The incident may be noticeable from the facility perimeter; however, no outside assistance is required and no evacuation outside the incident scene has occurred.
Value:	This classification allows for immediate reporting of an incident to the appropriate regulatory agencies. It also facilitates the organization's ability to augment its response at relatively low levels of security.

Alert

Criteria:	An incident with the potential to affect nearby off-site locations has occurred. Some outside assistance, such as mutual aid organization response, may be required. Any off-site assistance will generally be limited to a single jurisdiction and agency. The alert does not require off-site protective actions; however, on-site protective actions such as evacuation or sheltering may be implemented.
Value:	This classification allows for early assessment of the potential impact of the incident on off-site locations. Protective action recommendations are developed early to allow for their implementation by the appropriate off-site agencies.

Site Area Emergency

Criteria:	An incident has occurred, and the entire facility, with the exception of critical employees, has been sheltered on-site or evacuated. Off-site areas surrounding the facility may consider implementing protective actions. There is a potential threat to life, health, or property.

Value: This classification allows for early coordination of protective actions with the site and off-site locations. The geographic scope is expanded. Coordination and communications with off-site agencies is enhanced.

General Emergency

Criteria: An incident has occurred with off-site consequences. The affected community is implementing protective actions. Serious hazards or severe threat to life, health, and property exist. There may be a large geographic impact.

Value: This classification allows for immediate implementation of protective actions by off-site locations. Extensive resource management and allocation can be accomplished under a unified command structure.

INTERNALLY REPORTABLE EVENT

An internally reportable event is a small or minor incident that has occurred but does not meet the reporting criteria established for notification of off-site authorities.

When an internally reportable event occurs, the following actions are taken by the responsible party:

- The on-shift emergency manager and field incident commander will classify the incident in accordance with site EPIPs.

- On-site personnel will notify their supervision of the incident.

- The on-shift emergency manager and field incident commander will determine if additional staff are to be notified.

- The affected area supervisor will notify appropriate management and brief them on the situation.

- The event will be closed out with a log entry on an appropriate report in accordance with EPIPs and should be posted to the appropriate authority.

UNUSUAL EVENT

An unusual event is an incident which may be noticeable or detectable off-site but which presents no off-site threat. No outside assistance is required and no protective actions off-site are needed.

When an unusual event occurs, the following actions are taken by the responsible party:

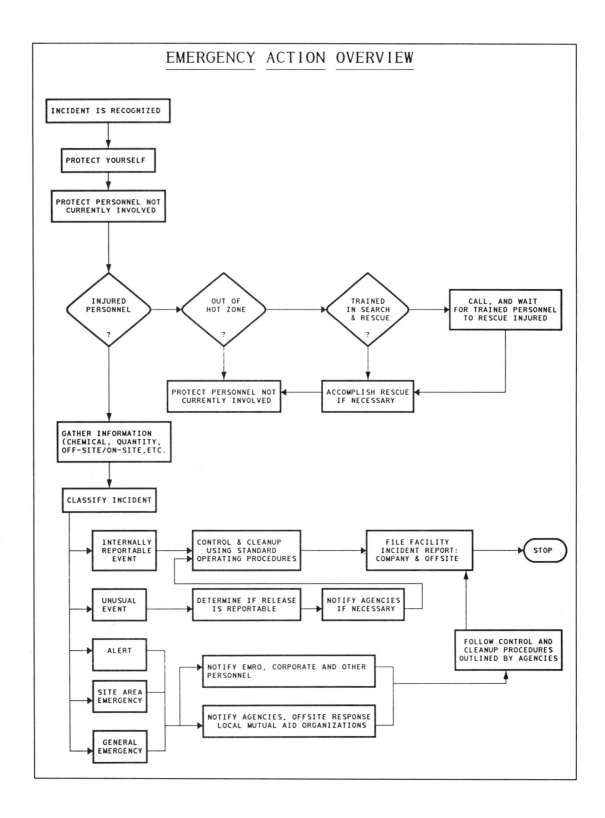

Figure 3–9

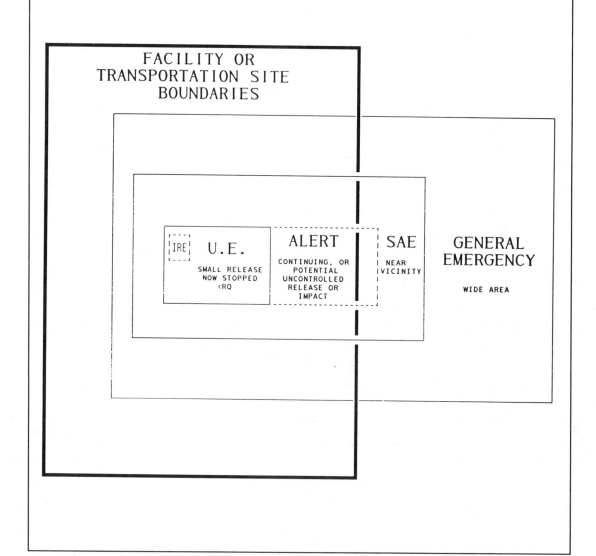

EMERGENCY CLASSIFICATION SYSTEM

BASED ON AREA OF IMPACT OR POTENTIAL IMPACT,
SEVERITY OF INJURIES AND IF PEOPLE OUTSIDE COMPANY ARE INJURED

FACILITY OR
TRANSPORTATION SITE
BOUNDARIES

IRE

U.E.

SMALL RELEASE
NOW STOPPED
<RQ

ALERT

CONTINUING, OR
POTENTIAL
UNCONTROLLED
RELEASE OR
IMPACT

SAE

NEAR
VICINITY

GENERAL
EMERGENCY

WIDE AREA

Figure 3–10

- The on-shift emergency manager and field incident commander classify the incident in accordance with EPIPs and activate the facility EMRO as needed.

- The affected area supervisor will complete appropriate report forms.

- The on-shift emergency manager and/or field incident commander will ensure that the incident support director is notified of the emergency classification and actions underway.

- The on-shift emergency manager and/or field incident commander will determine if additional staff are to be notified.

- The incident support director will notify the appropriate operations manager and brief him/her on the situation.

- For unusual operations procedures, refer to the EPIPs developed for these circumstances.

- The event will be closed out with a log entry on an appropriate report in accordance with the EPIPs and will be posted to the appropriate personnel. No further action will be required, with the exception of filing completed forms.

ALERT

At the alert classification, an incident has occurred and is not under control, but poses no threat to off-site locations.

When an alert occurs, all the actions associated with an unusual event are taken. As appropriate, the following additional actions are taken:

- The incident support director, or a qualified individual he designates, must call the appropriate company off-site personnel notifying them of the classifications and the actions underway.

- The field incident commander will ensure that mutual aid organizations are updated on the incident.

- Personnel assigned to the EMRO will be activated as prescribed in EPIPs.

- The incident support director may, at his discretion, contact the following EMRO staff and advise that they respond to the Emergency

Operations Center: the environmental coordinator, the public affairs director, and the emergency damage control director.

- The incident support director will notify the facility manager and advise him of the situation.

- The facility manager may, at his discretion, notify the rest of the facility management council and advise that they respond to the Emergency Operations Center to assume their emergency positions.

- The EOC assistant, status board plotter, and other EOC staff will:

  1. Prepare for EOC activation in accordance with EPIPs

  2. Test emergency communications systems

  3. Alert senior EOC staff and place them on standby for possible activation

  4. Obtain and post current weather information

  5. Review their emergency response duties, EPIPs, Emergency Management Plan and other supporting documentation and reference material

  6. Monitor ongoing incident status

SITE AREA EMERGENCY/GENERAL EMERGENCY

A site area emergency is a serious emergency that is not under control. Protective actions by off-site personnel may be required. A general emergency is defined as a severe emergency that is not under control and will require the affected community to implement protective actions. For these levels of emergency, the emergency management agency of the local community will be activated and become involved in implementing any required protective action for the affected community.

When a site area emergency or general emergency is declared, the following actions, in addition to those performed at lower emergency classifications, will take place:

- The facility EMRO will be fully activated so all emergency response facilities are staffed and operational.

- The incident support director and/or facility manager will notify the off-site emergency management agencies, informing the agencies that they will be the primary on-site contact. They may also wish to notify the Federal Aviation Administration (FAA) to clear the air space around the facility and prevent news agencies or other groups from dispatching aircraft near the affected zone.

- The field incident commander or his designee will prepare to assist mutual aid organizations in establishing mutual aid zones of control.

- Appropriate departments will respond to directives to evacuate or shelter as prescribed by the field incident commander.

- The public affairs director will activate the news center, remote media facility, employee injury/fatality tracking center, and rumor control system.

- The facility manager will remain in close contact with company management to provide additional briefings as dictated by the incident.

- EOC staff will gather field status reports from operational departments on an hourly basis. If deemed necessary, a shorter period may be implemented.

- The public affairs director will issue media briefings as necessary throughout the emergency, in accordance with prescribed EPIPs.

- Field and EOC staff will continue to monitor the incident.

- Based on the best available information provided by hazardous materials reference guides and technical experts on the scene, the field incident commander will advise the facility manager on the perceived need to implement protective actions. The decision to implement these actions will be transmitted to the appropriate off-site emergency management agencies.

- If off-site protective actions are warranted, the incident will be classified as a general emergency. If the nature of the incident warrants identification as worst-case scenario, response will be in accordance with EPIPs addressing worst-case scenario response.

- Following the completion of any necessary unit evacuation, a controlled ingress/egress point will be established.

- The public affairs director will continue to issue media releases from the news center as the situation warrants.

- EOC staff will coordinate with the appropriate mutual aid organizations to track patient transfer from affected areas to appropriate medical facilities.

- The environmental coordinator will coordinate with appropriate state and federal agencies and industrial representatives regarding ongoing scene assessment and air quality monitoring.

- Following a determination that a hazardous condition no longer exists, the emergency manager will recommend a downgrade in classification.

- Following the downgrade recommendation, the emergency manager will announce a staged reentry process to any evacuated areas. This reentry will be in accordance with EPIPs for reentry and recovery operations.

- Upon determination to allow unrestricted reentry, the emergency manager will terminate the emergency classification.

- The recovery support director will monitor the progress of cleanup activities, until such activities have been completed.

- The facility manager will ensure that reports are filed with the appropriate agencies, following the conclusion of the emergency.

EMERGENCY PLANNING ZONES (EPZS)

EPZs are the areas for which planning is needed to assure that prompt and effective actions can be taken to protect the public in an emergency. The size of the EPZ represents a judgment based upon detailed planning performed to assure an adequate response.

Dependent upon the severity of the incident, protective actions will generally be limited to operations in designated sectors; should the need arise, actions can be undertaken for the entire zone.

EPZs should be developed to assist the EMRO in determining protective action recommendations for the potential off-site consequences of an incident. The EPZ will vary in size according to the material involved. However, a 360° area should be established. This planning zone should be subdivided into sectors, either according to terrain features, noticeable boundaries (roads, fence lines, etc.), or into 22½° sectors. In this way the EMRO can plot the path of a plume and relate it to specific areas. As discussed in the facility hazard analysis, the EPZ size and area of coverage should be selected based upon knowledge of the potential consequences, timing, and release characteristics of a spectrum of incidents, regardless of their extremely low probability of occurrence. Figure 3–11 depicts EPZs as associated with the five classifications.

The size of the zone is based primarily on the following considerations:

- Projected release estimates for most incidents will not exceed exposure Protective Action Guide (PAG) levels outside the zone.

- Detailed planning within this area will provide a substantial base for expansion of response efforts in the unlikely event expansion is necessary.

- Planning within this area recognizes all the jurisdictional restraints imposed by the zone designation.

Major industries and special population facilities located near the facility should be listed and shown on maps.

INCIDENT ASSESSMENT

The initial response to any emergency condition at the facility should be based upon an assessment of the severity of the emergency condition. All abnormal events observed in or near the facility should be immediately reported by facility personnel. Figures 3–11 through 3–14 depict workpapers that can be used to classify the severity of an incident.

Upon receipt of the telephone call, appropriate actions for response can be initiated by the on-shift emergency manager.

Assessment activities can be subdivided into two phases.

Initial incident assessment consists of:

- Identification of the emergency condition

- Classification

- Notification (site, off-site, emergency response organization)

- Recommendation of initial protective actions

Ongoing incident assessment may include, as appropriate:

- Computer assessment of incident conditions

- Meteorological data assessment

- Effluent release data assessment

- Atmospheric dispersion calculations

- Environmental pathway assessments

- Assessment of on-site conditions

- Assessment of off-site conditions

- Environmental and industrial hygiene monitor data

PROTECTIVE ACTION RECOMMENDATIONS

Protective actions are measures taken to protect emergency workers, site personnel, and the public, based upon classification of the severity of the emergency and its potential effects with regard to health and safety. Protective action recommendations from the facility require prompt notification of off-site agencies and the public regarding the emergency situation. Typical protective action recommendations from the facility may include, but are not limited to:

- Evacuation

- Sheltering

- Respiratory protection

- Protective clothing

- Restrictions on foodstuffs/water

The protective action recommendations listed in the Emergency Management Plan are generally concerned with minimizing the exposure of the general public to deposition from or inhalation of an airborne plume. In some cases, however, the recommendations may also concern liquid spills or serious fire/explosion hazards.

The off-site emergency management agency director has the final

INCIDENT REPORTING SYSTEM FORM

Message #:_____

Page 1 of 1

1) COMPANY NAME, FACILITY, INCIDENT LOCATION and
   BRIEF DESCRIPTION of EVENT:

   _____
   _____
   _____
   _____
   _____
   _____
   _____
   _____

2) STATUS: Actual Event _____
            Drill   _____
            Terminated   _____

3) CLASSIFICATION:

   (IRE) ____
   (UE) ____
   (A)   ____
   (SAE) ____
   (GE) ____

4) TIME DECLARED:_____(a.m./p.m.)

5) INCIDENT INFORMATION:
Hazardous Material Involved (Yes) (No)
Trade/Common Name:_____
_____
Chemical Name:_____
_____

INCIDENT

INCIDENT CLASSIFIABLE — NO → ABNORMAL OPERATING PROCEDURES → CLOSEOUT — NO

YES ↓   CLOSEOUT — YES → END

INTERNALLY REPORTABLE EVENT

UNUSUAL EVENT

ALERT

SITE AREA EMERGENCY

GENERAL EMERGENCY

CLOSE OUT WITH LOG ENTRY

Activate EMRO   (EC) _____
Call Agencies   (EC) _____

EPA EXTREMELY HAZARDOUS SUBSTANCE LIST (Yes) (No)
PROTECTIVE ACTION RECOMMENDATION:(Evacuate) (Shelter) (Restrict Foodstuffs)(See DOT Emergency Response Guidebook)
HEALTH RISK/MEDICAL ADVICE: (Refer to MSDS)(See DOT Emergency Response Guidebook)
FATALITIES: (Yes) (No) Number:_____   INJURIES: (Yes) (No) Number:_____

TYPE OF RELEASE: (Gas) (Vapor) (Liquid) RELEASE MEDIUM: (Air) (Land) (Water) ESTIMATED QUANTITY:_____(Gal./Lb.)

RELEASE TO ENVIRONMENT: (None) (Potential) (Occuring) (Terminated)

WIND DIRECTION (From): A: North B: Northeast C: Northwest D: South E: Southeast F: Southwest G: West H: East

AGENCIES NOTIFIED: REMARKS:_____
Facility EMRO:_____ LEPC:_____ MUTUAL AID :_____   _____
Fire Dept. :_____ SERC:_____ OTHER(list):_____
Police Dept. :_____ NRC :_____ _____   _____

          Initial Call:_____(Time) Print Name:_____ Title:_____

FIGURE 13 Follow-up Call:_____(Mins) Signature:_____ Date:_____

Figure 3–11

decision-making authority regarding off-site protective actions, and is responsible for the implementation of those actions. Other officials, upon request from the local authority, may provide assistance to ensure proper implementation of these actions. The facility has no authority to impose or enforce protective response options beyond its boundaries.

The protective action decision-making process requires an understanding of the emergency classification system as well as the types of protective actions discussed in this section. An EPIP, Protective Action Recommendation Guides, should be developed to provide some of the guidance used to determine protective actions at the facility.

Deciding which area requires protective actions will depend on several variables, each of which will have to be evaluated at the time of an incident. The most significant variables include the facility process conditions and existing meteorological conditions.

EVACUATION

Evacuation of the population-at-risk is the most effective protective action. Off-site emergency management plans should detail off-site protective action decision making and implementation. The decision to recommend an evacuation requires that several influencing factors be considered; these include, but are not limited to:

- Timeliness of the recommendation

- Time required for evacuation to be complete

- Plume arrival and plume passage time

- Protection offered by buildings, shelters, or other structures

EPIPs for on-site evacuation should outline the criteria and method for partial or total evacuation of the facility. The procedure is based on several variables, including the type and quantity of the hazardous material released, the area subject to evacuation, various areas of congregation of the evacuees, and various methods to notify refinery personnel that an evacuation will take place.

An appendix on evacuation routes contained in the emergency management plan should provide site and facility maps for evacuation.

Since there are several variables involved in the evacuation procedure, it is evident that the situation will dictate the need for and extent of any evacuation.

FIXED FACILITY
EMERGENCY CLASSIFICATION SYSTEM

	Safety Injury/Fatality Protective Action	Environmental Impacts	Facility Status	Geographic Area/Location	Commodity Quantity (RQ) Volume & Toxicity	Meteorological Conditions/ Considerations	Response Capability/ Actions
UNUSUAL EVENT	Minor first aid treatment. Presents no threat. No PAR	Non-environmentally sensitive area.	Minor disruption to system. Facility shutdown facility systems	May be visible from facility boundaries.	Minor material release. Not Reportable	Not a factor.	Minimum ERO activation. notifications.
ALERT	Local area near scene evacuation. Injuries require EMS/hospital care.	Release on water. Potential impact to environmentally sensitive area.	operational. Affects facility/location operations.	In or near populated area. Media involved.	Reportable release.	Potential to influence release and/or plume coverage. Potential to impact response time.	ERO fully activated. EMO partially activated.
SITE AREA EMERGENCY	Injury/Fatality (single/multiple) Company personnel. PAR for emergency workers.	Environmentally sensitive area impacted. Major impact to environmentally sensitive areas.	Significant impact on operations.	Impacts large geographic area. Population impact. Media involved.	Release reportable, with voluntary callout of national spill response contractor.	Impacts response activities. Impacts release zone.	EMRO activated. External support activated. Agencies respond/ takeover command of operations.
GENERAL EMERGENCY	Injury/Fatality (single/multiple) Non-company and/or general public. PAR for general public.	Natural resources habitat impact.	Major impact on operations. Long-term cleanup required.	Interdicts major population group. Infrastructure (roadway, rail, waterway, etc.) impacted	Worst case scenario event/ discharge.	Significant impact on response activity Significant impact on plume zone coverage.	

Note: All seven columns do not have to be satisfied for a particular classification to be invoked.
Outside assistance may be required at any classification level.
PAR = Protective Action Recommendations

Figure 3-12

This decision will be made by the field incident commander and/or emergency manager, and will include the following:

- Areas to be evacuated

- Distance to be evacuated from the leak, spill, or other hazard

- Who, if anyone, will remain to take control of the emergency

Personnel need to be notified and instructed on appropriate actions to be taken. Each unit of the facility should develop Standard Operating Instructions (SOI) for specific unit actions.

If evacuation is necessary, the following guidelines are to be followed, along with instructions from the emergency response organization that will determine the safest and quickest route for personnel movement to assigned assembly areas. Note that:

- The quickest route may not be the safest.

- In the event of a toxic vapor release, always move upwind and/or at a 90° angle.

- Report to the assembly area designated by your supervisor. If no instructions are provided, select the safest preassigned area and proceed to that area.

Since the objective of evacuation is to protect the health of the threatened population, the main goal will be to safely move the population out of the threatened area. Transportation for evacuees should be considered. Commercial and/or private transportation may be required to move the population-at-risk. Prior to and during evacuation, the evacuation routes in the Emergency Planning Zone (EPZ) will have to be surveyed to ensure that routes are passable.

SHELTERING

Sheltering involves members of the population-at-risk seeking shelter in homes and/or buildings. It is specifically noted that, while evacuation (if accomplished before plume passage) minimizes chances of exposure, it also entails certain risks of injury and inconvenience. Consequently, serious consideration should be given to sheltering, if the desired result is reduction of population exposure to hazards. Sheltering is suitable as a protective action alone, or may be used in lieu of evacuation in two cases:

TRANSPORTATION EMERGENCY CLASSIFICATION SYSTEM

	Safety Injury/Fatality Protective Action	Environmental Impacts	Property Damage	Geographic Area/Location	Commodity Quantity (RQ) Volume & Toxicity	Meteorological Conditions/ Considerations	Response Capability/ Actions
UNUSUAL EVENT	Minor first aid treatment. Driver only. Presents no threat. No PAR.	Non-environmentally sensitive area.	Power equipment only, drivable.	May be visible to public.	No product is released. Not reportable.	Not a factor.	Driver and Supervisor. no notifications.
ALERT	Driver only. May need emergency room treatment.	Release on water. Potential impact to environmentally sensitive area.	Power equipment only, not drivable.	In or near populated area. Media involved.	DOT reportable release.	Potential to influence release and/or plume coverage. Potential to impact response time.	Driver and Supervisor. no HAZMAT team necessary. Local HAZMAT Team onscene.
SITE AREA EMERGENCY	Injury/fatality (single/multiple). Company only. PAR for emergency workers at the incident scene.	Environmentally sensitive area impacted. Major impact to environmentally sensitive areas.	Product vessel damage or minor containment loss. Immediate area impacted.	Impacts large geographic area. Population impact. Media involved.	DOT reportable release, with voluntary callout of HAZMAT or local spill response contractor.	Impacts response activities. Impacts release zone.	EMRO activated. company in charge at scene.
GENERAL EMERGENCY	Injury/fatality (single/multiple). Non-company and/or general public. PAR for general public in the vicinity of the incident scene.	Natural resources habitat impact.	Product vessel containment loss. wide area impact. extended cleanup.	Interdicts major population group infrastructure. (roadway, rail, waterway, etc.) impacted.	Worst case scenario event/ discharge.	Significant impact on response activity. Significant impact on plume zone coverage.	Agencies respond/ take over command of operations.

Note: All seven columns do not have to be satisfied for a particular classification to be invoked. Outside assistance may be required at any classification level.

PAR = Protective Action Recommendations

Figure 3-13

- Severe incidents when an evacuation cannot be implemented because of inadequate lead time due to the rapid passage of the plume ("puff" release)

- When local constraints such as inclement weather or road conditions dictate that sheltering is more feasible and effective than evacuation

While evacuation is preferred, some refinery buildings can become secured facilities, allowing occupants to shelter in place *if evacuation cannot be accomplished in the available time.* A building is secure when the doors and windows are closed, and ventilation/air conditioning systems, or other systems that would force or induce outside air into the building, are shut down. Shelter-in-place procedures/facilities are described in the EPIP on sheltering.

SECTION 6: EMERGENCY FACILITIES AND EQUIPMENT

Section 6 describes any on-site and off-site emergency facilities available to the EMRO. A brief overview of available emergency equipment can also be provided. The emergency equipment, emergency facilities, and any maintenance schedules are addressed in detail in Appendix P and associated EPIPs. The overview of various emergency response facilities, includes:

- Mobile command center

- Incident support center

- Emergency Operations Center (EOC)

- Staging areas

This section also describes emergency response equipment owned and operated by the location, or equipment available from contractors. The types of equipment discussed include:

- Fire fighting equipment

- Spill containment equipment

- Decontamination and cleanup equipment

- Portable test equipment

- Personal protective equipment

PIPELINE COMPANY
EMERGENCY CLASSIFICATION SYSTEM

	Safety Injury/Fatality Protective Action	Environmental Impacts	Pipeline System Status	Geographic Area/Location	Commodity Quantity (RO) Volume & Toxicity	Meteorological Conditions/Considerations	Response Capability/Actions
UNUSUAL EVENT	Minor first aid treatment. Presents no threat. No PAR.	Non-environmentally sensitive area.	Minor disruption to system. System shutdown pipeline system operational.	May be visible from ROW/site boundaries.	Minor material release. Not reportable.	Not a factor.	Minimum ERO activation. notifications.
ALERT	Local area near scene evacuation. Injuries require EMS/Hospital care.	Outage on water. Potential impact to environmentally sensitive area.	Affects pipeline/ facility/location operations.	In or near populated area. Media involved.	Reportable release.	Potential to influence release and/or plume coverage. Potential to impact response time.	ERO fully activated. EMO partially activated.
SITE AREA EMERGENCY	Injury/Fatality (single/multiple) Company personnel PAR for Emergency workers.	Environmentally sensitive area impacted.	Significant impact on operations.	Impacts large geographic area. Population impact. Media involved.	Reportable release, with voluntary callout of national spill response contractor.	Impacts response activities. Impacts release zone.	EMRO activated. External support activated.
GENERAL EMERGENCY	Injury/fatality (single/multiple) Non-Company and/or general public. PAR for general public.	Major impact to environmentally sensitive areas. Natural resources habitat impact.	Major impact on operations. Long-term cleanup required.	Interdicts major population group infrastructure. (roadway, rail, waterway, etc.) impacted.	Worst case scenario event/ discharge.	Significant impact on response activity. Significant impact on plume zone coverage.	Agencies respond/ take over command of operations.

Note: All seven columns do not have to be satisfied for a particular classification to be invoked. Outside assistance may be required at any classification level.

PAR = Protective Action Recommendations

ROW = Right-of-Way

Figure 3-14

Section 6 also briefly touches on the Hazardous Materials Identification System (HMIS) in use by the location, which is used to help pick appropriate protective equipment for personnel safety during an incident.

SECTION 7: PUBLIC INFORMATION

Section 7 describes the basic approach to public notification and public information releases during emergency conditions. Emergency news releases and instructions for the spokespersons are also discussed. This section introduces the concepts needed for effective communication to the community-at-large during incidents which may impact them. Included in this section are topics on:

- Emergency notification

- Public notification

- Facilities (news center, rumor control, etc.)

- Company guidelines (clearances, etc.)

Getting the facts out to the public is one of the fundamental tenets of emergency management. Regardless of how well an incident is handled, in fact, the *perception* of the public will depend on how well-informed they are, and how timely the information is. This section deals with the general aspects of information management to the public.

PUBLIC INFORMATION PROGRAM

The public information program should be developed to inform and educate the public within the area around the plant site that has been assessed as having potential for being impacted by an emergency. This program can be very effective when coordinated with the local response agencies and authorities.

An information package should be developed and distributed at least annually to the affected population. This package should contain generic information about the plant, the emergency response program and where to call for more information. Mailing lists for the package can be coordinated with the telephone company, electric utility office, and local authorities.

The public information program should also contain specific information regarding protective action and actions the public should take in the event of notification of an emergency. Information on sheltering and other protective actions, evacuation maps, and lists of radio and television stations to tune to in the event of an emergency should be included. A list of telephone numbers to call for information, such as the sheriff's department or rumor control, may be included in this package.

Self-addressed mailers for the handicapped or special care facilities should be developed and distributed. This subsection should describe the plan and procedures for maintaining the documentation in a secure and restricted access location. Revisions to the public information package should be made as often as needed.

Transient populations in the affected area should be addressed in this chapter also. Plans should be described for the posting of information in public areas, such as post office, telephone booths, telephone books, and recreation areas.

A description of the evacuation routes and the posting of signs indicating these routes should be provided in this chapter and in the public information packages. Occasional public meetings, designed to answer questions of the local residents, should be planned for and encouraged.

Depending on the size and scope of the anticipated crisis, plans should be developed to provide facilities for the news media, have enough trained spokespersons, and set up an internal network to obtain accurate information regarding questions from the media.

Considerations for the news center should be described. These will include:

- An adequate number of telephones connected to outside lines

- Electrical outlets for radio and television equipment

- Desks, typewriters, and stationery supplies

- Transportation to and from the news center

- Foodstuffs and other logistical considerations

A high-level spokesperson should be available for important on-the-record news conferences, interviews, and statements. In addition, the plan should address the need for lower level spokespersons to provide background information and guidance to the reporters, and to assist them and their technical crews in moving about the property.

Senior public relations executives, legal counselors, and other appropriate officials should be on hand for consultation. In addition, a network of information sources should be established throughout the affected areas, including sources in outside agencies.

JOINT NEWS CENTER OPERATIONS

This subsection of the chapter describes the activation and operation of the joint news center. It is advisable to colocate the site news center with the local, state, and federal authorities. In this way a coordinated and unified presence will be presented. This will also reduce the potential for confusion resulting from inaccurate flow of information.

Specific EPIPs should be developed to augment the discussion presented in this chapter. These EPIPs will help the personnel assigned to the news center in the activation and operation of the center.

RUMOR CONTROL

This subsection describes the activation and operation of the rumor control center. It is advisable that dedicated telephone lines be provided to the rumor control center. These lines should be accessible to the public. In this way a channeling of the flow of information can be accomplished while not interfering with the emergency response organization's efforts to mitigate the emergency. The rumor control center should receive all of the news releases from the site and joint news center. Personnel should have specific instruction to respond to questions with the information available and not to speculate. Specific EPIPs should be developed to detail the information discussed in this subsection.

NEWS MEDIA

During an emergency the news media will have to be controlled. This subsection of the plan describes the methods for controlling access and movement of the media. It should be emphasized that the control aspect is intended for the safety of the media, and not for limiting their access to information.

SECTION 8: POST-INCIDENT OPERATIONS

Section 8 describes the reentry and recovery aspects of the plan. Detailed in this section are the recovery organization, post-incident operations, incident investigation, and humanitarian assistance aspects of the plan.

Areas covered in this section include:

- Recovery plan

- Reentry operations

- Recovery operations

- Recovery organization

- Humanitarian assistance

- Outside support

Humanitarian assistance operations are introduced in this section, as they apply to employees and the general public. A recovery organization is formed when the emergency has been mitigated, and this organization derives its structure from the Emergency Management Organization (EMO). The focus of this organization is on effective recovery from the crisis. The areas of concern for this group include process operations, both short term and long term, and the human factors which emerge as a result of the crisis.

The purpose of reentry and recovery operations is to:

- Determine the extent of damage/cleanup required

- Restore the affected area to operational conditions

- Remove contaminants and other hazardous materials

This subsection on reentry also describes the recovery organization. The recovery organization should be composed of on-site and off-site personnel. The emergency plan should detail the key positions in the recovery organization, describing their functions, duties, and tasks. Interfaces should be depicted by using diagrams or charts to depict the interfaces.

A subsection should be devoted to the concept of operations, including:

- Activation

- Organizational structure

- Method of operations

- EPIPs

A plan for the documentation of the investigative follow-ups should be outlined. Key paragraphs in this subsection should include:

- Affected population

- Extent of damage

- Long-term health care concerns

- Extent of cleanup effort

- Plan for cleanup

- Reentry of evacuated populations

- Interfaces with other groups

- Reentry operations

- Techniques for spill containment and cleanup

- Resources for cleanup and disposal

- Recovery operations

- Recovery organization and plan

The documentation and investigation effort should be conducted with the support of the off-site organizations to the extent possible.

In addition to the documentation and preparation for reentry and recovery operations, you should consider the following nonoperational issues as you develop this section of the Emergency Management Plan. You should establish and maintain a separate facilities recovery and business resumption plan. As with the Emergency Management Plan you should construct this plan with appendices and EPIPs as support and implementation documents.

Information you may want to consider when preplanning reentry and recovery operations:

1. Facilities recovery plan

   Activation procedures

   Emergency Operations Center (EOC)

   Facilities recovery team telephone list

   General office occupancy list—by floor

   General office contact list—by floor

   Assigned recovery sites

      Floor-by-floor site assignments and requirements

Company/department site assignments

Floor plan of room assignments in [recovery site] building

Facilities and services departments

Facility recovery requirements, by floor

2. Relocation sites for shared quarters

Assigned relocation sites

Floor-by-floor site assignments and requirements

Company/department site assignments

Floor plan of room assignments in relocation site building

Facilities and services departments

Facility relocation requirements, by floor

3. Specialty furniture and equipment requirements

Listing of requirements

4. Special purpose rooms or areas

Requirements for rooms or areas

Requirements for locked rooms or security areas

5. Building documents/records required in emergency

Architectural drawings and blueprints

Lease information

Floorplans

6. Emergency teams—name of members and designated responsibilities

List of emergency services and responsibilities

Facilities recovery plan manager

Facilities recovery operations team

    Manager leasing

    Administration group

    Security group

    Operations group

    Architectural services group

    Leasing group

    Tape retrieval group

    Audiovisual equipment group

    Surface transportation group

    Aviation group

    Performance and cost management group

    Information services group

    Computer equipment acquisition group

    Meeting services group

    Executive services facilitator

7. Services

    Copy/office machine services

    Forms design and distribution

    Inactive records retrieval

    Library services

    Lodging and travel arrangements

    Mail services

Photography

Real estate

Records restoration

Reprographics

Mail services

Photography

Records restoration

Inactive records retrieval

Tape retrieval

Copy/office machine services

Reprographics

Forms design and distribution

Library services

Lodging and travel services

8. Critical requirements checklists and questionnaire

Critical requirements questionnaire

Departmental business resumption contacts

Hazard potential analysis: Floor-by-floor listing of critical requirements and recovery locations for each critical business function

9. Personnel skills requirements

Secretarial/clerical

Administrators/analysts

Security officers

Operations personnel

    Building engineers

    Maintenance supervisors and carpenters

    Electricians

    Painters

    Laborers

    Furniture specialists

    Carpet installers

    Safety and environmental specialists

    Telephone system specialists

Architects/designers/CAD technicians

Transactional real estate people

Restoration contractor list

10. Public sector contacts

    City of [YOUR LOCATION]

    [YOUR LOCATION] County

    State of [YOUR LOCATION]

    Federal government

11. Telephone/utility company contacts

    Telephone companies

    Electric utilities

    Gas utilities

12. Forms and supplies

Incident report form

EOC activation form

EOC emergency situation log

Damage assessment form

Emergency acquisitions form (purchase order)

Insurance claim form

Listings of [YOUR COMPANY] forms and supplies

13. Associated plans and information

Prefire plan

Drawings

Environmental, health, and safety manual

Humanitarian assistance plan

Purchasing acquisition plans

Telecommunications plan

Crisis communications plan

Security communications

Law department plan

Insurance and risk management plan

Treasury contingency cash plan

Controller's system for tracking recovery expenses

Community maps

Newspapers and radio and television stations

Vendor/supplier/consultant list

Floorspace alternatives outside main office

Business recovery center

Local hotels

Mass transit information

Landlords and noncompany tenants

Stress management/monitoring guidelines

Performance and cost management

Property operations

Building administration

Building operations

Building protection services

Communications facilities and services

Design and construction services

Tape retrieval

Library/information center

Meeting and travel services

Forms administration

Forms and records storage center

Graphic services

Mail service

Records planning, storage, and retrieval

SECTION 9: MAINTAINING EMERGENCY PREPAREDNESS

Section 9 describes the responsibility for training, the training program, and drill and exercise programs. This section focuses on the training, drill, and exercise program needed to maintain the proficiency of the EMRO. It also assigns responsibility for the training, drill, and exercise program needed to maintain readiness.

General details for training are provided here, with specifics deferred (appropriately) to EPIPs. This section also discusses the drill and exercise program needed to hone skills required during emergencies. Chapters 4 and 5 provide a detailed discussion of the training, drill, and exercise programs.

SECTION 10: EVALUATION

Section 10 describes the program for continued plan development and maintenance. The commitment tracking system, update policy, and audit elements are also presented. Responsibilities are assigned to appropriate individuals for developing and maintaining elements of the Emergency Management Plan. The need for regular review and update is brought into sharp focus in this section, since no program can remain viable if left on the shelf for long.

The update policy is described in this section, along with audit elements, audit planning guidelines, and commitment tracking.

Establishing and maintaining accurate and orderly files and records is essential to the emergency management compliance program. In order to facilitate regulatory requirements a record of compliance initiatives must be retained. These records document the accomplishments, requirements, commitments, and reports relating to various regulatory requirements. Identifying commitments to regulatory compliance for the emergency management program is vital to documentation. The establishment of a defined information management system structure can ensure that documentation will be available when needed.

In order to assure compliance with various regulatory guidances and state and local ordinances, it is extremely important to have a system in place that serves to identify, catalog, set priorities, and track commitments that relate to the Emergency Management Plan and supporting materials. The use of computer data bases to track the type and quantity of chemicals stored on-site, health hazards, location of storage, and other reporting requirements levied by the federal and state regulatory agencies is one method.

The information management system should provide a dynamic framework for the establishment of the necessary files required to accurately document various regulatory compliance initiatives. This also serves as a starting point from which a detailed file system structure can be established to ensure the accurate recording of vital information.

A computerized commitment tracking and information management system can be designed to monitor the status of compliance commitments. Such a system provides a user friendly structure which lets an individual track commitments, perform data entry, and perform routine data base maintenance. Additionally, the commitment tracking system provides a reminder that allows for the prompt scheduling and completion of regulatory requirements and other periodic commitments.

The commitment tracking system allows for verification that regulatory commitments (federal, state, local) are adhered to by the appropriate organizations and elements. It also allows for the evaluation of commitments against new requirements, expanded regulations, changes to old requirements, and addition/deletion of the scope of these initiatives.

The commitment tracking system must provide tracking against 11 distinct entry categories:

- Plans
- Procedures
- Facilities
- Equipment
- Communications
- Training
- Drills
- Organization
- Administration
- Public information
- Off-site coordination

The data base structure consists of a categorical breakdown of commitments as follows:

Item No: A chronological numeric listing of the commitments is maintained in the data base file. In this manner, the number of records contained in the data base is easily ascertained by the user. Additionally, recurring items have been provided a unique identifier to assist in identification and sorting.

Responsibility: Identification of the specific individual responsible for completion of the action item/commitment or the individual with overall authority for ensuring completion of the commitment.

Com-Date: Lists the month, day, and year that the commitment is anticipated to be completed.

Status: Open, closed, or recurring are used to identify the status of a commitment/action item.

Topic: See the 11 entry categories mentioned above.

Resolution: A brief description outlining the various deliverables and the resolution of the item.

Eleven subject categories represent the data base. The following subsections provide a discussion of each of the eleven subject categories in greater detail.

1. *Plans:* All commitments stated in the Emergency Management Plan are cited under this subject category. The commitments deal with the design, development, implementation, and maintenance of the plan.

2. *Procedures:* All commitments stated in the EPIPs are cited under this subject category.

3. *Facilities:* All commitments relating to the facility emergency response facilities are cited under this category.

4. *Equipment:* All commitments regarding equipment will be input under this subject category. Equipment commitments primarily deal with stocking, inventory, operability, operability checks, manufacturer information, and replenishment of expended or expired equipment and supplies.

5. *Communications:* Commitments concerned with communications hardware, lines of communications, notification systems, communication systems tests, and system availability are cited in this subject category.

6. *Training:* All facility commitments to provide training for the various Emergency Management/Response Organizations (EMROs), identified emergency responders, and various response organizations are listed under this heading.

7. *Organization:* Commitments concerned with the EMROs, its composition, personnel qualifications, and staffing are cited in this category. Additionally, nonfacility emergency response organizations may be represented in this category as well as commitments by the facility that impact these organizations.

8. *Drills:* All commitments for drills, exercises, tabletop, scenario development, and critiques are presented under this subject heading.

9. *Administration:* Commitments focusing on the continuing operations and maintenance of the emergency response capability for the facility and other EMROs are provided under this heading.

10. *Public Information:* This category deals with public awareness, public education, and news media commitments that the Emergency Management Plan has defined for the safety of the public in the emergency planning zone (EPZ).

11. *Off-site:* This category deals with commitments by various response organizations (state, county, local, federal, and private) when it is determined that they impact the emergency response capability of the facility.

You need to address another critical issue: resource tracking. It is essential to your ability to respond to an emergency. The ability to know the status of your resources can greatly improve the ability to respond and mitigate the emergency before it becomes a full-blown crisis. The responsibility for developing a resource tracking system should be assigned to someone in management with a broad base of knowledge in the areas of human resource identification, organizational planning, operations, public affairs, and emergency management planning. To find a person with all these skills may be quite rare; therefore a team may need to be established to assemble the needed expertise. You will want to coordinate your efforts with external sources such as your local emergency planning committee or mutual aid organizations. Once completed, the resource tracking system can be administered by a single group or department.

Critical to the mitigation of an emergency is the ability to allocate resources where they are needed. Internal resources from within the site, from the corporate level, and from other company facilities should be compiled to provide a ready reference in the event of an emergency. Your resource tracking should include human resources, equipment resources, information systems, technical data, and other information key to your operation.

Additionally, a listing of outside resources should also be compiled to ensure verification of capabilities and prompt notification, as well as maintaining a list to provide ready access to accurate and current information when it is most needed. Additional lists can be created to monitor the availability of health care facilities, status of schools, retirement homes, and other facilities and institutions that can impact the emergency management planning effort.

APPENDICES TO THE EMERGENCY MANAGEMENT PLAN

Appendices to the emergency plan provide information to the planners that is subject to frequent change. The appendices should include:

APPENDIX A: LETTERS OF AGREEMENT

All letters of agreement for support between agencies, company entities, local, state, federal, and private organizations should be documented. These agreements should be kept in a separate appendix to the emergency plan, entitled Letters of Agreement. The letters of agreement should be renewed on an annual basis or reviewed annually to ensure that they are still valid. Cross-references to related emergency response plans can be included in this appendix.

Examples of typical letters of agreement are:

- City, town

- Laboratories

- Hospitals

- Sheriff, law enforcement agencies

- Fire departments

- Ambulance services

- Private doctors

- Industry assistance organizations

- Other companies

- State, federal agencies

APPENDIX B: EMERGENCY PLAN AND EMERGENCY PLAN IMPLEMENTING PROCEDURES CROSS-REFERENCE

A cross-reference of the emergency plan and EPIPs provides a means to check the plan and procedures to ensure that they correspond. The cross-reference should cite specific sections of the plan and tie them to the corresponding procedures. When the plan or procedures are updated or revised, a check should be made to ensure that changes are made to other affected documents.

APPENDIX C: LIST OF EMERGENCY PLAN IMPLEMENTATING PROCEDURES

A listing of the EPIPs with the latest revision dates should be included in this appendix.

APPENDIX D: LIST OF ASSOCIATED EMERGENCY PLANS

A list of the supporting emergency plans and their sources should be included in this appendix. The latest revision date of each supporting plan should be included.

APPENDIX E: LIST OF RECOGNIZED ACRONYMS, ABBREVIATIONS, AND DEFINITIONS

All acronyms, abbreviations, and definitions used in the emergency plan should be referenced in this appendix.

APPENDIX F: LABORATORY, CONSULTANT, AND OTHER TECHNICAL SUPPORT RESOURCES

A list should be provided of technical support resources. The list should include:

- Name

- Location/address

- Telephone number

- Special access numbers

- Special information/comments

APPENDIX G: TECHNICAL LIBRARY

A listing of any specialized technical documents should be referenced in the technical appendix.

APPENDIX H: HAZARDS ANALYSIS SUMMARY

The hazards analysis summary may well be the largest of the appendices. It should contain all relevant data concerning the hazards analysis survey results. A list of the emergency types that could have disaster potential should be included at the beginning of this appendix. Examples of the evaluations included in this appendix are:

- Hazardous materials evaluation

- Chemical process evaluation

- Physical operations evaluation

- Equipment design evaluation

- Plant location and layout evaluation

- Operator practices evaluation

- Employee training evaluation

APPENDIX I: CROSS-REFERENCE TO SITE/FACILITY SECURITY PLAN

A cross-reference to the site/facility security plan is an important aspect of the emergency planning process. The site/facility security plan will have to be implemented for emergencies requiring off-site assistance. It is important to ensure that the emergency plan and site/facility security plan correspond and reflect the most current information available.

APPENDIX J: COMMUNITY AND FACILITY MAPS

The best available types of maps depicting the area and facility layout should be included in this appendix.

APPENDIX K: CHEMICAL INFORMATION

A listing of Material Safety Data Sheets (MSDSs), chemical lists, and other pertinent information on potentially hazardous materials should be included in this appendix.

APPENDIX L: OFF-SITE EMERGENCY MANAGEMENT/RESPONSE AGENCIES

This appendix should include the key off-site agencies and a listing of their addresses, telephone numbers, and key point of contact.

APPENDIX M: EMERGENCY
RADIO CHANNELS

A list of all available emergency radio channels to be used by the facility should be placed in this appendix.

APPENDIX N: LOCAL RADIO
AND TELEVISION STATIONS

A listing, including the mailing address, telephone listing, key contact, and other pertinent information should be provided in this appendix.

APPENDIX O: HOSPITALS

This appendix contains a complete list of hospitals to be used, including a discussion on capabilities, number of beds, special services, and physicians.

APPENDIX P: EMERGENCY
RESPONSE EQUIPMENT

A complete list of the available emergency response equipment by type and function should be provided in this appendix.

APPENDIX Q: CROSS-REFERENCE
TO REGULATORY REQUIREMENTS

A cross-reference to applicable regulatory requirements should be provided in this appendix. This will also assist in identifying commitments.

APPENDIX R: EMERGENCY MANAGEMENT/RESPONSE
ORGANIZATION POSITION DESCRIPTIONS

Detailed descriptions of personnel assigned to the Emergency Management/ Response Organization should be provided in this appendix.

APPENDIX S: FORMS

A listing of forms and a master copy of all forms used in emergency response operations should be included in this appendix.

THE STRUCTURE OF EMERGENCY PLAN IMPLEMENTING PROCEDURES (EPIPS)

As defined earlier, Emergency Plan Implementing Procedures (EPIPs) are written instructions specifying the actions to be taken by the Emergency Management/ Response Organization (EMRO) in the event of an emergency condition. The EPIPs contain specific detailed instructions and guidance for all aspects of the model Emergency Management Plan. They assign responsibilities to personnel, and include flowcharts and checklists, where appropriate, to improve emergency management and response. The Emergency Management Plan introduces concepts which are expanded upon and supported by appendices. EPIPs are the tools used to implement the Emergency Management Plan. They are grouped, roughly into four categories, as discussed below. The specific numbers appearing in each series are associated with the 10 key plan sections, and may vary from location to location. Regardless of where the plan is implemented, however, there will be consistent naming conventions and structure for the EPIPs. The EPIPs can be categorized as follows:

ADMINISTRATIVE

Administrative procedures consist of management guidelines. These procedures provide guidance for the key EMRO positions. Administrative EPIPs also prescribe the manner in which activities such as monthly calibration tests or communications tests are to be accomplished. EPIPs in the 100 series (110, 120, 130) cross-reference to Section 1 of the Emergency Management Plan and deal with a variety of administrative issues, from preparation of emergency plans to control of emergency-use vehicles. EPIPs in the 900 series cross-reference to Section 9 of the Emergency Management Plan (910–920) and deal with training and drill operations for maintaining emergency preparedness. EPIPs in the 1000 series cross-reference Section 10 of the Emergency Management Plan (1010–1020) and address those operations necessary to maintain and improve the Emergency Management Plan. Audits, reviews, updates, and procedures for these activities are thoroughly detailed in this series.

EMERGENCY CLASSIFICATION

Emergency classification procedures provide step-by-step immediate action procedures for the identification and classification of the severity of an emergency. Emergency classification procedures are extremely important as they are used to:

- Determine the severity of the emergency

- Determine the extent of activation of the emergency organization

- Determine the notification requirements

- Determine the protective action recommendations to be given to the off-site authorities

EPIPS in the 500 series cross-reference to Section 5 of the Emergency Management Plan (510–570) and address classification and personnel action operations during the period from onset of emergency conditions through mitigation.

EMERGENCY MANAGEMENT/RESPONSE ORGANIZATION (EMRO)

EMRO procedures provide task-oriented guides for each position in the EMRO. Duties are described in these procedures as well. EPIPS in the 200 series cross-reference to Section 2 of the Emergency Management Plan (210–280) and address organizational issues. Duties of various personnel who play management or response roles in an emergency are delineated in this series. Organization charts and functional descriptions are provided for key personnel, on-site and off-site.

EMERGENCY OPERATIONS

Emergency operations procedures provide guidelines for conducting operations focused on incident mitigation. Step-by-step instructions to direct specific personnel activities during an emergency are presented. EPIPS in the 300 series cross-reference to Section 3 of the Emergency Management Plan (310–380) and address operations and incident response issues during emergency conditions. EPIPS in the 400 series cross-reference Section 4 of the Emergency Management Plan (410–420) and address communications operations for emergency situations. EPIPS in the 600 series cross-reference Section 6 of the Emergency Management Plan (610–630) and address the activation operations of emergency facilities and deployment of personnel to the facilities.

REENTRY AND RECOVERY

Reentry and recovery procedures include step-by-step task-oriented sequences for personnel responsible for the recovery of the facility and its return to preaccident operating conditions. These procedures assure that appropriate recovery organization personnel and equipment are available when reentry and recovery operations commence. EPIPS in the 700 series cross-reference to Section 7 of the Emergency Management Plan (710–750) and address public and governmental affairs and human resource operations during emergencies. EPIPS in the 800 series cross-reference to Section 8 of the Emergency Management Plan (810–840) and address postincident operations, including humanitarian assistance.

EPIP FORMAT

Each EPIP should be sufficiently detailed so as to guide designated individuals or groups during emergencies or potential emergencies. The EPIPs should be written so that these individuals or groups will know in advance the expected course of events that identify an emergency condition and the immediate actions that should be taken.

Since emergencies may not follow anticipated patterns, the EPIPs can provide sufficient flexibility to accommodate various situations. The EPIPs should include the following provisions:

- Detailed instructions to cover step-by-step actions to be taken by designated individuals or groups for the implementation and subsequent use of the EPIP(s).

- Supplemental background information to further aid designated individuals of groups in the implementation of the EPIP(s).

All EPIPs should contain the following elements:

- A title descriptive of the emergency task to which the procedure applies.

- An EPIP identifying number.

- The EPIP revision number.

- A brief statement of the purpose or intent of the EPIP.

- A description of the individuals and/or groups to whom the EPIP applies.

- A Definitions section in which any applicable item or condition clarifying the EPIP will be described.

- An Instructions section that provides the guidance to initiate or complete the activity and may include precautions, initial actions, and subsequent actions as applicable.

- A list of applicable references.

- A list of any attachments, if applicable.

- The attachments themselves, which contain information pertinent to the accomplishment of the function or task described in the EPIP. This information may include drawings, telephone lists, data sheets or forms, checklists, and maps. If there are none, the EPIP should say so.

Each page of an EPIP should contain the following information:

- Cover page with title, EPIP identifying number, and authorization signatures.

- Title or EPIP identifying number.

- Revision number.

- Issue date.

- Page number as part of the entire procedure.

The attachments contained in each EPIP will contain the following information:

- EPIP identifying number.

- Attachment number.

- Revision number

- Issue date.

- Attachment page number as part of the entire attachment.

Each EPIP should have a header containing the following information: name of the facility; issue date of the EPIP; procedure number; title of the EPIP; revision number; and page identification (for example, page 3 of 12 pages). An example is provided below. It is imperative that all EPIPs be identified so that users can determine the currency and completeness of the copies issued to them. Like the headers, each page must be identified with the procedure title, procedure number, revision number, and date of issue. In addition, the last page of each procedure should be clearly identified. That is, it should be marked in one of the following ways: *Page ____ of ____; Final Page; Last Page.* This identification is particularly important because the last page of a procedure is the one most vulnerable to loss. If it becomes detached from the procedure, this fact must be made immediately apparent to the user.

A sample EPIP header is shown below.

XYZ Company Emergency Plan Manual	Issue Date	Procedure No. EPIP–110
Preparation, Revision, Approval, and Control of the Emergency Management Plan and Emergency Plan Implementing Procedures		Revision No. 0 Page 1 of 7 Pages

Please note that the procedure number should correlate to the section of the Emergency Management Plan to which it relates. Thus, EPIPs will fall into series. The 100 series relates to Section 1.0 of the Emergency Management Plan, the 200 series to Section 2.0 of the Emergency Management Plan, and so forth. This is important, as one will want to ensure an adequate cross-reference between the Emergency Management Plan, appendices and EPIPs. The suggested format for the body of the EPIPs is as follows:

1.0 *PURPOSE* - The purpose statement indicating the basic purpose of the EPIP. It should include sufficient leeway in the wording to provide flexibility for the user. For instance, a statement such as, "This procedure provides guidance and instructions..." allows the user some latitude to adjust decision making to the vagaries of the situation.

2.0 *APPLICABILITY* - The applicability section describes to whom the procedure applies. It also should have a one-line paragraph indicating the date of the procedure becomes effective. A statement such as, "This procedure becomes effective when issued," is sufficient. All of the EPIPs should be reviewed at least quarterly so it is likely that any individual EPIP will contain errors.

Revision dates and review intervals are not necessarily valid indicators of the accuracy or currency of an EPIP. A careful and detailed assessment should be carried out annually.

3.0 DEFINITIONS - With the overwhelming number of acronyms, abbreviations, and shortened wordings, it is advisable to define any new or unusual terminology. This section of the procedure also clarifies any terms as to their meaning.

4.0 INSTRUCTIONS - Section 4.0, on instructions, is broken down into subparts. These may include, but are not limited to: Responsibilities, General Information, Initial Actions, and Subsequent Actions.

5.0 REFERENCES - References to the Emergency Management Plan, other EPIPs, appendices, technical documents, and other sources of information should be listed in this section.

It is a very common practice for the instructions in one EPIP to refer users to other procedures for additional instructions concerning some part of the activity. Also, the referenced procedure may contain instructions that experienced persons are expected to know and, consequently, there is no apparent need to repeat it within the procedure. However, it is also known that persons are less likely to obtain information if they must seek it in a document other than the primary one they are using. As a consequence, they are apt to overlook needed information. Also, surveys suggest that referencing to other procedures is overused. Thus, as a general rule, all of the information necessary to accomplish the immediate actions should be provided by one EPIP to ensure, among other objectives, that all necessary information is indeed reviewed periodically in accordance with facility policies.

6.0 ATTACHMENTS - The attachments section contains information pertinent to the accomplishment of the function or task prescribed in the EPIP. This information may include applicable drawings, telephone lists, data sheets or forms, checklists, flowcharts, and maps. If there are none, the EPIP should say so.

The cover page of each EPIP should contain the following information: company name, facility location, full title of the EPIP, EPIP number, revision number, party responsible for preparing and submitting the EPIP, date of submittal, approving authority, and date of approval/issue.

CONTENT OF INSTRUCTIONS IN EPIPS

The instructional statements in the EPIPs should be reviewed for several characteristics: complexity, level of detail, and provision for contingencies.

COMPLEXITY OF STATEMENTS

One indicator of the complexity of an instructional statement is the number of actions the user is directed to perform by the statement. The more actions directed by a statement, the more likely one of them is to be overlooked and, consequently, omitted. Ideally, an instructional statement should contain a single verb followed by the object of the action; for example, "Open valve," "Observe gauge," or "Depress switch." Additionally, a statement should contain object identifiers (nomenclature, part numbers) and verb modifiers (for example, "Slowly open, adjust _____ until flow rate is _____ gpm."). In general, a numbered step should consist of one instructional statement or sentence. Instructions risk being too complex to ensure reliable comprehension during stressful conditions if they contain four or more actions per step. In fact, reliability of comprehension will be greatest for steps that direct only one action, and even then, a controlled, consistent, and limited vocabulary is required to achieve highest reliability.

Actions generally expressed in instructions consist of five categories:

1. *Verification.* For the most part, these instructions direct users to verify that listed symptoms were observed or that specified automatic actions occured.

2. *Communication/Coordination.* These instructions deal with informing other personnel that actions were taken or should be taken. Also, they include requests for assistance from others (off-site), or information from personnel at remote locations.

3. *Calculations.* The instructions direct personnel to perform calculations.

4. *Monitor/Control.* These instructions direct personnel to observe displays and manipulate controls.

5. *Other.* This category consist of negative actions; for example, "Do not open valve ____ if ____," and other forms of action statements not easily grouped.

LEVEL OF DETAIL

Instructions can be grouped by their level of detail. The following three levels of detail are generally consistent with the degree of complexity of the instruction.

Level 3. Instructions in this category are the most detailed. They meet three criteria:

    a. The specific action to be performed is stated.

    b. The object on which the action to be performed is clearly and unambiguously identified; for example, part number is specified, or nomenclature appearing on a label is specified.

    c. The conditions or limits of action are specified; for example, limits are expressed in quantitative rather than qualitative terms.

Level 2. Instructions in this category meet two of the above criteria.

Level 1. These instructions were the least detailed. Only one or more of the above criteria are met.

Ordinarily, it is extremely difficult to define the correct level of detail of information that must be provided to ensure acceptable reliability in the performance of an activity. Highly experienced personnel will generally need less information than less experienced personnel. However, it is extremely important to identify correctly the activities to which their experience applies. A member of the EMRO may have years of experience in plant operations, but little or no experience in responding to some of the conditions described in the EPIP. Furthermore, the EMRO member may have limited experience in performing or rehearsing the activities (either specific or generic) prescribed by the EPIP procedures. Or extended time periods may have intervened between experiences. These factors, combined with the detrimental effects of stress on recall and comprehension, support the position that more detail (checklists and flowcharts) should be provided in EPIPs.

CONTINGENCY INFORMATION IN INSTRUCTIONS

It is highly unlikely that any two emergency conditions will ever exhibit the same pattern of events, either in terms of their actual occurrence or the sequence of their occurrence. The course of events is dependent upon material, equipment, and other personnel inputs, and these will vary. EPIPs must be developed in combination with a formal analysis process or they are very likely to be incomplete.

CHECKLISTS FOR EPIPS

Checklists for EPIPs facilitate the implementation of instructional steps contained in the body of the EPIP (Section 4.0). Additionally, checklists help the individual/group implementing the procedure to visually ensure that items are being addressed by indicating completion of an item with a check mark (✓) next to each listed item. The addition of time-completed indicators also serves to enhance the value of the checklist.

DEVELOPMENT OF CHECKLIST ITEMS

Checklist items should be easily measurable and observable. These characteristics permit decisions to be made on the basis of measurable quantities rather than subjective judgments.

In many cases, subjective judgments might vary greatly among different persons. Even the judgment of one person can vary from time to time (particularly in view of stress-induced perceptual distortions). This subjectivity can prevent consistently acceptable decisions and resultant actions.

Checklists are typically developed using a combination of the following:

1. *Document Review:* This method consists of obtaining the checklist items of interest from related documents and evaluating them with respect to emergency response action criteria.

   Typically, related documents consist of (1) drawings, procedures, schematics, etc., specifically referenced by the EPIP, and (2) technical specifications and other basic requirements documents which might affect the content of the EPIPs. In some cases, it might also be necessary to examine corporate policies and directives having an impact on EPIP contents.

2. *Inspection Walk-Through:* Some checklist items, such as determining the correspondence between equipment nomenclature or identification numbers used in an EPIP and the nomenclature or numbers actually displayed on equipment, can be obtained by an inspector or only by walking through the facility with the procedure in hand and comparing the two. During the walk-through, it might be desired to make selected human factors observations of the work environment, the facility layout, and the equipment, all of which bear upon the effectiveness and safety of personnel performance.

3. *Test Walk-Through:* Unlike the preceding methods, the checklist is evaluated under simulated conditions to judge whether the amount and kind of information provided by the checklist is complete with respect to the information needs of the user. That is, the checklist is evaluated on its adequacy and level of detail of the EPIP. Judgments of adequacy of level of detail are based on assumptions about the qualifications of the personnel for whom the EPIP is provided.

Such assumptions are often tenuous at best because of the wide differences between groups of personnel with respect to training for emergencies, and the relatively unknown effects of these differences in training.

WEIGHTING OF CHECKLIST ITEMS

The final task in constructing a checklist will be to assign a weight to each checklist item. The weight is intended to indicate the impact of the characteristic referred to in the item and to prioritize each step as it relates to the quality of human performance.

If an EPIP cannot be accurately observed and measured, performance deviation is more likely to occur. Each checklist item should be rated and prioritized. The rating indicates the relative importance of the item.

FLOWCHARTS

The use of flowcharts to supplement the EPIP written instructions and checklists can be very helpful. Flowcharts allow the EPIP user to visually orient themselves to the tasks to be performed. This will generally allow for quicker implementation and prevent steps from being skipped. The combining of flowcharts and checklists will enhance the ability of EMRO personnel to perform under emergency conditions. Sample flowcharts are provided herein.

OTHER CONSIDERATIONS

Having consistent emergency management plans at diverse company locations makes good business sense, and provides the most cost-effective means of assuring that proactive safety programs are implemented company-wide. The model presented herein is suitable for use at various locations. This model employs an enhanced Incident Command System (EICS) for emergency management and response. Some other considerations for using a standardized format are:

Standard Terminology and Naming Conventions: It is essential to use terms and naming conventions consistently throughout the organization. Often referred to as the Emergency Management Plan Standard, it serves as a basis for implementing standard planning concepts and conventions throughout the enterprise.

Facility-Specific Procedures and Information: Specific techniques, procedures, and training materials related to the mitigation of hazards at the facility. Such information includes facility personnel names, phone numbers, maps, and information related to local outside agencies, including fire and police departments, hospitals, mutual assistance organizations, and news media.

4

Training:
The Critical Process

CHAPTER HIGHLIGHTS

"Now that I've got a plan, what do I do with it?"

In this chapter we present an overview of some essential considerations for personnel assigned the task of establishing a training program or developing effective training programs. The focus here is to help you make the transition from the plan development phase. It is critical to the success of your emergency management program that you have effective training program to ensure personnel can implement the plan in the most effective way.

INTRODUCTION

Training of personnel is an important component of the *all hazards* emergency management planning approach. The training of the Emergency Management/

134

Response Organization (EMRO) is one of the critical success factors that must be addressed to achieve an adequate response to a crisis.

Consider the effort involved in the preparation of the emergency management program. You have designed a dynamic organization structure that address management and response activities. You have developed a plan supported by appendices and Emergency Plan Implementing Procedures (EPIPs). It has been a painstaking process. You have high expectations of your plan's ability to help personnel address emergency situations. If you do not train these personnel, can your expectations, your company's expectations, or those of off-site authorities be met?

A well-designed training program is a necessary component of the all hazards approach. It is necessary because we want to be able to implement the plan in a timely fashion, with a minimum of disruption, by personnel who know their roles and are comfortable in the knowledge that they can adequately fulfill their obligations.

Our approach to preparing effective training programs consists of four elements.

1. *Task analysis:* The skills, knowledge, and procedures required for satisfactory performance of tasks must be determined at the time the training program is designed.

2. *Lesson development:* Learning objectives are defined from skills, knowledge, and procedures developed during task analysis. Instructional plans are then prepared to support the learning objectives.

3. *Instruction:* You need to systematically present lessons using appropriate instructional methods. Instruction may include lecture, self-paced or group-paced mediated instruction, simulation, and team training.

4. *Evaluation:* Performance standards and evaluation criteria will need to be developed from the learning objectives. Each trainee's performance will need to be evaluated during training and during field performance testing (drills/exercises).

One of the critical items in the success of your training program is the instructor. The following information is provided as a guide to assist you in preparing for and presenting training to your personnel.

This chapter includes guidance on:

1. Design and development of training

2. Implementation of training

3. Evaluation of training

DESIGN AND DEVELOPMENT: THE INITIAL STEPS

You have just been assigned the responsibility for preparing and implementing the training portion of the emergency management program. You are excited because this means a promotion. You have been recognized as a rising star. You want to do well; however, you've never designed, developed, or implemented a training program. You think to yourself, "I've been to training classes before. It didn't seem too difficult. The instructor just read from a text and we watch a tape." Sound familiar? How much did you retain from the training? Maybe, and I mean maybe, a few good jokes; and only if they were good ones! Keep this in mind as you work your way through this material. Really good training is not something slapped together the night before it is to be presented. It is a well-thought-out process, a process that is critical to the effectiveness of your emergency management program.

Let's turn our attention to how we go about developing effective training programs. Instructional System Development (ISD) is a methodology that has been used effectively to prepare training programs. The ISD approach consists of five components:

- Analysis

- Design

- Development

- Implementation

- Control

Each component builds upon the output from the previous component. It is a continuous cycle. Once complete, you can begin again with the Analysis component. In this manner, your training program is maintained concurrently with changes/improvements to the emergency management program.

Where a particular ISD program begins depends on what has been done before. For example, if you or someone else recently completed an adequate job and task analysis for the particular job for which you intend to provide an ISD training program, you should not need to perform another analysis.

The ultimate purpose of ISD is to produce a properly trained person; that is, a person who can do the job for which he was trained. This means that to design and carry out effective training, you first must know the job in considerable detail. The ISD process begins with specific questions about the *job*. Some of the things you must find out about the job to develop adequate training are:

1. What kinds of people will be doing this job? How many will be doing the job? Where will they be located?

2. What major duties does the job include?

3. What tasks make up the position?

4. Exactly how is each task accomplished? What work elements make up the task? In what order must these be performed?

5. Under what conditions must each task be performed? What tools, equipment, or other facilities are required to perform each task?

6. What cues cause a job holder to perform a particular task in a particular manner? (How does he know when to start a task, when to perform each element that makes up the task, and when the task is completed?)

7. To what standard of proficiency must each task be performed?

Requirements for trained people originate from a number of sources:

1. Introduction to new duties and systems.

2. New EPA, OSHA requirements, company-specific needs, and social problems.

3. Realignment of organizational responsibilities, assignment of additional duties, and assignment of emergency management/response duties.

4. Quality control reports indicating a training need is not being adequately met.

While training needs can and will arise from any and all of these sources, the first step in the ISD process is to identify the *discrepancy* that exists between whatever training is being given currently and the training that must be given to satisfy the newly identified needs. Discovery of this discrepancy begins by asking the question, Does anyone do the job now? If the answer is "yes," there is a second question: Is there now a training program for this job?

If the answer to both questions is "yes," you will have to look further to discovery the discrepancy. In the ISD model, finding the *first* discrepancy indicates only where you should begin. Finding and correcting the first discrepancy probably will not result in an acceptable training program. Instead, it will most likely require a series of changes that will affect every part of the program.

If the answer is "no" to either of the above questions (that is, if no one does the job now or no training programs for the job exist), you have found the discrepancy. If no one does the job now, the job undoubtedly is just being created because of some new or modified requirement, such as, expanded emergency management roles. A discrepancy is certain to exist between the ability of existing courses to train personnel, and the training requirements of an as-yet-undefined new job. If there is no existing training program for either a new or existing job, the discrepancy is obvious. Therefore, the correct place to begin in the ISD process is to analyze the job to determine exactly what the job holder must do when he does the job right. This is the foundation for all sound training programs. If this step is not done and done well, there will be no basis for development of effective, efficient instruction.

Some outputs of this analysis are:

1. A validated list of tasks that make up the particular job being analyzed.

2. Conditions under which each task must be performed, cues that initiate performance of the task, and standards to which each task must be performed.

3. Details of how each task is performed; that is, a listing of the work elements that make up each task.

A decision must be made about which tasks will be trained and which tasks will not be trained. Job Performance Measures (JPM) will need to be developed to determine whether someone is capable of doing the job. This step may require input from some of the same people who provided input in developing the listing of duties and tasks for the EMRO position. You cannot develop JPMs for tasks selected for training until you know what the tasks are from which you are to choose.

Other than such obvious, logical restrictions, the ISD process does not restrict you to a specific job analysis approach or to a specific sequence of steps in training program development.

The only requirement is that your approach be well-planned, logical, and consistent with the needs and resources of the EMRO.

DEFINITION OF JOB ANALYSIS TERMS

We have already used some terms that many people use to mean different things. It is essential that those involved in the development of training for the EMRO define such terms as *job, duty, task* and *element* in the same way. Since one of the purposes of analyzing jobs is to provide information for developing instruction, there must be clear communication between the ones who analyze the job and the ones who use the job analyst's findings as a basis for developing instruction. Because of this, we will spend some time here defining job analysis terms and pointing out how the terms can be effectively used to describe exactly what a person does when he does his particular job right.

JOB

The duties and tasks performed by a single individual assigned to the EMRO constitute the *job*. If identical duties and tasks are performed by several individuals, they all hold the same job. The job is the basic unit used in carrying out the personnel action of selection, training, classification, and assignment. In the EMRO, such groupings or jobs are defined as Emergency Organization Specialties (EOS). These specialties form the occupational basis of the assignment of personnel to the EMRO. That is, they identify work requirements and individual qualifications, facilitate assignment and distribution of personnel, provide for trained replacements, and facilitate more accurate estimates of staffing requirements.

Some examples of jobs are emergency manager, incident support director, field incident commander, and safety officer.

DUTY

A *duty* is one of the major subdivisions of work performed by one individual. A job is made up of one or more duties.

The following are some of the characteristics of duties:

1. A duty is one of the job incumbent's main functions. It sometimes may be a particular job incumbent's total job.

2. A duty is a grouping of closely related tasks.

3. Duty requirements often are the basis for initial assignment to a job, for determining the qualifications required to perform in the job, or for determining requirements for training.

Duties can usually be defined by analyzing the five or six most critical factors of a job or assessing the demand on the person being considered for a job. In the case of the Field incident commander, for example, you may say, (1) ability to assess the emergency situation, (2) ability to coordinate large organizations, (3) ability to communicate clearly, and (4) ability to classify the severity of an incident.

Selection of duty titles often is somewhat arbitrary and subjective; however, they should, whenever possible, reflect industry terminology. Duty titles often are used in job analysis for categorizing groups of tasks under identifiable headings to help in organizing lists of tasks. At other times, duty titles are assigned for convenience after tasks have been identified and grouped. In either case, the duty title serves to clearly identify closely related groups of tasks.

A good way to write duty statements is to use action words ending in *-ing* to describe duties. This wording fits the intent of the duty statement in the job inventory since the *-ing* relates the word to an entire function rather than to an individual action. The action word generally is followed by an object. For example,

Approving

Briefing

Calibrating

Developing

Gathering

Informing

Reading

Scheduling

TASK

Job analysis actually is accomplished at the *task* level. As you will recall, duties are actually clusters of tasks, the performance of which constitute the duties. Job analysis goes more deeply into job activity descriptions at the task level than it does with the more general duty statements. A task is the lowest level of behavior in a job that describes the performance of a meaningful function in the job under consideration. Examination of the job at task level allows the job to be described in sufficient detail to serve as the basis for a complete instructional system.

Task statements must be constructed carefully to assure that the final analysis yields usable job performance data. The following are characteristics of tasks and task statements:

1. A task statement is a statement of a highly specific action. The statement has a verb and object.

2. A task has a definite beginning and end.

3. Tasks are performed in relatively short periods of time, i.e., seconds, minutes, or hours, but rarely, if ever, days, weeks, months, or years. Although no definite time limit can be set, the longer the period of time between the beginning and the completion of the activity, the greater the probability that the activity is a generality or goal rather than a task.

4. A task must be measurable and observable; that is, in the real world, a technically proficient individual can observe the performance of the task or the product produced by the task, and be able to conclude that the task has or has not been properly performed.

5. Each task is independent of other actions. Each task statement must describe a finite and independent part of the job. Tasks are *not* components of a procedure. In the eyes of the job holder, a task is performed for *its own sake* in the job situation. A task is either performed or not performed for only *part* of a task. If he is responsible for only a part of a work activity that would otherwise be defined as a task, the part of which he is responsible *is* the task.

ELEMENT

An *element* is the smallest package of behavior that has practical meaning to the instructional designers. *Has practical meaning* means that further subdivision of the element is unnecessary since the instructional designers fully understand the element without further subdivision. To be useful as a basis for developing instruction, step-by-step direction and guidance is required as to how the task is performed. The work activities that make up this step-by-step direction and guidance are the elements that make up the task.

The elements that make up each task must be determined for two reasons. First, since many tasks will be selected for training, the instructional designer must have sufficient details of the tasks to provide a solid basis for training. If individuals are going to be trained to a task or be provided with job aids to help them perform a task, those who develop the training or Job Performance Aids (JPAs) must know exactly how the task is done. JPAs are manuals, checklists, or any other devices—often attached to equipment—that assist individuals in performing certain operations.

The second reason for determining the elements that make up a task is that some task statements look alike, although the tasks are quite different. Some task statements may have the same verb and object and only appear different when the elements are added. Table 4–1 provides an example of the breakdown of tasks into easily definable terms.

Table 4–1
Task Statement Requirements

Requirement	Task Statement	Example
Clarity	Use wording that is easily understood.	"Compare written description to actual performance," but not "Relate results to needs of field."
	Be precise so it means the same thing to all personnel.	Use words such as check, coordinate, and assist with caution—they are vague.
	Write separate, specific statements for each task. Avoid combining vague items of skill, knowledge, or responsibility.	"Supervise files," or, "Maintain files," but not "Have responsibility for maintaining files."
Completeness	Use abbreviations only after spelling out the term.	"Inventory emergency equipment" may be followed by, "Prepare requisitions for emergency equipment."
	Include both form and title number when the task is to complete a form, unless all that is needed is the general type form.	Complete emergency classification worksheet (Form No. XXX).

Requirement	Task Statement	Example
Conciseness	Be brief.	"Write incident notification and response report," but not "Accomplish necessary reports involved in the process of notification and response procedures."
	Begin with a present-tense action word (subject "I" or "you" is understood). Indicate an object of the action to be performed. Use terminology that is currently used on the job.	Use "complete" or "call," as in, "Complete checklist," or "Call National Response Center." Use most recent regulatory documentation.
Relevance	Do not state a person's qualifications.	"Load tape," but not, "Has one year of training."
	Do not include items on receiving instruction, unless actual work is performed.	"Prepare lab report," but not "Attend lecture."

This step-by-step description of the task must be detailed enough to be followed by those who need to understand how the task is performed. Each position in the EMRO must have a completed job and task analyses. This means a great deal of judgment must be used to list elements. There is a lower limit to the degree that elements can be subdivided. This limit is the point at which further subdivision would result in breaking the elements into such basic work units as the separate motions, movements, and mental processes involved. There is also an upper limit to the degree that elements must be subdivided. This limit is the point at which less subdivision would certainly fail to present a clear description of how the task is performed. The practical limit is usually somewhere between two extremes. You should subdivide the element to the point necessary for communicating with those who will use the information, and no further.

CONDITIONS

Conditions, as used in this book, refer to on-the-job conditions that significantly influence performance of a task. These significant on-the-job conditions provide the basis for determining JPM conditions and the necessary training conditions.

CUES

A *cue,* as used in this book, is the state of affairs or the occurrences that determine when the job incumbent performs a particular task according to a particular procedure.

OVERVIEW OF JOB ANALYSIS

Job analysis begins with the recognition of a discrepancy between job performance ability and job performance needs—a discrepancy that cannot be corrected by existing training courses, either because no such course exists, or because analysis of existing courses indicated that no acceptable course exists.

The first step in developing adequate training is to collect valid and reliable data about the job. The original source of valid and reliable job data is job analysis. Various methods can be used to obtain necessary data. Figure 4–1 provides an example of a job analysis workpaper. Some suggestions are:

- Reviewing available job information

- Develop data collection plan

- Review job requirements with technical experts

- Review job acquirements with incumbents

- Develop survey/questionnaire instruments

- Review existing literature

The ISD process does not dictate a specific procedure. The basic requirement is that you make logical decisions based on the resources and constraints with which you must work. The guidelines that follow will assist you in making those logical decisions.

Regardless of the route that you take to accomplish the job and task analysis, the ultimate end product, or output, must include a validated list of tasks that make up the job. These tasks must be described in sufficient detail to permit collection of valid and reliable data for use in making decisions about which tasks will be trained.

JOB ANALYSIS INFORMATION SOURCE

DATE _____

A. Identification Information:

   1. Name _____ Title: _____

   2. Present Work Assignment _____

   3. Primary Duties _____

                             _____

                             _____

B. Job Location Information:

   1. Facility Mailing Address _____

                             _____

   2. Telephone Number and Extension _____

   3. Present Geographical Location _____

C. Experience and Other Job Related Information:

   1. Total Months in Present Work Assignment _____

   2. Total Months in This Career Field _____

   3. Total Months at Present Facility _____

   4. Total Months in EMRO _____

   5. Reassignment Plans _____

   6. Highest Education Level Completed _____

   7. Number of Subordinates Supervised _____

   8. Primary Job Interest _____

   9. Training Received for Present Work _____

Figure 4-1

DEVELOPING TRAINING OBJECTIVES

Job tasks for which training must be provided have been identified in the first phase of the ISD model. Job Performance Measures (JPMs) have been developed to measure performance on these tasks. In those cases where it was impractical to measure actual job performance, the JPMs were designed to provide practical, high-fidelity measurement alternatives. Since the primary objectives of training are to produce individuals who can adequately perform the job, and since the JPMs are the best practical measure of performance, the JPMs are the basis for developing module objectives.

Some JPMs closely resemble the actual task, and the Terminal Module Objectives (TMOs) written for them will closely resemble the actual task statement. Other JPMs will only approximate the actual task, but the learned behavior should be virtually identical to the behavior on the job.

The first step in developing training objectives is to prepare TMOs which are direct translations of the JPMs into objectives for training. These TMOs describe the actions, conditions, and standards to be met in training to prepare the person for their EMRO position and functions.

A TMO is:

1. A specific description of the action the learner is to exhibit after training.

2. The conditions under which the action will take place.

3. The standard or criterion which must be reached.

TMOs are intended to be directly related to the job task performance even when the action, conditions, and standards cannot be identical. In many tasks, these will be identical and there will be no need to sacrifice fidelity. The TMOs should be documented on a form similar to the one shown at the end of this section.

The Training Objective (TO) provides a more precise action statement which presents a word picture of what the individual must be able to do. This approach avoids vague terms and stresses the actions that the individual must perform to be satisfactory in a field environment.

TMOs and TOs should have all the characteristics listed below. They will be evaluated by these same criteria:

1. Objectives must be a statement of student behavior (action), such as the creation of a product or some other overt act, which can be accepted as

evidence that the intended outcome has occurred.

2. The behavior must describe specifically all outcomes that will demonstrate that learning has occurred.

3. The required student behavior must be capable of being observed and evaluated within the learning and testing environment.

4. The objective must be stated in learner, rather than teacher, terms. That is, it must describe actions which the student will perform rather than what the teacher will say or do.

5. There must be a standard against which the student behavior will be measured. It must be fully specified.

6. The statement of the conditions under which the student behavior will occur must be fully specified.

One must determine applicable learning guidelines to specify learning activities that must take place in the training environment to help. These guidelines will make sure the instruction is as effective and efficient as possible, and is directly related to task performance as possible.

All learning objectives do not require the same specific learning guidelines for optimum learning to take place. Information is not best learned the same way as a physical skill. This section provides guidance for separating learning objectives into subcategories that may require different instructional treatment. Specific instructional guidelines are matched with the different subcategories of objectives so the instruction can be as effective as possible.

There are four general guidelines that are appropriate for most learning objectives. These are:

1. Inform the learner of the objectives.

2. Provide for active practice.

3. Provide guidance and prompts for the learner.

4. Provide feedback to the learner.

These learning guidelines will assist students in learning a variety of new knowledge, skills, and attitudes. In determining exactly how to implement these general guidelines, consider their application in each of the TMOs for each module.

EVALUATING PERFORMANCE: TESTING

Testing is used after training to determine whether or to what degree trainees learned what they were intended to learn. In addition, entry tests are used to reject people for training or to prescribe remedial training. Pretests that match posttests are used for placement within a training program or for exempting trainees from a program, and within-course tests are used to determine trainee progress and need for assistance during the training.

Each Terminal Module Objective (TMO) is derived from a Job Performance Measure (JPM). The training test for the TMO may be identical to the JPM, or there may be additional constraints in the training setting that decreases the level of fidelity of the training test. The change may be in the action, the initiating cues, conditions, or standards. Each Training Objective (TO) must be tested under simulated conditions in the training setting. For the same reason mentioned above, these tests may or may not be identical to related parts of the JPM. The Learning Steps (LSs) may or may not be tested individually; however, they are often tested as part of the TMO or TO test.

In the learning analysis of the TMO, many TOs and LSs may be listed. Some of these are steps in the original task or JPM; however, some of them represent other skills or knowledge that must be obtained to master the TMO. Generally, these other skills or knowledge, once mastered, are of no particular further concern to the evaluators (testers).

How detailed and inclusive a test should be depends upon its intended use. If the need is to place trainees in remedial courses, place them at various points within a course, or exempt them from a course, the test must be sufficiently broad to cover all the course prerequisites, entry behavior, and all the TMOs and TOs. It must be detailed enough to discriminate between those who can perform and those who cannot.

If the test is to be used to decide whether to reject or accept someone in a training course, it should be a relatively narrow test that discriminates between those who have the necessary entry behavior and those who do not.

If the purpose of the test is to give trainees information on their progress, the test should include test items on TMOs, TOs, and possibly LSs, that can be scored either mechanically or by the student to give him feedback. This feedback can also be used to recycle the student, prescribe remedial instruction, or place the trainee ahead.

When a course is being developed, there is an additional use for test results. If students are tested frequently, the scores provide a record of how well the instruction is working. Errors by students pinpoint failures in the instruction.

Early achievement of goals or higher than expected standards are indications that the instruction should be shortened. Testing for validation should be detailed and should have a detailed scoring procedure. A complete discussion on the construction of written achievement tests is provided in this section.

Particular learning events and activities must occur in the learning environment in order for instruction to be effective and efficient. Some general learning guidelines are applicable for a variety of training objectives. Other guidelines are unique to each category of learning. The objectives of this block are to classify training objectives according to the appropriate subcategory within their learning category; to identify for each subcategory those learning guidelines necessary for optimum learning to take place; and to specify activities that must take place in the learning environment to provide training most directly related to task performance.

CONSTRUCTION OF WRITTEN ACHIEVEMENT TESTS

An achievement test must meet certain requirements if it is to serve as an effective measuring device. These are described in the following sections.

THE TEST MUST BE VALID

A test is said to be valid when it actually measures what it is *supposed* to measure. This is the most important feature of a good examination. A test designed to measure the student's ability to use and apply certain facts learned in technical courses is not valid for that purpose if it measures only the student's ability to recall and write these facts on paper. It must measure application of facts rather than mere memorization. As part of the process of standardizing a formal test, an index of its validity can be obtained by computing the coefficient of correlation between scores on the test and measures of some predetermined criterion of validity.

However, the usual method of estimating validity of an informal instructor-constructed test is to have several competent individuals carefully go over the contents and test results to determine how well the examination does what it is supposed to do. Although the test maker may have only subjective means at his disposal, he must give careful consideration to the extent to which the test actually measures what it is designed to measure.

THE TEST MUST BE RELIABLE

A test is said to be *reliable* when it measures accurately and consistently what it *does* measure. If the test measures the student's abilities in exactly the same manner each time it is administered, and if the factors that affect the test scores affect them to the same extent every time the test is given, the test is said to be high in reliability. A highly reliable test, then, should yield essentially the same score when administered twice to the same student, providing, of course, that no learning occurs while the test is being taken for the first time, or no learning or forgetting takes place between testings.

Although treated separately, reliability and validity are closely related. Reliability is considered a factor in validity. A test cannot be extremely high in validity and low in reliability.

Presumably, if the test does not measure accurately and precisely, there must be variable factors other than achievement that affect the score. High reliability does not ensure high validity, however. A test can measure with extreme accuracy but fail to measure what it is *supposed* to measure. Validity is sometimes decreased by an overemphasis upon reliability.

Again, validity, because it is related to the test's purpose, is the most important feature of a test. It is particularly important to let the trainee know the role he is playing in the ISD effort. The particular course being conducted may still be in the development stage, and the trainee can help make it a better program. You need him and his cooperation. If you tell him this, he is likely to respond in a positive way. Most likely, the evaluation plan will require numerous responses from the trainee that are not listed in the student's manual. You must supplement the manual by providing the trainee with clear instructions, not only about what is expected of him, but also how the information will be used. This instruction may be developed for the trainees in any suitable manner, including an oral presentation.

Whereas the validity of an informal written examination is usually determined by more or less subjective means, an accurate estimate of the reliability can be determined by a precise mathematical procedure—if a sufficient number of test papers are accumulated.

THE TEST MUST BE OBJECTIVE

For the test to be objective, the personal judgment of the individual who scores the test must not be a factor. Different individuals scoring the same test paper or the same individual scoring the same paper at different times must arrive at the same score if the test is to meet the full measure of this requirement.

It is obvious that the essay test, as usually constructed and scored, registers poorly when measured by this standard. Instructors competent to judge rarely agree on the score that should be recorded for a given essay test paper. They do not have a common objective basis for marking.

Instructors often notice that students are making higher marks than usual and begin to grade the tests "harder," that is, they begin to take off points for errors. Such a system of scoring is not objective and should not be tolerated in a testing program.

To get an appreciation of the subjectivity of the ordinary essay or discussion type test, one has only to select several competent instructors of the subject and have each score independently the same test paper covering materials that they teach. There will be considerable variation in scores recorded for the single test paper. If the same instructors score the same test paper again one week later, the difference between the first and second set of scores will again be considerable. It is not to be assumed that the essay should be eliminated altogether from tests. When carefully constructed, it measures well the ability of the student to organize and express his thoughts.

The aspect of objectivity which has been described is concerned with the scoring and marking of test papers. Another aspect, equally important but more subtle, and therefore more frequently neglected, has to do with the students' interpretation of the items in the test.

Well-constructed test items should lend themselves to one and only one interpretation by students *who know the subject matter involved*. That is, a given test item should mean essentially the same thing to students who know the point in question. Items should be stated clearly so that students will know what information is desired.

Items that are ambiguous or have double meanings should be carefully "weeded out" if the test is to be objective from the student's point of view.

THE TEST MUST DISCRIMINATE

To be discriminating, the test must be constructed so that it will detect or measure small differences in achievement or attainment. This is an absolute essential if the test is to be used for ranking students on the basis of achievement or for assigning marks.

Three things will be true of a test that meets this standard of discrimination:

1. There will be a wide range of scores when the test is administered to students who are actually at significantly different levels of achievements. If the *full range* of achievement is to be measured, scores are likely to vary from the lowest to the highest possible score. However, for practical purposes, and for most subject-matter fields, scores should vary from near the highest possible score to a score that is less than half the total number of points on the test.

2. The test will include items at all levels of difficulty. That is, the items will vary uniformly in difficulty from the most difficult, which will be answered correctly only by the best students, to an item so easy that practically all of the students will answer it correctly.

3. Each item will discriminate between low achievers and high achievers. Each item will be missed more frequently by poor students than by good students.

   As is true with validity, reliability, and objectivity, the discriminating power of a test is increased by concentrating on and improving each individual item in the test. After a test has been administered, a simple item analysis can be made which will readily show the relative difficulty of each item, and of greater importance, the extent to which each discriminates between good and poor students.

THE TEST MUST BE COMPREHENSIVE

A comprehensive test must sample liberally the objectives that are being measured. A test should be comprehensive enough to be valid, that is, it should be long enough to do what it is supposed to do.

THE TEST MUST BE READILY ADMINISTERED AND SCORED

Consideration must be given to the feature of the test which makes it readily administered and scored. It must be so devised that a minimum amount of student time will be consumed in answering each item. The test items must also be constructed so that they can be scored.

THE TEST MUST BE FAIR

A fair test gives as accurate an appraisal of the student's knowledge in the area tested as possible. A test which does this provides the student with useful knowledge of his own performance, of strengths as well as weaknesses. The test must not include material not adequately covered in the course, although it may include material from outside assignments.

The test must not be made so simple that those who have put forward only minimal effort can pass, since this penalizes those students who have worked at their studies. Simple tests tend to reduce the level of motivation of the students and ultimately to degrade the course itself.

On the other hand, the test must not be made so difficult that only the best students can pass any items at all. This type of tests tends to discourage the student whose performance has suffered only through lack of proper motivation toward his studies. A fairer test must tend to provide additional motivation needed to move him in the direction of more satisfactory performance.

Finally, the test should be fair to the instructor. It should help provide him with evidence of the success (or lack of same) of his efforts. It can provide guideposts to direct his further teaching of the material. It can indicate to his administrators the adequacy with which the group taught has taken on the material. It can provide a point of reference for coordinating the teaching of the same subject by more than one instructor.

If a test is to be valid, reliable, and objective—that is, if it is to be comprehensive, discriminating, and easily administered and scored, a definite systematic procedure must be followed in its construction. One such procedure is itemized briefly below:

1. Decide on the specific points or objectives that are to be measured.

2. Write each objective on a separate sheet or card.

3. Determine which type of test item will measure best the extent to which the student has attained each specific objective.

4. Construct one or more test items for each objective listed.

5. Assemble the items for the test. List all items of the same type (completion, matching, multiple choice, and so on) together. Arrange questions within each type so that those concerning related material appear together.

6. Write clear and concise directions for each type of question.

7. Study every aspect of the assembled test.

8. Have others criticize and actually take the test.

9. Make any necessary revisions.

10. Construct the key.

11. After the test has been administered to one or two groups of students, study carefully the student responses. Correct any weaknesses that they reveal. Continue to revise and improve the test from time to time.

There are many specific points that must be kept in mind as an effective test is constructed. Some of these points are listed below. Others will be presented later in the discussion of the various types of test items.

1. Make the mechanics of taking the test as simple as possible.

2. Include several types of test items.

3. Do not include one item that supplies the answer to another.

4. Make each item independent of the others. Do not have the correct response to one item dependent upon the responses to another.

5. Make the test comprehensive, but exclude trivial and insignificant items. Sample the whole range of instruction up to the time of the test.

6. State questions clearly; eliminate ambiguous items.

7. Include a large number of items in the test. This tends to increase reliability.

8. As far as possible, arrange the items in the order of their difficulty.

9. Keep the method of recording responses as simple as possible. The technique for answering test items can easily become more difficult for the student than recalling or recognizing the information he or she needs to answer. Complicated methods of indicating responses tend to measure general intelligence rather than achievement.

10. Arrange the items so that it will not be necessary for the student to refer to more than one page in answering a given item.

11. Include no item from which the answer is obvious *to a person who does not know the subject matter*.

12. Arrange blanks for responses along one side of the page if possible. This makes scoring easier.

13. Arrange items so that responses will not form a particular pattern, such as, TTFF or 1234.

14. Make certain that the types of test items used for measuring each objective is the one that will measure that objective the best. Remember that certain types of test items have advantages over others, but that these are *specific* advantages in *specific* situations.

15. Leave sufficient space for all responses without crowding.

16. Number the responses consecutively from the beginning to the end of the test.

17. Avoid the weighting of such items. Each single response should be numbered and should count as one point. The number of points that a test item should count will depend on the number of responses required in that item. If a particular point is highly important and you wish to stress it in a test, call for several responses concerning it. Measure the student's knowledge of it by setting up several situations in which the point is involved.

18. Use as many questions as possible that require the student actually to apply things learned, rather than merely recall or recognize facts.

19. The practice of underlining crucial words tends to increase the objectivity of test items if not done too frequently and indiscriminately.

20. Directions should be complete. They should state clearly and concisely:
    a. *what* the student is required to do
    b. *how* the response is to be indicated, and
    c. *where* the answer is to be placed.

21. The directions should include at least one example of an item correctly answered. Many incorrect responses can be traced directly either to the student's failure to understand the intent of the directions or his failure to read them carefully. Make the test fair to the student.

22. Examples accompanying directions should be taken from the subject matter of the test. Make the examples meaningful. Use them to teach certain points.

23. If a penalty for guessing is to be made when scoring the test, this should be explained for the directions.

24. Concentrate on individual items in the test. Improve them.

25. Word questions in the simplest manner possible. Confine the terms used to the vocabulary level of students.

26. Keep in mind that it is not possible to measure all outcomes of instruction with written tests. The performance test is much more effective.

27. Avoid trick or "catch" questions.

28. A card file can be used effectively to accumulate new items for both daily and final tests.

29. Avoid questions to be answered by *yes* or *no* when other types of items can be substituted.

30. When possible, keep the responses short.

31. Include items at all levels of difficulty to ensure a significant range of test scores.

32. In designing recall questions, determine what information is to be supplied, write out the answer, and then construct a test item that will test the student's knowledge of the answer.

33. Make out the key or the answers to the questions while the test is made.

34. Any test given to anyone for any reason which will affect that person's job, pay, or status in the company, either present or future, *must* be tried out or validated before being given.

TYPES OF TESTS

TRUE–FALSE

The unmodified type of true/false test item consists of a simple statement that may be either true or false. The student is required to indicate whether or not the statement is true. This type of test item has been used extensively and often indiscriminately by instructors. The plain true/false item is not recommended for use in achievement tests. However, variations or modifications can be used effectively.

Uses, Advantages, and Limitations are listed below.

1. The true/false item can be used effectively as an instructional test item to promote interest and to introduce points for discussion.

2. It can be used to sample effectively wide ranges of subject matter.

3. It can be made a factual question or a thought question that requires reasoning.

4. It can be scored readily in an objective manner.

5. It can be used to sample a wide range of subject matter.

6. It has doubtful value as an item for measuring *achievement.*

7. Difficulty is encountered in constructing items that are either completely true or false without making the correct response obvious.

8. It encourages guessing. The student has a 50 percent chance of marking an item correctly without any knowledge of the subject matter involved.

9. A true/false test is likely to be low in reliability unless it includes an extremely large number of items.

There are a number of critical points to be observed in constructing the true/false test items.

1. Make approximately half of the items true and half false.

2. Do not make one part of a statement true and the other part false.

3. Do not make the true statements consistently longer than the false statements.

4. Direct students to indicate responses by one of the following methods: (1) encircle "T" of true and "F" if false; (2) mark true items with a plus sign and false items with a zero, not a minus sign; (3) write "True" or "False" before the statement; (4) encircle or write yes or no as the answers to direct questions.

5. Avoid negatives and involved statements.

6. Make application of things learned in as many of the items as possible.

7. Avoid using such words as all, none, never, and so on, in such a manner as to make them "specific determiners."

8. Where possible, make the crucial elements come near the end of the statement.

MULTIPLE CHOICE

The multiple-choice item consists of an incomplete statement followed by several phrases, words, or clauses from which the student must select one that will complete the statement in accordance with directions.

The multiple-choice test item in its various forms is one of the most valuable types that can be incorporated in a written test.

1. *One right answer.* This is the simplest kind of multiple-choice item. The student is required to identify the one correct response listed among several items that are totally wrong but not obviously wrong.

2. *Multiple right answer.* This is more complex than the one right answer multiple-choice test form. The multiple right answer allows for the student to choose a combination of correct answers.

MATCHING, LIST-CORRECT-ORDER, COMPLETION TESTS

The matching test includes two lists or columns of related topics such as words, phrases, clauses, or symbols. The student is required to match each item in one list with the item in the other list to which it is most closely related.

Classification, a type of matching test, requires the student to classify several terms, phrases, or clauses and so on, in terms of certain definite categories. The same points should be observed in constructing this type of test. The classification type can and should be substituted for the matching when several things listed in the exercise bear a definite relationship to other things listed. Many variations of this type of test item can be used effectively.

The listing or enumeration test requires the student to supply a list of terms, rules, or factors, and so on, that have been taught and emphasized in a given course. It is used frequently, but is often abused. The student may or may not be required to list in a particular order the things called for.

The correct-order-of-rearrangement test requires the student to indicate the order in which items listed should occur. The list may include a few items in addition to those that are to be arranged in a certain order. If extra items are included, the student is required to do two things: (1) pick out the items that apply, and (2) arrange them in a given order.

The simple completion test requires the student to recall and supply one or more key words that have been omitted from statements. The words, when inserted in the appropriate blanks make the statements complete, meaningful, and true. The statements may be isolated and more or less unrelated, or, they may be combined to form short paragraphs that carry a continuous line of thought.

There are several variations of the completion test. The simple completion item requires the student to *recall* certain information. The controlled completion is a variation that merely requires the student to recognize and select from a list of possible responses the correct answer for each blank. The controlled completion item has not been used extensively but is coming into more common use.

ESSAY

In the essay test, the student is required to make a comparison, write a description, or explain certain points over which instruction has been given. Although it has been criticized severely, it can be designed to provide an effective measurement of certain important outcomes of instruction.

EMRO TRAINING PROGRAM

Once the job task analysis has been successfully completed, you can begin to develop the training program for the EMRO.

The establishment of a comprehensive training program will ensure appropriate training of EMRO staff in emergency response and implementation of the Emergency Management Plan.

OSHA 29 CFR 1910.38, 1910.119, 1910.120 and 1910.156; 40 CFR 112; and 40 CFR 261 delineate training requirements for emergency response personnel for implementing chemical emergency plans, and require that they be provided training opportunities that enhance emergency response capabilities.

Personnel assigned specific duties during an emergency should receive training appropriate to their assignments. Satisfactory completion of the required training should be mandatory prior to an individual assuming an EMRO position assignment.

A modular approach to training should include:

- Lesson plans (Figs. 4–2a-b)

- Audiovisual aids

- Presentation notes (Figs. 4–3a-b)

- Student materials (readings and handouts)

- Tests

- Training documentation forms

An overview of the plan should be provided to all personnel assigned to the EMRO and should be offered to local emergency response organizations. The objectives of the training should include familiarization of the attendees with the background for emergency planning, the Emergency Management Plan, its activation and implementation, emergency communication skills, record keeping requirements, and an overview of the concept of operations.

As appropriate, personnel assigned to the EMRO will be provided training in their assigned emergency response functions. Within the scope of this training the following topics may be discussed:

- Emergency communications

- Hazards assessment overview

- Emergency classification

- Damage assessment

- Protective action recommendations

- Off-site support agencies

- Reentry and recovery operations

- Emergency damage control operations

- Search and rescue operations

- Assembly area operations

LESSON PLAN MODULE:	TIME ___	MONTH/YEAR ___/___	CLASS CODE ___	PAGE ___ OF ___

LESSON TITLE

_____

LEVEL OF INSTRUCTION   COGNITIVE   PRACTICAL

                                                          _____   _____

BEHAVIORAL OBJECTIVES

TRAINING AIDS AND EQUIPMENT	REFERENCE MATERIAL

PREPARATION

PRESENTATION	INSTRUCTOR NOTES

Figure 4–2a

The lesson plan (Figs. 4–2a and 4–2b) is a blueprint that will guide you in teaching the course material. The purpose of the lesson plan is to:

- *Standardize* training

- Present material in proper *order*

- *Emphasize* material in relation to importance

- Avoid *omission* of essential material

- Run class on *schedule*

- Provide for trainee *participation*

- Increase *confidence* of instructor, if new

The Lesson Plan consists of the following basic elements:

- *Lesson plan module number:* Appearing on the top left of the lesson plan, this indicates the number order of the module.

- *Time:* This item provides the estimated time associated with presentation of the training module.

- *Month/year::* This block provides you with the date of creation of the lesson plan materials.

- *Class code:* The class code provides information on the level of instruction. For example: A = Awareness Level, O = Operations Level, S = Specialist Level, T = Technician Level, IC = Incident Commander Level. You may see more than one code in this block if the material applies to several levels of proficiency.

- *Page ___ of ___:* Provides you with the page number and total page count of the lesson plan.

- *Lesson title:* Provides the lesson title of the module.

- *Level of information:* This block indicates the level of instruction **cognitive**, for knowledge-based instruction. **Practical** for skill based instruction.

- *Behavioral objectives:* This block describes the lesson objectives in terms of what the student should accomplish upon completion of the instruction.

PRESENTATION	INSTRUCTOR NOTES	PAGE ____ OF ____

Figure 4–2b

- *Training aids and equipment:* This block provides a recommended list of equipment and training aids required to present the module.

- *Reference material:* This block provides a listing of the sources of information used to prepare the lesson materials.

- *Preparation:* This block provides information on instruction preparation.

- *Presentation:* This block provides an outline of the dialogue for each portion of the presentation. It highlights key points and focuses on critical aspects of instruction.

- *Instructor notes:* This block provides a reference to specific training aids to be used with the associated presentation text.

The responsibility for the coordination of the emergency preparedness training program should be assigned to a specific department within the company, preferably one that has a vested interest in ensuring the quality of training for personnel who are assigned EMRO duties. This may entail some senior management oversight and/or the assignment of an audit function to a nonbiased third-party group.

Instructors are a vital part of any instructional system, and the effort put into helping prepare them to undertake the functions expected of them will be effort well spent. Many instructors are not accustomed to instruction that emphasizes how the student performs rather than how the instructor performs.

However, instructors are just as critical to the ISD team as in a traditional setting. A clear understanding of the critical functions that they must perform will help them fit into their role. Since instructors will contribute heavily to the planning and carrying out of the implementation phase, they should be brought into the team as soon as practical.

Instructors often will be someone other than the designer, developer, or evaluator of instruction. They must be trained for their role as an instructor, and must be able to demonstrate their ability to work effectively in the particular training setting.

IMPLEMENTING A TRAINING MANAGEMENT PLAN

One of the critical items in the success of the training program is an instructor's manual that describes the course and gives directions for administering the course. You should develop a comprehensive document. As a minimum, it should contain the following:

LESSON NOTES

Figure 4–3a

1. A clear, complete description of the course.

2. A description of the target population.

3. Directions for administering and scoring tests.

4. Directions for administering the course.

The instructional program should include guidance on:

1. What you wish to accomplish (in the form of learning objectives).

2. How you intend to accomplish it (in the form of lessons plans, instructional materials and delivery system, and

3. How you will know if you meet your objectives (in the form of tests and other appraisal instruments).

Be sure the basic information you need is included in the training manual. You will have to add any site-specific material you deem necessary. If you are not satisfied with the manual, get back with those who developed it and attempt to resolve differences or obtain the missing information. If you still do not have adequate information to carry out your responsibilities, do what the manual says—even if you disagree. But document what you think should have been different; the training process is never complete, so there will be time for changes in any or all parts of your program.

In addition to a thorough review of the instructor's manual, you may need supplementary information as cited above. The reasons for this are:

1. Unless the instructor's manual was prepared with your particular facility in mind, some necessary details may be missing. You may have to provide details of how the Emergency Management Plan will be integrated with the rules and regulations of your particular state and local area, and with your equipment, or personnel. You will need to make sure of such essentials as scheduling, equipment locations, personnel assignments, and any other details peculiar to your particular situation.

2. As an instructor you may be required to complete forms or perform other activities not included in the manual.

Most of what has been said about the instructor's manual is also true of the student materials you will develop. The trainee must have a clear idea of what he/she is supposed to be doing in order to make optimum use of the learning material. Again,

LESSON NOTES

SLIDE #

SLIDE #

SLIDE #

Figure 4–3b

you will want to thoroughly review the student manual and go through the proper channels to clarify or modify any unacceptable areas. And again, as you did for the instructor's manual, you may need to provide supplementary materials describing unique characteristics of your facility and the local regulations.

After you have been oriented to the instructional materials, and have mastered the necessary skills, you will conduct instruction in accordance with the instructor's manual. As a part of the instructional activity, you should document any required changes and other observations and participate in follow-up activities.

From a practical point of view, it is almost impossible to design instruction that will provide solutions to all possible problems. Some students will always have trouble mastering certain objectives and performing certain tasks. The trouble spots will be different for different people. One of the major duties of the instructor is to identify such problems and to provide assistance where needed. There will be students who are unusually fast or slow. The more capable students must be kept from becoming uninterested and bored, and the problems of the less capable students must be diagnosed and appropriate action taken. Your emergency management program should be flexible enough to make certain provisions for training individuals of varying capabilities and degrees of motivation; however, it continues to depend on classroom managers or instructors to meet unexpected requirements.

Included at the end of this chapter are sample checklists and guidelines that you may find useful as you develop your training program. In the next section we will review some instructional techniques you may wish to apply as you implement your training program.

INSTRUCTIONAL TECHNIQUES IN TRAINING

There are two kinds of groups which use participation for learning: discussion groups and conference groups. Discussion groups merely "discuss" predetermined subjects with the objective of explanation, problem solving, and the possibility that some new thinking may develop.

With conference groups, the instructor *has predetermined all the objectives and other relative data and leads the group to agreement on the data through the participation method.* The instructor's role is to stimulate and clarify discussion. *You are not a lecturer.*

The success of a conference depends on the instructor's knowledge of the subject and his ability to use the following techniques and tools.

ENCOURAGING PARTICIPATION

Seemingly minor points of technique in conference teaching are actually of major importance. For instance, you should condition your reflexes to give credit at all times for any offering, good or bad, by participants. Analysis will show that offerings and questions by group members are largely psychological and not always objective. The subconscious desire of a group member to establish himself or be recognized is greater than he realizes. Grasp every opportunity to show individuals in their best light. Nothing encourages participation more.

You should never miss the opportunity to build up any of the participants, but be cautious about overbuilding any one member of the training group. The reasons are obvious.

Another way to encourage participation is to ask a question. The question is the basis for holding group attention and serves many purposes:

1. It can keep people on the subject. (The mind tends to dwell on the subject of the question to the exclusion of extraneous information.)

2. It can keep attention at a high level by generating thought on the subject of discussion.

3. It can place ideas firmly in the minds of members of the group.

4. It can test the progress of information flow.

5. It can control participation within the time limits and schedules set by the conference leader.

Use an "overhead" question directed at the entire group. This is one of the most effective ways to get discussion started. Don't be alarmed if the group is slow to answer. This is common. Another way of getting discussion started is with "Let's suppose" type questions, based on a hypothetical situation or a "case history" question related to an actual experience. A direct question, aimed at one participant, should be avoided until discussion has started.

To keep discussion going, use questions like these:

1. "Can anyone add anything to that?"

2. "Does anyone disagree/agree?"

3. "Can anyone give us an actual example?"

4. "Anyone like to comment on that?"

5. "(Individual by name), how do you feel about this idea or point?"

6. "Anyone thought about this part of the problem?"

7. "Would this idea or technique work in all situations?"

THE IMPORTANCE OF ALERTNESS AND MEMORY

Two good assets for an instructor are alertness and memory. You should be alert to facial expressions and suppressed desires of participants. You should also possess the memory to carry your training objectives in mind as well as the details of ideas offered by students. For instance, a student raises a question which causes some discussion. Three hours or a day later, when that subject comes up again, you can remind the group that "Jim Smith" brought this up yesterday. Here again, you are reminding the participants that their offerings are meaningful. In being alert to small signs and group reactions, you use your eyes and thus accomplish another purpose—holding attention.

GAIN ATTENTION STEP

A gain attention step is something that the instructor does to either gain or to maintain the attention of the students. Often, a gain attention step is used for the introduction of the presentation. Items such as little-known facts, startling statements or a question directed at the entire class is effective in gaining attention. Visual aids are also exceptional tools for instructors to utilize. Brightly colored charts and overheads spur student interest, allow everyone to focus on the same item, and also aid in student comprehension. An effective method is to use a gain attention step in your introduction. This is simply a mechanism whereby you are able to capture your audiences initial attention.

Examples of a gain attention step, include but are not limited to:

- A dramatic opening slide

- Having the attendees introduce themselves and state what they expect to take away from the presentation

- Verbal or other visual clues (flash the lights)

- Dramatic gestures

Generally speaking, the gain attention step is anything you use to draw the focus of the attendees to you—the instructor.

SPEECH AND MANNER

You should, of course, enunciate clearly, use a good choice of words and good grammar.

Good instructional technique appears effortless, fun, and informal. To help promote this kind of atmosphere, your manner should be informal and natural throughout the training session. Your attire and that of the participants should be informal whenever possible.

To what degree should you use humor? Every training session needs light moments—you should inject humor whenever the opportunity presents itself. However, don't overdo it. Humor is like salt on a steak: a pinch or two enhances the flavor, but too much can ruin the whole meal!

TRAINING SESSION TOOLS

LESSON PLAN

The lesson plan provides you with a sequence of objectives and details of what you must cover and when. An effective lesson plan should be easy to read from a distance with large type or print. The layout should be simple: cues in the right column; questions and statements in the left column; colored pen or pencil can be used to highlight or emphasize cues. Allow for plenty of space between ideas. The lesson plan should be housed in a three-ring binder.

TEAR-OFF CHART PAD EASEL

The easel helps you to gain and hold attention and stimulate and clarify discussion. It has many advantages over a blackboard. It's neater, cleaner, and easier to read. Completed sheets can be referred to later or put up on the wall. Wax crayons are easier to work with than magic markers—they don't squeak or dry up.

The following points should be kept in mind when using the chart pad:

1. Write your statements or questions so that they can be read by the partici-

pants in the back of the room. Write big and don't labor your writing. Get the idea on the sheet, then step back and say what you wrote.

2. If you are a "lefty," the easel should be positioned to your right—vice versa if you are a "righty." Allow plenty of room to move from the podium to the easel.

3. When you have no further use for the idea you have recorded on a chart pad page, flip the page. In other words, always have a clean page ready to go when you start a new topic.

CHARTS

Charts play a role similar to the chart pad. They are also effective in introducing, clarifying, or summing up a topic. Keep your charts simple—one idea to a page using as few words as possible. Most legible color combinations are:

- Black lettering on yellow stock

- Green lettering on white stock

- Blue lettering on white stock

- White lettering on blue stock

- Black lettering on white stock

Lettering should be easy to read from a distance: letters 2" high and ¼" wide project 55 feet; letters 1" high and ¼" wide project 30 feet.

When using charts, always prepare the group for the chart you are about to unveil. For example: "Ladies and gentlemen, you are all aware that our Emergency Management Plan..." or, "In appendix... Here it is." (Unveil the chart or diagram). Avoid competing with your own chart for the group's attention. Pause after you expose the chart and give the group some time to digest it. Then, highlight, amplify, or summarize what's on the chart. And above all, make sure that each chart you show *serves a specific purpose.*

HANDOUTS

Handouts provide students with reference material. Handouts are effective in bringing in nonparticipants. They also eliminate the need for note taking and can be used for written exercises. Handouts should not be distributed until after the topic has been discussed.

CAUTION

A caution: always check your handouts well in advance of the training session. If they are out of sequence or are the wrong handouts, you'll have real problems during the training session.

THE TRAINING ROOM

The training room is an important tool and should be selected and set up with careful thought given to size, seating arrangement, atmosphere, and location. You should make it a point to seat the participants so that participation is balanced—with both sides of the table participating. The horseshoe or "U" seating arrangement is ideal for the students and for you.

STUDENTS' PLACE CARDS

(table tents) Place cards help you remember the students' names and establish a particular seating arrangement.

COFFEE BREAKS

Coffee breaks at the right time in the morning and afternoon (usually 10 am and 3 pm) relieve group fatigue and make your job of holding attention and interest easier. Three-to-five-minute stretch breaks in the morning and afternoon also help to relieve fatigue and restlessness.

THE CLOCK

The clock can work for or against you. If it works against you, remember, the pressures of time are solely yours and should never be evidenced by any outward show to the group. If the group feels this pressure, participation will be unnatural and limited. It may even cease completely!

INSTRUCTOR'S SELF EVALUATION CHECKLIST

The checklist enables you to objectively measure the quality and quantity of your performance during and after the training session (Appendix A and Appendix D).

HANDLING TRAINING SITUATIONS

1. Irrelevant offerings can be turned to the advantage of the member making the offering if the leader merely says, "That is an interesting thought, Jim." Then, if you can transpose the thought into something more constructive and logical by using at least some of the words of the originator and then give credit to the originator for this thinking on the subject, you accomplish two things: You establish a good point, and you gain the respect and further participation of the originator.

2. If open discussion is wanted and time is available, the following question might be asked to bring out uninhibited participation. "What do you think of this?" (Write the idea on the chart pad.)

3. If you want to establish a *positive* conclusion, a question can be asked that generates a positive agreement, such as, "What advantages do you see in this?" Obviously, the group will compete in contributing further *advantages* and therefore establish the required positive concept.

    If you require a negative conclusion to establish his point, you might ask the opposite, "What disadvantages do you see in this?" It is surprising how experts use of the question can channel group thinking. You might ask, "Suppose one member challenges either vein?" By then, of course, the group reaction is so overpowering that the dissenting member's challenge can be thrown to the group and free you from taking sides.

4. To prevent discussion from wandering from the point, say, "Can someone tell me what bearing this has on our problem?" Or, "Your point is an interesting one, but let's get back to our subject."

5. To suggest that no new information is being added, say, "Can anyone add to the ideas already given on this point?"

6. To register steps of agreement and disagreement, say, "Am I right that we all agree or disagree on this point?"

7. To bring the *generalizing* speaker down to earth, say, "Can you give us a specific example of that point? Your general idea is good, but I wonder if we can't make it more specific."

8. In order to maintain the focus/direction of the class, say, "I wonder what bearing this has on the question."

9. To suggest there are some talking too much, say, "Are there those who haven't spoken who have ideas they would like to present?"

10. To suggest the value of compromise, say, "Do you suppose the best course of action lies somewhere between those two points of view?" (Show the two points on the chart pad.)

11. To draw the timid but informed member into the discussion, say, "Melvin has experience in this area. Suppose we ask his opinion."

12. To handle questions asked of the leader, say, "I don't know. Who does?"

13. To help the member who has difficult expressing himself, say, "I wonder if what you're saying isn't this?" or, "Doesn't what you said tie in with our subject something like this?"

14. To encourage further questions by friendly comment say, "That's a good question. I'm glad you raised it. Anyone have an answer?"

15. To break up a heated argument, say, "I think we all know how Harry and Fred feel about this. Now, who else would like to get in on it?" (The leader can also state that 100 percent agreement is not expected.)

In using questions to call attention to weaknesses in discussion or procedure, you must be careful to avoid statements that might indicate your own opinions on the question under discussion. There is seldom a conference that does not have one or more characters in the group as well as awkward situations.

The *know-it-all* wants to impose his opinion on everyone else. To handle them effectively, check off his opinions with other members of the group. Encourage the group to comment on his/her remarks freely. *Let the group take care of him.*

The *arguer* tries to get you into an argument. *Keep cool.* You can never win an argument. Always make him back up his opinions. Draw out other students' opinions and turn them back to the arguer. Avoid getting personal.

The *meek* is in every group and must be brought out. Call him by name and ask for an *opinion.* Or, ask him an easy question, one he/she is sure to be able to answer. Then praise him. Have him read handouts. This person is worthy of your attention.

If you have come up against a *so-whatter*, point up something he has done as a good example of the point you are trying to make. Bring up things you know he is interested in.

To take the play away from a *long-winded participant* say, "You raise a number of interesting points which should keep us busy for a good while. Would anyone else like to comment on one of them?" or, "While we're on this point, let's hear from some others."

The *pinner* works at pinning you down to an answer. When he does, simply bounce the question to the group by saying, "I don't know. Who does?"

To help the fumbler, the student who has difficulty expressing a point, say, "I wonder if what you're saying isn't this?" or, "Doesn't what you said tie in with our subject something like this?"

To a silly or illogical statement by a student, say, "All right, John, that's one way of looking at it." or, "I've never looked at it that way." Then, if you can transpose the thought into something more constructive and logical by using at least some of the words of the originator and then give credit to the originator for their thinking on the subject, you accomplish two things: You establish a good point, and you gain the respect and further participation of the originator.

If occasional whispering between two people gets bothersome, you can stifle it for good by abrupt silence and a friendly stare at the "whisperers." At *no* time should you indicate any displeasure with the group or any outward show that things are out of control. Never publicly remonstrate a group member. It should not be necessary and can be a source of dissension for other students.

To bring the *generalizing* speaker down to earth, say, "Can you give us a specific example of that point? Your general idea is good, but I wonder if we can't make it more specific."

The *free for all* is the greatest deterrent to most instructors and creates an inward panic caused by fear of losing control of your group. If, in the course of discussion, the entire group breaks out in confused participation, talking to each other rather than to you; step away from the center of the teaching area. You can nonchalantly stare out of the window or examine your schedule, with two purposes in mind: one, to give each member a chance to express himself; and two, to set the stage for reentry to the teaching area where your presence will be a factor in reorienting the group to more controlled procedures.

Even if you give up two full minutes of your time (and the length of time will depend upon the enthusiasm of the total discussion), you have gained considerably by freeing the minds of the individuals for future discussions.

POINTS TO REMEMBER

1. If you can't measure it, don't train for it: There must be a standard observable performance against which to measure trainee's progress *and* the means to make that measurement.

2. Training represents an investment, not solely a cost to a company. The proper question to ask of a training function is *not* "What is the cost of training?" but rather, "What is our *return* on the training investment?"

3. The lead time to produce qualified people (especially supervisors and managers) is long. The wise trainer *anticipates* needs. He or she begins planning with a manpower requirement forecast for one, three, and five years.

4. All company problems are *not* necessarily training problems. The effective trainer first reviews alternatives to training before making the decision to train.

5. Training program evaluation must be checked (measured) at three points in the training cycle: trainee's performance at entry into training, at close of training, *and* back on the job. A baseline is central to proper evaluation: otherwise how do you know if any change took place as a result of training?

6. Don't confuse knowledge with understanding. For example, a student can define delegation, explain how it works, discuss its effects, and pass a test *but* still not be able to delegate.

7. Don't confuse symptoms with cause.

8. Don't assume the latest training technique is a *panacea* for all company training programs.

9. Don't undervalue your worth or become passive, reactive, or apologetic for being a trainer.

10. Understand how to sell training. What do errors cost? What does above-average performance represent in dollars and cents?

11. Don't miss the opportunity to get into line for a year or so. Don't miss the opportunity to attend seminars on management (not on training).

INSTRUCTOR PRESENTATION CHECKLISTS

Two checklists are provided to aid you in preparing for and presenting an effective presentation.

Figures 4–4a-c deal primarily with the physical aspects of the presentation. Personnel, logistics, room appearance, audiovisual equipment, lesson plan, lighting, curtains, sound, and special effects are the items listed. You should review this checklist prior to the presentation to ensure the appropriate equipment is in working order and to avoid time-consuming disruptions which will reduce the effectiveness of your presentation.

Figures 4–5a-d concentrate more on the actual instruction by giving advice on how to maintain class interest and ensure understanding of the material. Items listed include control of interest, lesson organization, establishing a good learning environment and training aids.

Figures 4–6a-d provide an evaluation form for trainees who have finished the program.

PRE PARING FOR THE TRAINING SESSION

A successful training session requires a certain amount of advance planning. In addition to audiovisual equipment and a place to meet, you will need to determine the appropriate number of students, schedule a time convenient for all, and so on.

NUMBER OF STUDENTS

The best range is between 4 and 25 group members. Ideally, you'll need at least 4 students to generate a good group interaction. If more than 25 people will attend, you should schedule two (or more) sessions.

TIME

The session provides for at least eight hours of instruction; the time noted after each activity in the lesson plan is the *minimum* time that should be spent on it. You may conduct the entire session in one intensive day, or you may divide it up over several days.

As you plan the session, look over the estimated times and determine when you may need more—for example, a site visit scheduled as part of the training activity may take more than an hour. This will influence how you schedule the session.

SCHEDULE

Depending on your organization, you may need to make arrangements with participants, supervisors, or management to schedule the session without disrupting work routines.

ROOM

Arrange for a room at your schedule time(s) that is large enough to comfortably seat all the participants. Make sure enough chairs are available. Participants will do some writing—tests and note-taking—so arrange for writing surfaces, either tables or note pads. You may also want to provide coffee or soft drinks, particularly if the session will run longer than two hours on a given day.

EQUIPMENT AND MATERIALS

You will need audiovisual equipment as well as a stand or table so that the materials (overheads/slides) can be viewed by all participants. Don't forget extension cords. Make sure they are the right configuration (that is, three-prong) to work with the outlets and equipment.

You will also need a flip chart and marker, to record points made during the discussion. (A chalkboard may also be used.) Ask participants to bring their own pencils or pens, but provide extras just in case.

PHOTOCOPYING

Master copies of the handbook and tests are included in your training packet. Prior to the seminar, make enough photocopies of these for all participants, plus a few extra copies.

PRE-SEMINAR CHECKOUT

Make sure everything is in place at least two hours before the session is to begin. Is the room ready? Are there charts, a flip chart, a marker? Does the audio/video equipment work? Refer to the accompanying checklists.

FINAL CHECK BEFORE START OF SESSION

Classroom Management

_____ **Item A: Personnel and Logistics**

_____ Communicate the goals and objectives of the training session.

_____ Structure training hours.

_____ Schedule times with participants and managers.

_____ A list of participants is available.

_____ Beverages and/or food arrangements have been made.

_____ Extra pencils/pens/pads of writing paper.

_____ Training facility instructions are available (i.e., location of restrooms, etc.)

_____ **Item B: Room Appearance**

_____ The room has been reserved.

_____ The classroom is clean.

_____ Desks and/or tables are arranged neatly.

_____ There is adequate seating.

_____ There are adequate writing surfaces.

_____ Class-in-Session lights are turned on.

Figure 4–4a

FINAL CHECK BEFORE START OF SESSION

PAGE 2 OF 3

_____ **Item C: Audio/Visual Equipment**

_____ Ensure that equipment works.

_____ Set audio level.

_____ Videotape(s) advanced to appropriate segment(s).

_____ Compatible videotape player, monitors, extension cords.

_____ Monitor stand is available.

_____ Flip chart (or chalkboard).

_____ Marker (or chalk).

_____ **Item D: Lesson Plan**

_____ Lesson plan is arranged in current order.

_____ Lesson plan is customized.

_____ Copies of tests are available.

_____ **Item E: Lighting**

_____ Lights can be turned up when the instructor is the focus of attention or the students are working on a particular module.

_____ Lights can be turned down when modified lighting is necessary to highlight a film, slide, or some other training aid.

Figure 4–4b

FINAL CHECK BEFORE START OF SESSION

_____ **Item F: Curtains**

    _____ They are to be kept closed except when opened for a video presentation or to expose a training aid.

    _____ When opened, only the area necessary is exposed, i.e., only the blackboard or screen in use.

_____ **Item G: Sound**

    _____ The sound is adjusted so that all personnel in the classroom can hear the presentation clearly.

    _____ The sound level is adjusted so that there is no "feedback" (high pitched squeak) in the system.

_____ **Item H: Special Effects.**

    _____ Special effects can be used to add emphasis to a key point or retain attention without creating a "dog and pony show" atmosphere.

Remarks:

_____

_____

_____

Figure 4–4c

KEYS TO EFFECTIVE PRESENTATION

PAGE 1 OF 4

Control of Interest

_____ Item A: Student Involvement. The students are involved in the teaching process through maximum use of questions and practical exercises.

_____ Item B: Humor. Humor used in the presentation is appropriate (no religious, racial, or sexual overtones).

_____ Item C: Training Aids. Training aids are used where the subject requires visual or audio support.

_____ Item D: Interest Factors. Interest factors are used to contribute to the class.

Lesson Organization

_____ Item A: Introduction

_____ A Gain Attention step is used.

_____ The subject is tied in to previous and subsequent instruction.

_____ The training objectives are fully explained.

_____ Item B: Body

_____ The class is broken into meaningful segments.

_____ The segments of the class are presented in a logical sequence.

_____ Transitions are used to move from one segment to another.

Figure 4–5a

KEYS TO EFFECTIVE PRESENTATION

_____ Item C: Conclusion

    _____ The students are alerted for the review.

    _____ All main points are reviewed in a logical sequence.

    _____ There is a strong concluding statement.

Establish a Good Learning Environment

    _____ Item A: Communicate an OPTIMISTIC, HIGH STANDARD OF EXPECTATION to the group.

    _____ Item B: The lesson objectives are EXPLAINED until all the students see them as valid, important, attainable, and personally valuable.

    _____ Item C: Provide at least one INCENTIVE (tangible or intangible) for good performance.

    _____ Item D: "REINFORCE" any (and all) behavior(s) in the lesson objective(s) occurring during the practice portion of the lesson.

    _____ Item E: "EXTINGUISH" any (and all) inappropriate actions of the group.

Training Aids

    _____ Item A: The training aid(s) used:

    _____ Reinforce the spoken word.

    _____ Make things clearer.

    _____ Aid in retention.

Figure 4–5b

KEYS TO EFFECTIVE PRESENTATION

PAGE 3 OF 4

_____ Item B: The training aid(s) are:

    _____ Appropriate, simple, accurate, necessary, attractive.

    _____ Not a distraction.

    _____ Large enough to be seen by everyone in the classroom.

    _____ Not used as a crutch by the instructor.

    _____ In the proper position on the platform.

    _____ Removed or covered when no longer required.

_____ Item C: If an overhead projector is used:

    _____ The slides are neat and attractive.

    _____ Slides do not contain too much material.

    _____ The lettering is large enough to be seen by all learners.

    _____ The projector is turned off when no longer required.

_____ Item D: If the chalkboard is used:

    _____ The lettering is of proper size to be seen by all learners.

    _____ The lettering is neat.

_____ Item E: If a flip chart is used:

    _____ The lettering is of proper size to be seen by all learners.

    _____ The lettering is neat.

    _____ Color of markers is appropriate to distinguish key points.

Figure 4–5c

KEYS TO EFFECTIVE PRESENTATION

PAGE 4 OF 4

_____ Item F: If a 35mm projector is used:

    _____ The projector is of the type needed for presentation (sound/ silent).

    _____ The lens provides sufficient size to enable all personnel to see the slides.

    _____ Slides used are:

        _____ Professionally done

        _____ Created in-house

        _____ Other

_____ Item G: Videotape/Projector

    _____ Projector is easily seen by all personnel.

    _____ Sound is adjusted to meet the size of the room.

    _____ Professional tapes are used.

    _____ In-house tapes are used.

_____ Item H: Demonstrations

    _____ Actual item/equipment is used.

    _____ Safety precautions are provided.

    _____ Item/equipment check is accomplished prior to demonstration.

    _____ Simulation/Model used.

    _____ Comparison to actual items is provided.

Figure 4–5d

[YOUR COMPANY]

Emergency Management Program (EMP)

Training

Post-Evaluation

Page 1 of 4

For each of the items on the following, please indicate your opinion by circling a number from (5) to (1). Space is also provided for any comments you may have which will assist us as we plan for future training sessions.

5	=	Strongly Agree with Statement
4	=	Agree
3	=	Uncertain
2	=	Disagree
1	=	Strongly Disagree

PROGRAM CONTENT, STRUCTURE

1. The program was well organized.   5   4   3   2   1

2. The purpose of the program was clear.   5   4   3   2   1

3. The program achieved its purpose.   5   4   3   2   1

4. The program had real-life applications.   5   4   3   2   1

Additional comments:

_____

_____

_____

Figure 4–6a

[YOUR COMPANY]

Emergency Management Program (EMP)

Training

Post-Evaluation

Page 2 of 4

COURSE MANUAL

5. Course materials supplemented the   5   4   3   2   1
    instruction.

6. The course materials were well organized. 5   4   3   2   1

Additional comments:

_____

_____

_____

FACILITIES

7. The classroom arrangement was good.   5   4   3   2   1

8. The number of participants was   5   4   3   2   1
    manageable.

Additional comments:

_____

_____

_____

Figure 4–6b

[YOUR COMPANY]

Emergency Management Program (EMP)

Training

Post-Evaluation

Page 3 of 4

INSTRUCTORS

9. The instructors were knowledgeable   5   4   3   2   1
   about the subject matter.

10. The instructors encouraged participant   5   4   3   2   1
    input.

11. The instructors tailored their presentations 5   4   3   2   1
    to meet the needs of the audience.

12. The instructors interacted well with the   5   4   3   2   1
    participants.

Additional comments:

_____

_____

For each statement below, please respond to "YES" or "NO" and briefly explain your response.

13. I found particular topics of the course more useful than others.

    Yes _____   No _____

Please list below:

_____

Figure 4–6c

[YOUR COMPANY]

Emergency Management Program (EMP)

Training

Post-Evaluation

Page 4 of 4

Comments: (Which ones and why?)

_____

_____

_____

14. I would recommend particular topics to be added to the course.

    Yes _____   No _____

Comments: (Which ones and why?)

_____

_____

_____

15. I would recommend that the program could be improved in the following ways:

_____

_____

_____

Figure 4–6d

5

Demonstrating Proficiency:
Establishing and Maintaining Performance Standards

CHAPTER HIGHLIGHTS

You've planned, you've trained; now it's time to demonstrate proficiency under simulated emergency conditions. In this chapter we present a practical approach for conducting drills. Initially, we will define various types of drill/exercise activities. Please note, the terms used herein are not exclusive to the system discussed. Nor are they inclusive of all the terminology currently used to describe the various stages of drill/exercise activity.

The degree of sophistication you desire is based entirely on where you and your organization are in the development of your emergency management program. You should consider several variables before embarking on your drill/exercise program. We will discuss many of these variables in this chapter.

INTRODUCTION

Simulated emergency conditions can provide a measure of an organization's ability to respond to a real incident. However, as is often the case, there may be long periods of inactivity after initial training. Should an incident occur, personnel may find it difficult to respond appropriately. Periodic drills and exercises will help you maintain a high state of preparedness and test and validate your program before it is activated during an actual incident.

A coordinated drill and exercise program should include a variety of management and response proficiency demonstrations, each with varying degrees of complexity. Segregation of these functions into categories based on degree of complexity and participation allows for the application of common terminology and stresses the purpose and usefulness of such activities in an all hazards emergency management program. Drill and exercise activities can be defined by establishing a tiered system based on complexity, level of participation, intent of the activity, functions, and the physical locations involved. Each higher tier of activity should build toward the demonstration and assessment of an effectively integrated incident management program.

TYPES OF DRILLS AND EXERCISES

An integrated drill and exercise program ensures that the EMRO can successfully assume emergency roles and functions in accordance with the Emergency Management Plan (EMP). A drill/exercise program is essential for the success of the overall program.

Drills and exercises can be broadly classified in four major categories:

- Orientation/walk-through

- Tabletop/minidrill

- Functional exercise

- Full-scale exercise

Each of these drill and exercise categories require different resources and skill sets to implement. Some require minimal preparations and are simple to execute, while others may be more complex and require greater efforts and resources. Each provides its own benefits. The following subsections describe each in more detail. However, before we delve into a detailed discussion of the activity types, some definitions are provided to establish a common terminology.

DEFINITIONS

Orientation/walk-throughs: Orientations and walk-throughs are highly supervised sessions that follow formal classroom instruction and are aimed at developing and maintaining skills in a particular operation. All orientation/walk-throughs should be supervised and evaluated by a qualified drill controller. The designated drill controller should possess the necessary expertise in his/her functional area of responsibility.

Tabletop/minidrills: Tabletop or minidrills are supervised instruction periods aimed at limited testing, continued development, and maintenance of skills in a particular operation by individuals or teams. All tabletop/minidrills should be supervised and evaluated by a qualified drill controller. The designated drill controller should possess the necessary expertise in his or her functional area of responsibility.

Functional, Full-Scale Exercises: Full-scale exercises are designed to test major portions of the emergency management program and the implementation capabilities of the EMRO represented at various levels, facilities, and participating entities.

Scenario: A scenario is a script that describes various simulated emergency events.

Players: Players are those participating EMRO personnel, and other entities who have been assigned active roles in the management/response to incidents.

Controllers: Controllers are designated personnel assigned responsibility for providing drill/exercise messages and scenario-specific data to the players. Controllers also may initiate certain actions to ensure continuity in the developing drill/exercise scenario. They are generally used in minidrills and larger scale exercise activities. The control group is responsible for monitoring drill/exercise play to ensure that the scenario proceeds according to the schedule of events and that players' response activities are conducted within the intended parameters of the activity. They also ensure the level and pace of activity are realistic, given the limitations imposed by the type of activity and scenario. Controllers have responsibility for stopping play by the organization they are monitoring, as appropriate. Because of the nature of their duties, controllers may interact with players to ensure the integrity of the drill/exercise activity.

Specific responsibilities include:

- Being familiar with the Emergency Management Plan and specific Emergency Plan Implementing Procedures (EPIPs) of the individuals or groups being monitored;

- Maintaining a record of player activities throughout the drill/exercise;

- Monitoring the scenario timeline/message list to ensure the activity is proceeding as planned;

- Monitoring and regulating the pace of the drill/exercise in coordination with appropriate management;

- Addressing any perceived concerns with scenario information or player response by coordinating with drill/exercise management;

- Monitoring player actions to ensure their activities stay within the established guidelines of the drill/exercise;

- Conducting and participating in debriefing sessions for the participants and providing input to evaluators concerning their specific area of control.

Evaluators: Evaluators have responsibility for documenting and evaluating the actions of the players during the drill/exercise. Evaluators are a main source of input to the drill/exercise critique process. Evaluators should be used at all levels of drill/exercise activity. Their documentation provides the data to be used to critique the drill/exercise and evaluate the effectiveness of management/response activities. Evaluators should not interact with players or interfere with player responses.

Specific responsibilities include:

- Being familiar with the plan and procedures as well as with the organizational structure of the individuals or groups being monitored;

- Observing and recording player responses to exercise stimuli and other player activities;

- Evaluating player performance in light of exercise objectives and plan

194

and procedural requirements;

- Gathering all player notes, documents, or other visual or written materials used to support their activities following termination of the drill/exercise;

- Participating in debriefing sessions for the participants and providing input concerning exercise activities; and,

- Completing evaluation based on comparison of response activities to exercise objectives, performance criteria, Emergency Management Plans and implementing procedures.

Observers: Observers are nonparticipants invited to view a drill/exercise. Observers are usually interested individuals or organizations who observe exercise activities as a learning experience.

Simulators: Simulators are generally used in drills/exercises activities. Simulators act out the roles of individuals or organizations not actively participating in drill/exercise activities. They are responsible for stimulating response efforts through the use of prescribed messages or reacting to players' inputs. They must be technically knowledgeable to respond to player inquiries, and able to simulate credible and realistic responses.

Specific responsibilities include:

- Being familiar with plans and procedures of the individuals or groups being monitored;

- Creating the necessary messages to drive the scenario;

- Knowledgeably responding to requests for information from players;

- Coordinating simulated response activities and information, as appropriate and necessary, with other simulators;

- Maintaining communication logs;

- Tracking unresolved items and troubleshooting problems in coordination with appropriate exercise management; and,

- Participating in debrief sessions for the exercise organization.

ORIENTATION/WALK-THROUGH

Orientation/walk-throughs are used to acquaint personnel with policies and procedures developed in the planning process and material presented in the classroom setting, by providing a general overview of the Emergency Management Plan and its provisions. Orientation/walk-throughs are especially effective in ensuring that EMRO personnel understand their roles and responsibilities.

They also help to clarify vague and highlight critical plan elements. While an orientation/walk-through does not normally involve any explicit simulation or role playing, it can be used to review the Emergency Management Plan and EPIPs and informally apply them to potential emergencies or past events familiar to everyone.

Orientation/walk-throughs can be characterized by:

- Knowledge testing, rather than skill testing

- Individual and team training

- Team-building focus by a single management/response group

- A conference room or small group setting

- Interactive discussions among participants

- No mobilization of resources

- No simulation except as necessary to prompt consideration of issues as appropriate

- Response and management dialogue guided by a moderator

- Documentation of participant discussions

- The moderator's personnel's assessment of personnel's knowledge as compared to performance, in relation to a set of training objectives

TABLETOP/MINIDRILL

A tabletop/minidrill is primarily a learning exercise that takes place in a meeting room. Prepared situations and problems are combined with role playing to generate discussion of the plan, its procedures, policies, and resources. Tabletop/minidrills are excellent for familiarizing groups and organizations with their roles, and for practicing proper coordination. They also provide a good environment in which to reinforce the logic and content of the plan, and to integrate new policies into the decision-making process.

Tabletop/minidrills allow participants to act out critical steps, recognize difficulties, and resolve problems in a nonthreatening format. This tier of activity involves mobilization of personnel, and some equipment, and demonstration of incident response skills by the participants. Activities at this tier may range in purpose from demonstration of a discrete and narrowly defined aspect of incident response to a more comprehensive assessment of skill levels and interaction among representative elements of the EMRO. Simulation through the use of a drill support organization is introduced at this level.

These types of drills may encompass such activities as emergency response team drills, emergency facilities drills, fire drills, and notification call-outs. Additional drills might focus on the ability of multiple elements within the EMRO to work together effectively, as well as demonstrating each element's specific skills, decision making abilities, and knowledge of management/response operations.

Tabletop/minidrill activities are characterized by:

- Practice and testing of a specific functional response and a focus on demonstration of knowledge and skills, as well as management/response element interaction and decision making capability;

- Actual or simulated response locations and/or facilities;

- Involvement and interaction of a limited number of management/response elements, with optional involvement of external organizations;

- Mobilization by limited elements of the EMRO;

- Varying degrees of actual, as opposed to simulated, notification and mobilization of resources;

- Simulation, directed through a drill support organization, of nonparticipating essential activities that impact management/response efforts;

- Use of controllers to ensure that activity remains within intended parameters; and,

- Evaluation of performance against a set of drill objectives by the drill support organization or an evaluator.

FUNCTIONAL EXERCISE

A functional exercise involves emergency simulation designed to train and evaluate emergency operations management.

More complex than the tabletop/minidrill, it focuses on interactive decision making and agency coordination in a classical emergency management environment such as the Emergency Operation Center (EOC), mobile command center (field location), or with off-site groups. All field operations may be simulated activities, although messages and information are typically exchanged using realistic communications via radios and telephones. The functional exercise permits decision makers, command officers, and coordination and operations personnel to practice emergency response management in a realistic forum with time constraints and stress such as may be experienced during an actual incident. It typically includes several organizations and agencies practicing a series of interactive emergency functions for direction and control, assessment, and evacuation.

Functional exercises involve multiple organizational tiers and are more extensive than tabletop/minidrills in scope, scale, participation, and location. Therefore, functional exercises are significantly more complex. The primary focus of functional exercises is to assess the interaction of organizational elements to perform incident management and emergency response functions in an uninterrupted linkage of elements within a company.

Activities are characterized by:

- Operational demonstration of emergency management/response capabilities;

- Actual or simulated response locations and/or facilities;

- Involvement of multiple emergency management/response organizations and/or various organizational tiers of the company, with optional involvement of external organizations;

- Mobilization of personnel and resources at varied geographic sites;

- Varying degrees of actual, as opposed to simulated, notification and mobilization of resources;

- Simulation, through the drill support organization, of nonparticipating essential activities that impact response efforts;

- Use of controllers, evaluators, and observers to ensure that exercise activity remains within intended parameters; and,

- Evaluation of individual and team performance as compared to exercise objectives.

FULL-SCALE EXERCISE

A full-scale exercise evaluates several components of the EMRO simultaneously. The interactive elements of a community emergency management program may also be activated for a full-scale exercise. Similar to the functional exercise, the full-scale exercise is more complex, as it includes elements which are outside of the span of control of a single entity. A detailed scenario is used to simulate an incident which requires on-scene direction and operations and includes coordination and policy-making roles. Direction and control, mobilization of resources, communications, and other special functions are rigorously exercised. The full-scale exercise is reserved to distinguish those infrequent but important exercises involving all organizational tiers extending from the local facility level to corporate senior management.

This level of activity involves performance of crisis management activities and emergency management/response skills by representative elements throughout the company.

The primary focus of full-scale exercise activities is the integration of management/response efforts throughout the organization so that the response of the company is uniform and consistent. Full-scale exercise activities are distinguished from functional exercise activities by the involvement of *all* levels of the company in emergency management/response activities.

A second characteristic of a full-scale exercise is the extended duration of play. Because a large number of participants are involved, exercise play will generally be extended over a longer period to allow issues to fully evolve as they would during a crisis, and allow realistic play by all of the involved groups. A full-scale exercise is generally sponsored by the executive management of the company.

PROGRESSIVE DRILL AND EXERCISE PROGRAM

Recognizing that the drill and exercise types described in this book are intended to build on one another, each becoming more complex and comprehensive, a progressive exercise program is recommended. This program would first schedule basic orientation/walk-throughs for personnel. These orientation/walk-throughs introduce the plan, its components, and specific policies and responsibilities which apply to the EMRO and other elements represented in the Emergency Management Plan.

Tabletop/minidrills are then conducted to practice actual coordination and leadership provisions of the plan, including those emergency operations concepts which may be new to many personnel. These will be followed by functional exercises to integrate the Emergency Management Plan's more complex sections under simulated emergency conditions.

The entire Emergency Management Plan should be evaluated by an annual Full-Scale exercise. The annual emergency preparedness exercise scenario should include, as a minimum, the following elements:

- The basic objectives of the exercise and the appropriate evaluation criteria

- The date, time, place, and participating organizations.

- The simulated events

- A time schedule of real and simulated initiating events

- Arrangements for advance information and materials to be provided to evaluators

- A narrative summary describing the conduct of the exercise/drill. As appropriate, the summary should include descriptions of:

  Simulated casualties

  Off-site organization(s) assistance

  Rescue of personnel

  Use of protective clothing

  Deployment of industrial hygiene teams

  Public information participation

The exercise scenario should vary each year to ensure that all major elements of the EMRO and of the Emergency Management Plan of the participating organizations are tested within a five-year period. Provisions should be made to start an exercise between 4PM and 11PM, and another between 11PM and 7AM, once every six years. Exercises should be conducted under various weather conditions, when possible. Some exercises should be unannounced.

GENERAL EXERCISE ACTIVITY PROCESS

Design, Develop, Conduct, and *Evaluate* are the four cycles describing activities that are essential for the continual improvement and verification of management/ response capabilities.

DESIGN

The design process is essential to developing realistic drill/exercise activities and is critical to a successful proficiency demonstration program. The design process should begin with the selection of a designated group or team assigned responsibility for each phase of the drill/exercise process, or who will provide critical input to the process.

The design process includes, but is not limited to:

- Selection of a design team and controller organization

- Establish the basic parameters of the drill/exercise activity

- Determine drill/exercise objectives

- Determine drill/exercise scope

- Determine activity focus and format

- Determine simulation and activity levels

- Determine awareness policy

- Establish working groups for exercise development, conduct, and evaluation

- Determine means of assessment

- Establish a workplan and schedule

- Determine resource requirements

- Secure approval by management

DEVELOPMENT

The development phase consists of those steps taken to create, fully prepare, and organize the drill/exercise activity. The process of developing drill/exercise activities can be divided into several primary tasks. These include training development, scenario development, general management and administration, materials production, and predrill/exercise activities. These activities are interrelated and generally occur concurrently.

- Player and exercise organization training development

  Materials should include:

  Lesson plans

  Audiovisual aids

  Presentation notes

  Student materials (readings and handouts)

  Tests

  Training documentation forms

- Scenario development

  Develop scenario options

  Draft scenario

  Finalize scenario

- General management and administration

- Secure approval by management

CONDUCT

The actual conduct of the drill/exercise activity consists of initiating play, simulating, monitoring, controlling, or facilitating activities to ensure that play remains within the design parameters and issues that are raised. It also involves documentation of player activities and terminating play as appropriate.

- Initiating play

- Controlling the activity

- Terminating play

- Evaluation (for all types of drill/exercise activity)

EVALUATION

Evaluation of drill/exercise activities is critical to the continual improvement of crisis and emergency management/response capabilities. This phase of an exercise activity consists of collecting and analyzing data, documenting findings and recommendations for improvement, and ensuring information is integrated into the drill/exercise program planning activities. The evaluation process includes, but is not limited to:

- Data collection

- Analysis

- Documentation and presentation of findings

CRITIQUES

Drills and exercises provide the principal means for assessing the effectiveness of the Emergency Management Plan, its associated implementing procedures, and the state of preparedness of personnel and equipment. To evaluate the performance and lessons learned, a critique should be conducted in a timely manner following each drill or exercise. The critique should be initiated by the drill support organization with the assistance of an emergency preparedness oversight committee.

The objectives of the critique session should be to evaluate the management/response capabilities of the participating personnel, to assess the adequacy of dedicated emergency equipment, and to identify deficiencies in the Emergency Management Plan and EPIPs as they are written.

The purpose of a critique is to compare the observed response of the participants with the response anticipated in the scenario. Each evaluator should use a prepared evaluator's checklist to evaluate the observed response and compare it with the anticipated response. Each Evaluator's Checklist (Fig. 5–1) will be unique

EVALUATOR'S CHECKLIST

PAGE ___ of ___ PAGES

LOCATION/POSITION BEING EVALUATED:_____

TIME	EXPECTED RESPONSE	ACTUAL RESPONSE

SIGNATURE:_____ DATE:_____

Figure 5–1

to the drill or exercise and to the facility or personnel being evaluated. In addition, each evaluator should keep a chronological log using an evaluator's/controller's log sheet (Fig. 5–2).

The critique should include a discussion of both acceptable as well as unacceptable emergency responses. Observed deficiencies, as well as recommended corrective actions, should be recorded and documented by the drill support organization and maintained by the emergency preparedness oversight committee. Recommendations should include any provisions for additional training, assignment of appropriate personnel, suitability/performance of emergency equipment, and any changes in scope or completeness of the Emergency Management Plan and Emergency Plan Procedures.

The drill support organization and/or emergency preparedness oversight committee should be responsible for preparing a written summary of the exercise critiques. This summary should include the objectives of the drill/exercise and a list of participants, controllers, and observers. This summary should also include a list of any identified deficiencies, as well as recommendations for their resolution. This information should be provided to upper management for assessment and resolution.

CONTROL/CRITIQUE TECHNIQUES

Controllers should use the following techniques to control drill/exercise activities in accordance with the scenario.

EXERCISE MESSAGES

Exercise messages provide information to the participants and/or cause the participants to take actions needed to keep the exercise moving smoothly. The Controller will give a hard copy of the exercise message to the designated participant at the time specified on the exercise message. As appropriate, the controller will provide the essential information verbally. The controller will follow through and clarify the message by answering questions to ensure that the participants do not read extraneous meaning into the message. *Controllers should not tell participants what action they are expected to take.*

EVALUATOR'S/CONTROLLER'S LOG SHEET

PAGE ___ of ___ PAGES

LOCATION/POSITION BEING EVALUATED: _____

TIME	SUMMARY OF ACTIVITIES

SIGNATURE: _____ DATE: _____

Figure 5–2

CONTINGENCY MESSAGES

Contingency messages are used only if participants fail to take the major actions expected from the exercise messages by the time designated. Controllers should give the contingency message to the designated participant and explain, in as much detail as necessary, what actions the participant is expected to perform. Contingency messages are used to keep the drill/exercise on schedule though their use may indicate inadequate plan implementation. *Controllers should notify the lead controller prior to using a contingency message.*

SUPPLEMENTARY MESSAGES

Supplementary messages provide information and/or situations for specific EMRO (drill/exercise participants) personnel. Supplementary messages require the recipient to take some action to respond to the message. Controllers should give supplementary messages to the designated participant and explain, in as much detail as necessary, what action the participant is expected to perform. Supplementary messages are used to ensure participation by all personnel involved in the exercise. *Controllers do not need to notify the lead controller prior to issuing a supplementary message.*

CONTROL INFORMATION

Controllers, in designated locations, provide information upon a specific request for information or performance of a task. This can be provided either verbally or via hardcopy. Controllers will refer to the time span indicated on the sheet for applicability of the message. Control information exists under the categories of emergency facility information and maintenance-operating control information. Other categories may be devised for sub-scenario portions of the activity. Controllers may direct participants to simulate actions that are outside the scope of the drill/exercise. Supplemental messages are issued at the designated time and reflect the actual time unit status information would be received.

FACILITY/LOCATION INFORMATION

Controllers issue facility/location status information at designated intervals to drill/exercise participants. This represents key parameter information.

EMERGENCY MANAGEMENT/RESPONSE ORGANIZATION INFORMATION

Controllers utilize sample questions to test the reactions of the participants. Controllers may free-play questions to provide challenge to the participants. These questions simulate the presence of persons who would normally be involved in an actual event.

CONTROLLER GUIDANCE

Controller guidance is provided as needed to direct the participant's actions on complicated evolutions. This includes guidance on degree of simulation and actions that may be needed if an unexpected event occurs (a small actual fire for scenario purposes becomes larger than expected, for instance).

OBSERVATIONS OF RESPONSES TO MESSAGE

Controllers should be especially observant of participants' responses to the messages received. Controllers also rate areas in which the scenario information caused confusion, generated unexpected responses, or was incomplete. Records of these evaluations are maintained for the critique. Evaluations will be used on a real-time basis to decide if a contingency message will be needed.

OBSERVATIONS OF EMERGENCY PLAN IMPLEMENTING PROCEDURES (EPIP) USAGE

Controllers should observe the participant's usage of EPIPs. Notes should be taken on what procedures were referenced and if done appropriately to the existing conditions. No evaluation will be made in the final critique on correct usage of nonemergency procedures.

Evaluators use the following techniques to evaluate the performance of the EMRO.

OBJECTIVES

Evaluators evaluate participants' actions against the stated objectives. Controllers should ensure all objectives for the facility/location being evaluated are understood and included on the evaluator checklist sheets.

CHECKLISTS

Evaluators evaluate participants according to the criteria specified in the facility/location specific checklists. This should include all objectives. Additional criteria are represented to test general response of the organization.

GENERAL OBSERVATIONS/RECORDS

Evaluators observe and record all significant activities of participants. The time of each activity is recorded in the evaluator/controller journals. These journals will be used to evaluate the adequacy of the emergency response facility logs prepared by participants and assist with evaluations for the critique and written report.

DOCUMENTATION/CHECKLISTS

Documentation should be requested from all participants at the conclusion of the drill/exercise critique. All participant documentation, logs, controller records, and evaluation checklists should be used to prepare the written evaluation of the drill/exercise.

DRILL/EXERCISE PARTICIPANT ROLES

PLAYERS AND CONTROLLERS

As defined above, controllers have a very distinct role in a drill or exercise. While the players' responses are dictated by the developing scenario, it is the controllers' responsibility to ensure that the drill/exercise scenario develops in an orderly, coordinated manner to permit the adequate testing of the players. During a drill or exercise, controllers are the only personnel who will provide scenario information, in the form of messages and data to the players. Additionally, controllers are the only personnel who may prompt or initiate certain actions to ensure continuity in the developing scenario.

Furthermore, if a situation occurs during a drill or exercise which warrants an alteration in the schedule or sequence of events set forth in the scenario, controllers are the only personnel who can initiate such changes.

EVALUATORS

Evaluators do not possess any authority to control or alter the scenario during a drill or exercise. While documenting and evaluating the players' responses during the drill or exercise, evaluators may question the players to clarify actions taken or procedural concerns. Evaluators shall not prompt the players during a drill or exercise. If an evaluator has a concern regarding the scenario, that evaluator should discuss his or her concern with a controller, who will then decide if further action is required. Sometimes, a controller may perform a dual role as a controller/evaluator.

OBSERVERS

Observers also do not possess any authority to control or alter the scenario during a drill or exercise. Observers shall not interfere with the actions of the players, controllers, or evaluators. Any questions or concerns by an observer during a drill or exercise should be communicated to a controller, who will then decide if further action is required.

IDENTIFICATION OF PARTICIPANTS

During a drill or exercise, the various participants will need to identify themselves. Color-coded arm bands, vests, hats, and other means can be utilized to differentiate between the players, controllers, evaluators, and observers.

BASIC ORGANIZATIONAL ELEMENTS AND RESPONSIBILITIES

For the coordination and conduct of a drill or exercise to be carried out effectively and efficiently, a structured drill/exercise control organization must be established. Within this organization, responsibilities, authorities, interfaces, and lines of communications must be clearly delineated to ensure that the drill/exercise control function is precisely coordinated. The manpower level required to staff such an organization (also called the controller team) depends on the scope of the drill or exercise and the complexity of the scenario utilized. In some cases, the timing of certain events in the scenario may allow an individual to fill more than one controller position assignment. It is important to note, however, that for each assignment, the controller should be thoroughly familiar with his or her responsibilities; the players' expected responses; and the procedures they will utilize during that portion of the drill or exercise; and any actions that may have to be simulated to ensure the continued development of the scenario.

The following paragraphs provide descriptions of the key positions within the drill/exercise control organization, and the authorities and responsibilities associated with those positions.

LEAD CONTROLLER

The lead controller is responsible for the overall management and technical direction of the controller team. The lead controller monitors the progress of the drill or exercise to ensure that the scenario develops in an orderly, coordinated manner. During a drill or exercise, the lead controller coordinates the issuing of drill/exercise messages with the other members of the controller team. Should a situation occur during a drill or exercise that warrants an alteration in the schedule or sequence of events set forth in the scenario, the lead controller is the only individual who can approve the initiation of such changes. The lead controller also serves as the primary controller team interface with key players and evaluators regarding the development of, or alterations to, the scenario.

During a drill or exercise, the lead controller should be positioned at a location which is expected to be a central point for the drill/exercise activities. This point will provide for sufficient communications with the other members of the controller team. The lead controller will normally be stationed at the emergency operation center.

FIELD OR MOBILE FACILITY CONTROLLER

The field or mobile facility controller is primarily responsible for issuing drill/exercise messages and data describing the incident scene and facility/location conditions. Since most scenarios are constructed to allow the players, both on-site and off-site, to react in response to postulated events at the facility/location, most of the messages issued during a drill or exercise are issued from the field or mobile facility controller. In addition, all data related to facility/location operations or status, and current meteorological conditions, are issued from the field or mobile facility controller.

For these reasons, the field or mobile facility controller normally will not interface with any other member of the controller team other than the lead controller. The field or mobile facility controller should be an individual who possesses a thorough knowledge of the facility/location configuration and operations, and who also played a significant role in the preparation of the scenario.

Depending upon the scope of the drill or exercise and the complexity of the scenario utilized, the field or mobile facility controller may require one or more assistants to ensure that messages and data, including the simulated effects of potentially hazardous materials releases, are issued in a timely manner to support the developing scenario.

EMERGENCY RESPONSE FACILITY CONTROLLERS.

The emergency response facility controllers are responsible for monitoring the progress of the drill or exercise at designated on-site and off-site emergency response facilities, issuing messages as required by the scenario, and identifying and resolving potential problems that might adversely affect the progress of the drill or exercise. Each controller should be thoroughly familiar with the expected response of the players stationed at his/her assigned emergency response facility, and with the procedures the players will utilize. Controllers stationed at the various emergency response facilities routinely communicate with the lead controller, but may communicate among themselves as the situation dictates.

ADDITIONAL PERSONNEL

Depending upon the details of the scenario and the extent of play to be carried out in a drill or exercise, additional personnel may be required to act as controllers. For example, the scenario may require the assignment of controllers to issue messages and data to one or more of the following:

- Emergency repair and damage control teams

- Fire brigades

- Security teams

- First aid teams

- Hospital staff

DRILL/EXERCISE MESSAGES & METHODS FOR ISSUING

DRILL/EXERCISE MESSAGES

Throughout the course of a drill or exercise, messages will be issued by controllers to the players. Drill/Exercise messages (Fig. 5–3) contain information about the developing scenario, which the players will then utilize to determine their response actions.

EXERCISE MESSAGE   E-24

TO: *Field Incident Commander*

FROM: *Mobile Command Controller*

   TIME: 1045

CONTENT:

Facility status. Unit has been shut down. Work continues on securing the unit.

Emergency Damage Control Teams (2) are in staging area awaiting dispatch.

ACTION TAKEN:

_____

_____

_____

_____

_____

_____

_____

_____

_____

Figure 5–3

Besides the information describing the scenario events, each drill/exercise message should contain the following information:

The EMRO position title(s) of the player(s) to whom the message will be issued; the location(s) at which the message will be issued; and the time at which the message will be issued.

The time is normally given as the real clock time. Real clock time (such as 10:30 AM or 1030 hours) indicates the actual time at which the message will be issued if the scenario is developing according to its originally prescribed schedule. Should a situation occur where play is suspended and then resumed such that the real clock time indicated on the messages cannot be used, then the drill/exercise time (for example, H + 4:30) will be utilized. Drill/exercise time indicates the number of hours and minutes that have elapsed since the start of the drill or exercise (H + 00:00). Should the use of drill/exercise time become necessary, the lead controller will advise each controller of the correct drill/exercise time to be utilized when play is resumed.

Prior to a drill or exercise, assignment of responsibilities for issuing messages will be specified within the controller team. These assignments are specified according to the locations where the messages will be issued. During a drill or exercise, the lead controller will normally instruct the responsible controller to issue a message at a prescribed time. If more than one message is to be issued in rapid succession at the same location, the lead controller may instruct the responsible controller to do so.

Often a message will be issued at more than one location simultaneously. In such a case, the lead controller will coordinate the issuance of the message with all of the responsible controllers to preclude any mismatches in the transmission of information among the players. When a message is issued to a player, the responsible controller must be alert to the possible misinterpretation or misreading of that message. If the message is misread by the player, the controller should immediately convey the correct information to that player. *In a drill,* if the contents of the message are read correctly, but misinterpreted, the controller should discuss the message content and any expected response actions with the player to rectify the situation. *During an exercise,* controllers are not allowed to interpret messages for the players.

Sometimes, a message may be read and interpreted correctly, but the player's response action is incorrect. If this incorrect response action does not adversely affect the conduct, or the continuity of the scenario, the player should be allowed to proceed without further controller prompting. Errors in judgment and incorrect response actions are potential problems that must be dealt with under actual emergency conditions.

CONTINGENCY MESSAGE   C-7

TO: *On-shift Emergency Manager*

FROM: *Lead Controller*

TIME: 0735

CONTENT:

Field Incident Commander has called with the following information.

FIRE/EXPLOSION	*Facility operator reports vapor release. A leak has been detected on a sour fuel line from the depropanizer reflex drum. The operator cannot reach the isolation valve due to the release of sour gas which contains H_2S.*
FATALITIES/INJURIES/MISSING	*A moderate fire continues in the area of the facility. Four men are down and unaccounted for. Four men are seriously injured.*

ACTION TAKEN:

_____

_____

_____

_____

_____

Figure 5–4

SUPPLEMENTARY MESSAGE   S-64

TO: *Public Affairs Director*

FROM: *Media Controller*

                    TIME: 1050

CONTENT:

John Jones from Channel 15-TV, NBC, Chicago is on the air with a special report on the incident from Chicago. It appears that all of the national stations are running reports on the incident.

ACTION TAKEN:

_____

_____

_____

_____

_____

_____

_____

_____

Figure 5–5

CONTINGENCY MESSAGES

Contingency messages are utilized during a drill or exercise when a player's actions or lack of actions may adversely impact the conduct of the drill or exercise. Contingency messages, when utilized, document and call attention to the deficiency. Situations requiring the use of contingency messages may include the reporting of vital information that would affect or alter the response actions of other players or that might require the declaration or escalation of the emergency classification.

Figure 5–4 provides an example of a typical contingency message. The format for a contingency message is not significantly different from that of the drill/exercise messages previously described, with the exception that the contingency message is identified as such.

If a situation warrants the use of a contingency message, the responsible controller should discuss the situation with the lead controller and obtain his/her concurrence prior to issuing the message.

SUPPLEMENTARY MESSAGES

Supplementary messages are routinely used during drills and exercises to create "what if" situations which will provide additional training for specific players who may or may not have an active role in that drill.

The information contained in supplementary messages creates problems or miniscenarios that do not affect the conduct of the drill, but will provide the players with opportunities to resolve situations that might occur as a result of, or in conjunction with, the emergency. Figure 5–5 provides an example of a supplementary message. Again, the format for these messages is not significantly different from that of the other messages previously described. However, supplementary messages should be identified as such.

The use of supplementary messages is normally left to the judgment of the responsible controller. The issuance of supplementary messages usually is not time-dependent.

COMMUNICATIONS WITHIN THE DRILL/EXERCISE CONTROL ORGANIZATION

Once a structured drill/exercise control organization has been established, a communications network within the controller team must be established. Generally, communications within the controller team will be accomplished via telephone or radio or through direct face-to-face communications.

Specific methods for communicating with each controller have been established, including predesignated telephone numbers and radio channels for controller use. A directory of the controller assignments and associated telephone numbers or radio channels should be included as part of the controllers' instructions. Immediately prior to a drill or exercise, the lead controller will verify the predesignated telephone numbers and, if possible, radio channels to ensure that the communications network is intact and that all controllers are properly prepositioned.

During a drill or exercise, most communications within the controller team will occur between the lead controller and the other controllers via telephone. However, communications between the lead controller and those controllers assigned to the environmental monitoring field teams or any other controllers normally accessible by radio only can prove to be more difficult. Thus, these controllers must be capable of carrying out their assigned functions with a minimum of direction from the lead controller. Additionally, the entire controller team must ensure that the scenario develops according to its originally prescribed schedule to preclude any mismatches in data and message transmissions.

During a drill or exercise, all communications within the controller team should be kept short and to the point, particularly those communications with the lead controller.

PHONETIC ALPHABET

The Phonetic alphabet assigns a name to each letter so that when spoken the letter is clearly understood. The use of a phonetic alphabet can be invaluable when trying to communicate in high noise areas or over long distances. For example, the "A" may be phonetically communicated as "Adam" or "Apple," thus "A as in Apple." The phonetic alphabet should be used when transmitting letters of the alphabet to distinguish between similarly sounding letters. When necessary to identify any letter of the alphabet, a standard phonetic alphabet should be used.

Acronyms should be avoided as they may cause confusion. Always be sure to identify whether the message is part of a drill or if it relates to a real incident. To ensure this, at the beginning and ending of all communications say, "This is a drill" or "This is not a drill" as appropriate. This is especially important when communicating with off-site organizations or over an unprotected radio circuit.

An example of a phonetic alphabet is provided below:

A - Alpha	E - Echo	I - India	M - Mike
B - Bravo	F - Foxtrot	J - Juliette	N - November
C - Charlie	G - Golf	K - Kilo	O - Oscar
D - Delta	H - Hotel	L - Lima	P - PaPa

Q - Quebec	T - Tango	W - Whiskey	Z - Zulu
R - Romeo	U - Uniform	X - X-Ray	
S - Sierra	V - Victor	Y - Yankee	

SCENARIO DATA AND DISSEMINATION METHODS

OPERATIONAL DATA

Operational data, also referred to as facility/location parameters, is utilized by the players to evaluate facility/location conditions, assess the severity of an incident, and evaluate the extent of damage. The data is normally presented as it is available from the operating system computers. This data is usually provided in 15-minute increments throughout the duration of the drill or exercise, unless rapidly changing refinery conditions dictate smaller time increments. Operational data will normally be posted in the field or mobile location and emergency operations center at specific intervals, and interpolations of that data are provided upon request.

Since the field or mobile controller will often be asked to interpolate the data provided in the tables, and approximate other facility/location parameters not provided in the scenario manual, this individual should possess a thorough knowledge of facility/location operations and the specific facility/location configuration.

METEOROLOGICAL DATA

Meteorological data is utilized by the players to evaluate plume dispersion, plume travel, and plume washout in order to complete on-site and off-site projections.

CURRENT METEOROLOGICAL DATA.

Current meteorological data is normally provided to the players upon request, in a format consistent with the way that the data is obtained under normal conditions. Current meteorological data is normally provided in 15-minute increments. Since meteorological conditions usually change relatively slowly, interpolation of the data should not be necessary. The data values which are closest to the time of interest should be provided to the players. If the scenario dictates a rapid change in current meteorological conditions, the data would be provided at shorter intervals.

FORECAST METEOROLOGICAL CONDITIONS

Forecast meteorological conditions are normally provided to the players upon request in the form of one or more drill/exercise messages. Such messages simulate a U.S. National Weather Service forecast. Depending upon the procedures utilized under actual conditions, the location at which these messages are issued may be different from the location at which current meteorological data is issued.

ENVIRONMENTAL DATA

Environmental Release Data, utilized to determine exposure, is provided to the players upon request. This data is drawn from tables or graphs for material released. The data presented in tabular form is normally provided in 15-minute increments. If data is requested at times other than those provided in the tables, the corresponding graphs should be utilized to determine the correct data values.

Environmental release flow rate data, which is utilized in conjunction with environmental release data to determine release rates or verify that a release is actually occurring, is provided to the players upon request. This data for all key release points is normally drawn from tables or graphs. The data presented in tabular form is normally provided in 15-minute increments. If data is requested at times other than those provided in the tables, the corresponding graphs should be utilized to determine the correct data values.

Area monitoring data, which is utilized to evaluate in-refinery conditions and the extent of damage, will be provided to the players upon request. This data will be provided in tabular form in 15-minute increments. During periods of rapidly changing conditions, interpolation of the data may be required. If so, a linear relationship between the two nearest given data values should be assumed.

Personnel contamination data is utilized by the players to determine the methods for handling and treating an injured, contaminated individual. The data provided normally consists of a drawing indicating the location and severity of the injury and the areas and extent of contamination. To further test the ability of the players to locate the contaminated areas with their survey instruments, one or more tags may be placed on the injured victim. If a tag is utilized, precautions should be taken to protect the wearer from any unnecessary exposure to potentially hazardous materials and/or situations.

Once the surveys for contamination have been completed, the responsible controller should instruct the players to substitute those data values for the actual survey instrument readings. Any areas not identified on the drawing as being contaminated should be assumed to be free of any contamination.

Plume monitoring data is utilized to locate, track and evaluate the severity of the plume for the purposes of updating projected doses to on-site and off-site areas.

This data is presented in a tabular form for each affected predesignated monitoring location, for specific downwind distances at one-, one-half-, or one-quarter-mile increments, and for specific off-centerline distances. For data other than that provided for predesignated monitoring locations, area maps will be used to facilitate interpolation of the data during plume search operations. Data for those predesignated monitoring locations under consideration and specific downwind distances will be provided in 15-minute increments. In addition, conversion factors will be provided for converting the given count rate values, should an other-than-standard probe be used by the players. Data will be provided to the players upon request, but only after the field team has demonstrated their survey techniques and procedures.

FORMULATION AND IMPLEMENTATION OF CONTINGENCY ACTIONS

Unforeseen situations may arise during a drill or exercise that will require the controller team to prevent those situations from adversely impacting the conduct of the drill or exercise. An example would be the occurrence of an actual incident during an exercise at an operating facility/location. In such situations, a controller must be capable of making a rapid assessment of the situation and advising the lead controller immediately. The lead controller will then discuss what actions are to be taken with the key players and evaluators.

Once all parties have agreed upon the contingency actions, if any, to be implemented, the lead controller will advise the controller team accordingly. Under no circumstances should a controller interfere with any player's efforts to respond to an actual off-normal or emergency condition. If controller assistance is required, such as aiding injured personnel, such assistance shall take precedence over any other controller functions.

PREDRILL/EXERCISE BRIEFINGS

CONTROLLER TEAM BRIEFING

Prior to a drill or exercise, the lead controller will conduct a controller team briefing for the entire controller team to prepare for the drill or exercise, and to review any last-minute details. At this briefing the lead controller will review the following:

- The controller's instructions contained in the drill/exercise scenario manual

- The controller assignments, including locations for prepositioning

- The details of the drill/exercise scenario, including:

  The schedule of the expected sequence of events

  Controller responsibilities and methods for message handling

  Controller responsibilities and methods for disseminating operational data

  Methods for issuing contingency messages and implementing contingency actions

  The responsibilities and criteria for documenting drill/exercise activities

  The drill/exercise evaluation criteria

EVALUATION TEAM BRIEFINGS

In the evaluation team briefing, prior to an exercise, the controller team should review and discuss the guidelines for exercise coordination and conduct and the details of the exercise scenario. Exercise scenario details include the schedule of the expected sequence of events, controller responsibilities and methods for message handling, controller responsibilities and methods for disseminating operational messages, and methods for issuing contingency messages and implementing contingency actions.

Controller and evaluator assignments, including repositioning or rendezvous locations, must also be discussed.

BRIEFINGS FOR KEY PLAYERS

In the briefings for key players prior to a drill or exercise, the lead controller and other key members of the controller team should meet with the key players to review and discuss the following: drill/exercise control organization and controller responsibilities; guidelines for drill/exercise coordination and conduct; methods for message handling; methods for disseminating data; and methods for issuing contingency messages and implementing contingency actions.

DOCUMENTATION OF DRILL/EXERCISE ACTIVITIES

Throughout a drill or exercise, each controller should thoroughly document the activities of those players he/she observes. Normally, this information is logged on forms provided in the scenario manual. Following the conclusion of the drill or exercise, this information will be compiled to develop a written assessment of the conduct of the drill or exercise activities and the performance of the players and to prepare a drill/exercise chronology.

The types of information to be recorded, and the level of detail of the information to be recorded, should include:

- The times notifications are performed or received

- The times emergency classification is declared

- The arrival and departure times of players at the various emergency response facilities

- The times the various emergency response facilities are activated and deemed operational

- The times important briefings or other communications occur

- The times drill/exercise messages are issued

- The times contingency actions are implemented

- The times supplementary messages are issued

- The responses of the players to the developing scenario

In addition to their drill/exercise control functions, controllers may also serve as evaluators. The following criteria, (Fig. 5–6-5–12) also referred to as evaluation elements, should be used to evaluate exercises. Controllers' documentation of a drill or exercise should consider these evaluation elements as appropriate to the scope of that drill or exercise.

SUMMARY

An exercise is an event that tests the major portion of an Emergency Management/Response Organization (EMRO), while a drill is simply a supervised instruction period aimed at testing, developing, or maintaining skills in a particular operation. Players are participating emergency response organization members, while controllers are personnel who provide messages and scenario data to the players or prompt or initiate actions to ensure drill/exercise continuity. Evaluators are those personnel who document and evaluate player actions, while observers are personnel who simply view a drill or exercise and have no evaluation, control, or participatory function.

Drill/exercise messages are prepared materials given to players to ensure drill or exercise scenario continuity. Contingency messages are prepared during conduct of a drill or exercise when a player's actions or lack of actions may adversely impact the conduct of a drill or exercise. Supplementary messages are used during a drill or exercise to create "what if" situations for additional player training.

Unless the scenario calls for more rapid movement, operational data will normally be provided to the players in 15-minute increments. A controller may interpret messages for a player during a drill, but may not offer any interpretation during an exercise.

A picture with labels on it will normally be used to identify injuries and contamination levels of personnel. A controller's log should contain the logged time that every event in the controller's area occurs along with a description of the event and responses of the players to the developing scenario.

CONDUCTING A CRITIQUE: CHECKLIST

Fifteen minute break for players while evaluators and lead controller do quick overview of exercise.

Lead controller opens critique session with a few broad comments on performance, pointing out both good areas and problems. Sets the theme of professionalism and objective review of performance.

At conclusion of controller remarks, lead controller moderates a brief (two minutes is probably enough) report from each individual on performance in the exercise. Lead controller should try to keep a balance by asking the overly-negative person, "What went well," etc. Help players avoid fixing blame and concentrate on corrective comments about errors. Make a record of the comments.

After everyone has spoken, the lead controller distributes the critique sheet and asks everyone to sleep on their thoughts and fill out the critique sheet tomorrow. A date and method of return are provided.

The lead controller thanks everyone and the exercise is over.

Figure 5–6

CRITIQUE, EVALUATION, AND FOLLOW-UP CHECKLIST

_____ Examine general and specific objectives

_____ Select and train exercise evaluators

_____ Identify areas to observe

_____ Identify actions or decisions to observe

_____ Determine what performance is acceptable

_____ Observe exercise

_____ Attend immediate participants' critique

_____ Study the critique sheet submitted by participants

_____ Draft evaluation report (by critique group)

_____ Conduct evaluation and recommendations meeting

_____ Present recommendations and proposed follow-up

_____ Draft a follow-up memorandum for the Crisis

_____ Management Coordinator

_____ Monitoring implementation of recommendations

_____ Test follow-up with next exercise

Figure 5–7

EVALUATION REPORT CHECKLIST

_____ Evaluator's group observations

_____ Participants' debriefing comments

_____ Participants' written critique

_____ Comments received from controller and/or simulators

_____ Any subsequent clarification or discussion with participants

Reviewing the Draft Report

_____ Physical setting conducive to participation

_____ Agenda separating parts of the exercise into units for discussion (probably grouped by objectives)

_____ Ability to record comments of participants

_____ Participant interaction

_____ Consensus on recommendations (if possible)

_____ Summary of recommendations by chairperson

_____ Heavy emphasis on follow-up to implement recommendations

Figure 5–8

EVALUATION REPORT CHECKLIST

Preparing the Final Report

_____ Recommendations

_____ Objectives

_____ Summary of critique
session

_____ Scenario objective

_____ Major and detailed
events sequence

_____ Participant personnel

_____ Evaluation group report

_____ Directive,
announcements,
handouts

_____ Exercise development
group

Figure 5–9

(STRUCTURED EVALUATION QUESTIONNAIRE)

Please complete this form by placing an "X" in the appropriate box. Provide an explanation when you select the boxes "sometimes," "seldom," or "never."

NAME: TITLE:

DRILL POSITION (circle one):   Controller   Evaluator   Observer

1. Were the plans, procedures, and resources used during the exercise adequate?

    / / always   / / sometimes / / seldom   / / never

Explanation:

_____

2. Did the participants have access to the information they needed in carrying out their responsibilities?

    / / always   / / sometimes / / seldom   / / never

Explanation:

_____

3. Did the exercise address the exercise objectives adequately?

    / / always   / / sometimes / / seldom   / / never

Explanation:

_____

4. Were communication systems adequate for staff alert, notification, and emergency operations?

    / / always   / / sometimes / / seldom   / / never

Explanation:

_____

5. Was public information accurate and timely with respect to the actual play of the exercise?

    / / always   / / sometimes / / seldom   / / never

Explanation:

_____

6. Was the exchange of information among the participants adequate?

    / / always   / / sometimes / / seldom   / / never

Explanation:

_____

Figure 5–10

STRUCTURED EVALUATION QUESTIONNAIRE

In the left-hand column, record the five most important areas of concern raised by the exercise about the emergency management system. Give a reason for your choices in the center. In the right-hand column, write your recommendation for improvement or a solution.

KEY AREAS: REASON   RECOMMENDATIONS OF CONCERN

1.

2.

3.

4.

5.

Figure 5–11

PARTICIPANT EVALUATION QUESTIONNAIRE

Please take a few moments to fill out this form. Your opinions and suggestions will help us prepare better exercises in the future.

1. Please rate the overall exercise on the scale below:

   _____

   1   2   3   4   5   6   7   8   9   10

   Very Poor   Very Good

2. Compared to previous exercises, this one was:

   _____

   1   2   3   4   5   6   7   8   9   10

   Much Worse   Much Better

3. Did the exercise effectively simulate the emergency environment and emergency response activities?

   Yes _____   No _____

   If no, briefly explain why: _____

   _____

4. Did the problems presented in the exercise adequately test readiness and capability to implement the plan?

   Yes _____   No _____

   If no, briefly explain why: _____

   _____

5. The following problems should be deleted or revised:

   _____

   _____

6. I suggest you add the following problems to the next exercise.

   _____

   _____

7. Please add any other comments or criticisms on the remaining portion of this sheet or separate sheet.

   _____

   _____

Figure 5–12

6

Communicating in a Crisis:
The Management of Public Information

CHAPTER HIGHLIGHTS

In this chapter we focus our attention on the issue of crisis communication and the role it plays in how your emergency management/response efforts are perceived.

Today, more than ever before, effective crisis communication plays an integral role in successful emergency response. Furthermore, the opportunities for communicating are vast. There are approximately 1,150 television stations, 8,200 radio stations, 1,700 daily newspapers, 8,000 weekly newspapers, and more than 12,000 magazines in the United States.

Getting information about your company on the air or into print during an emergency isn't too difficult. But the sources and type of information are often not the information you want to convey to the public. Therefore, it is your challenge as a company to deliver a message that is simple, attention-getting, and memorable.

There are many issues—both positive and negative—relating to any crisis. This chapter provides guidance for supplementing Section 7, Public Information, and Section 8, Postincident Operations, of the Emergency Management Plan.

INTRODUCTION

Management is never put more strongly to the test than in a crisis situation. The objectives are immediate and so are the results. A crisis is an event requiring rapid decisions involving the media, which, if handled incorrectly, could damage your company's credibility and reputation.

That is why a company should develop a crisis communications plan as a supplement to Section 7 of the Emergency Management Plan and as part of its normal preparation for handling emergencies. The crisis communication plan should offer guidelines for immediate, effective, and responsible crisis communications. Such effective communications can help resolve a crisis and will help maintain a company's integrity and credibility.

The incident in Bhopal, India clearly demonstrated the inadequacy of the chemical industry's preparations for emergency communications. Management simply must devote sufficient resources to being able to communicate quickly, accurately, and effectively in response to any plant occurrence, large or small. A routine incident can be treated as front-page news by the media. We must be prepared to deal with public perception, as well as reality. You cannot allow the public communications functions to be a bit player, then expect a star performance when the going gets tough. The communications staff will not be ready, and the operations personnel are not likely to accept them as an integral part of the emergency response effort.

COMMON CHARACTERISTICS OF A CRISIS

A crisis can take many different forms with a variety of facets. But generally crises have some common characteristics. Some shared by most crisis situations are listed below.

- *Surprise:* We can never be certain when a crisis will occur or what form it will take. But a good plan will serve us in any situation.

- *Panic:* A certain amount of panic is inevitable. The degree of panic is inversely proportional to the degree of preparation. Plan now.

- *Rapid flow of events:* The early stages of a crisis can be confusing and chaotic. Reaction time at this stage is critical. Preparedness helps control the situation.

- *Lack of, or insufficient, information:* This creates uncertainty, but we must communicate. Early in a crisis, the media have neither the time to wait nor require a great deal of information. Give them what you have about the crisis as quickly as you can, dig for more, and provide background information on hand for this purpose.

- *Government involvement:* A crisis almost always concerns elected and appointed officials and government agencies. A good communications plan strongly considers important government audiences at every appropriate level.

- *Internal conflict and confusion:* This is inevitable. Whether it cripples action and stifles communication depends upon the level of preparation for, and cooperation during, the crisis.

- *Forgotten employees:* Our best allies often are left out, wondering what is really going on. Putting informed employees into action can help a lot.

- *Social ramifications:* Most crises affect the communities where we operate. But if we perform well during and after the crisis, we may even enhance our reputation.

- *Intense media scrutiny:* The media thrive on a crisis. If it is out of the ordinary, it is news. Since there are generally few eyewitnesses to the actual event, public opinion is formed by what is seen, heard, and read in the media. How well we perform with the media can have a great impact on public perception.

- *Siege mentality:* If planning has been poor, everybody heads for the bunker. But if there is a well-rehearsed crisis communications plan, there will be no need to hide.

When developing the crisis communication plan you need to understand and assess risk. Risk is the probability of something happening. Risk assessment is the science of determining those probabilities. Risk management consists of actions taken to reduce the risk to acceptable levels.

Both risk assessment and risk management rely on sciences of numbers. Risk communication, however, goes well beyond talking about numbers; it must address individual opinions, attitudes, and perceptions.

Risk is an everyday part of life in today's business environment. However, affected entities view risk differently. The company engineer may view risk as the probability of something happening. This is an analytical view using numbers to reflect the probability.

The company environmental staff may view risk in terms of the probable health effects related to exposure. The public, however, views risk in an entirely different fashion. The public response to risk is generally emotional. That is to say, the public perception of risk may not be in harmony with the results of the engineering or environmental models of risk.

The public, for example, uses many factors in addition to numbers in deciding whether something is risky. That is why communicating risk can be so difficult.

We often think facts and numbers of our risk assessments will convince the public to accept risk associated with the chemical industry. Instead, the public generally uses other factors to develop its perceptions and acceptance of the risks involved.

You may be tempted to dismiss the public's emotional reactions to the risks associated with your facility or its tendency to disregard numbers in favor of other considerations. But remember: *although the public perception of risk may not bear much resemblance to risk assessment, when it comes to their accepting the risk, perception is reality.*

RISK COMMUNICATION

An integral part of the crisis communication process is the communication of potential risk. Risk communication can either positively or negatively influence public reaction. Improperly presented data on risk can cause alarm, fear, rage, or even lead to an emergency or crisis. Remember, perception is reality.

Properly handled, communicating risk can reassure, lead to a better understanding, educate, and increase knowledge and confidence in the capability to handle emergency or crisis situations. In effect, good risk communication will diffuse a potentially explosive situation. Poor risk communication can shorten the fuse to the powder keg.

If viewed from a rational perspective, risk becomes logical, or nonpersonal. This is the risk analyst's perspective. However, if viewed from the irrational perspective, risk becomes an emotional issue, that is, it's taken as a personal matter. This is the public perception of risk.

When relating risk to the public there are eight primary factors that emerge as key in the acceptance versus nonacceptance of risk. The public will respond to the outrage value associated with their perception of risk. The greater the outrage value associated with an event, the greater the response from the public.

The risk must be perceived as:

Acceptable		Nonacceptable
Voluntary	vs.	Coerced
Familiar	vs.	Exotic
Nonmemorable	vs.	Memorable
Controlled by individual	vs.	Controlled by others
Fair	vs.	Unfair
Distance	vs.	Proximity
Trustworthy Source	vs.	Nontrustworthy Source
Low complexity of information	vs.	High complexity of information

Being aware of some of the factors that stand in the way of effective communication will help us plan for and overcome them.

- *No plan:* Being unprepared for a crisis causes confusion and a strong desire to remain silent. Instead, develop an operational Emergency Management Plan and balance the operational Emergency Management Plan with a crisis communications plan.

- *Normal fear:* Someone once described speaking publicly as an unnatural act. Under the best circumstances, it is unnerving for most of us. Communicating during a crisis can create a virtual adrenalin factory. Developing an Emergency Management Plan and implementing a viable, focused training program can significantly reduce fear and build confidence.

- *Fear of accountability:* When business people are interviewed by the media, their first concern is how their supervisors will judge them. Their next concern is how their peers will view them. Then they worry how they'll look and sound to their families and friends. Last of all is concern over how the public will feel in a crisis situation. The last concern must come first. If done well, the other concerns will take care of themselves.

- *Fear of revealing proprietary information:* Having a crisis communication plan and a well-trained crisis team can reduce the burden of this problem. When in doubt, get help.

- *Desire to avoid panic:* We often feel that if we communicate the real situation, we will cause panic among our employees or in the community. Consequently, some people clam up, which only makes people fear the situation is worse than it is.

- *Lack of a spokesperson:* If you don't have an Emergency Management Plan, there probably will not be a designated spokesperson. Valuable time can be lost spent scrambling to find someone in an incident. Designate a primary and at least two alternates to fill this critical position and get them placed in crisis communications training programs.

- *Legal implications:* Sometimes we are afraid to communicate because we might say something that could be used against us in court. During a crisis, you will have as much help as you need from company lawyers and public affairs people. They will guide you. If others are not available in the early hours of a crisis, your common sense and good judgment should guide you. *The liability concern should never stop you from taking responsible emergency actions and communicating about those actions.*

- *Protection of corporate and product reputation:* The best protection is a balanced Emergency Management Plan, supplemented by a crisis communications plan and trained personnel that can be implemented promptly.

- *Problem isn't solved yet:* Initially, people affected by the crisis are most interested in what is being done to contain the problem. The final outcome of the crisis may or may not be of immediate concern. Don't wait for a solution before you begin to communicate.

- *Desire to assemble all the facts quickly:* A crisis is often characterized by a rapid flow of events. There are times when information arrives like a flood and can't be processed quickly enough. There also are times when there is not nearly enough information to communicate. In both cases, we often feel the need to sort out everything neatly before we communicate. Reporters cannot wait. Don't expect them to. They will ask eyewitnesses, neighbors, or others.

COMMUNICATIONS BASICS

Communication may be defined as the transmission of information, ideas, emotions, skills, and other elements, by the use of symbols such as words, pictures, figures, and graphs.

Transmission is the ability to convey your message in a clear, concise, and understandable manner. How you convey your information in many respects is more important than the actual content of the information. The property of transmission in the communication process is probably the most prevalent property of communication, as is the use of symbols (verbal and nonverbal cues) in the transmission process. Communication also includes all of the procedures by which one mind may affect another.

Effective communications within groups as well as between pairs of individuals always requires a correct reading or interpretation of both explicit verbal cues and the more subtle, nonverbal cues. In an emergency, the ability to communicate quickly, accurately, and effectively is of unparalleled importance, as many communications must be made over radio or telephone without benefit of nonverbal cues.

Emergency communications should be a natural extension of the normal operating communication procedure. Before you begin, know your data. Work with key technical and management resources to analyze and assess relevant plant information. Crisis communications can be successful when focused on:

- Personalizing the message—don't use jargon

- Knowing your audience

- Controlling the size of the audience

- Involving community leaders

- Being conservative, and not overstating or understating the facts

- Working with the media

- Accessing outside resources

- Being organized

Accurate, timely, and complete communications form the basis for all emergency actions. More problems result from poor communications than any other single factor during emergency situations. Standard terminology and formality are important considerations regarding communications during normal plant operations and emergency situations.

All communications should follow the acronym FACT: formal, accurate, concise, and timely.

- *Formal:* Treat the person on the other end of the line as an official rather than a friend. Experience has shown that formality in communications eliminates confusion during emergency situations and adds to the overall efficiency of the Emergency Management/Response Organization (EMRO).

- *Accurate:* Ensure the facts are accurate, complete, and all units are provided. To ensure the communications are *accurate,* give only the facts, be sure the information is complete, and provide all measurement units. You should also get a complete repeat-back of the message. Request a repeat-back if one is not given immediately.

- *Concise:* Get your message across with as few words as possible.

- *Timely:* Late or overdue information can expand the problem. Timely information is essential. However, the quality of a task should not be sacrificed just to do it quickly. Poor or wrong information can be worse than late information. When making initial contact, especially with off-site organizations, identify yourself and find out to whom you are speaking. Ensure that you are speaking to the correct person.

The following suggestions are provided to assist you when you have to communicate during an emergency. Develop and practice these skills in nonemergency situations and you will find that you can respond more efficiently during an emergency.

Here are the skills you'll need to get the job done:

- *Prepare:* Think ahead and plan your communication. Give your communication a beginning, middle, and end. If you are briefing, and time permits, prepare good visual aids and arrange the briefing room in advance.

- *Clarify:* Make the communication clear and understandable. Unravel the difficulties in your own mind first. Evaluate the competencies of the person who is receiving the communication—is he technically knowledgeable? Avoid obscure ways of putting things. Seek clarifying questions—ensure accurate communications. Avoid acronyms and the use of jargon.

- *Simplify:* Put complex matters into simple form. Use analogies—relate the familiar to the unfamiliar. *Avoid complicated terminology.* Give an overview or outline first. Summarize the key points at the end of the communication.

- *Animate:* Make the subject come alive. Use vivid language and be enthusiastic regarding the communication. Treat all communications as if they were the single most important thing to be accomplished at the time.

- *Be yourself:* Foster the ability to cope with stress, nerves, and tension and behave naturally. Breathe deeply, eliminate nervous habits, and think confidently.

During the initial stages of a crisis, reporters generally will ask basic questions. Reporters feel compelled to ask many simple questions because they are generalists who need to educate themselves quickly. If you don't have the answer to a question, admit that you don't but explain that you'll try to get the answer. If you can't answer a question, explain why. Figures 6–1 through 6–9 provide examples of workpapers that can be used to prepare your response.

Reporters are taught to ask who, what, where, when, why, and sometimes how. Prepare accordingly, and you can respond quickly to such questions as:

- What happened?

- Is there any danger to the community?

- What are you doing to contain the danger?

BACKGROUND FACT SHEET

COMPANY:

FACILITY:

ADDRESS:

Township: _____   County: _____

PHONE #s:

Office _____

Fax _____

Emergency _____

Other _____

PRINCIPAL BUSINESS ACTIVITY:
AT THIS FACILITY

_____

_____

FACILITY FACTS:

Occupies: (in acres) _____ Under Roof (in sq. ft)_____

Items Produced or Processed: _____

Volume or Material Processed: _____

Number of People Served: _____

Value of Production: _____

Appoximate Annual Payroll: _____

EMPLOYEES:
Hourly Salaried Total:

1ST SHIFT _____

2ND SHIFT _____

3RD SHIFT _____

HISTORICAL BACKGROUND:

Facility Opened: _____   Previous Owner(s): _____

Major Modifications: _____   Year(s): _____

_____

Previous Incident(s): _____   Year(s): _____

_____

_____

OPERATES UNDER AUTHORITY OF:

At This Facility: _____   Issued: _____   Agency: _____

At This Facility: _____   Issued: _____   Agency: _____

At This Facility: _____   Issued: _____   Agency: _____

Revision Date: _____

Figure 6–1

PERSONNEL DIRECTORY

FACILITY	Name	Home Address	Office Phone Home Phone
Manager	_____	_____	_____
		_____	_____
Assistant Manager	_____	_____	_____
		_____	_____
Operations Manager	_____	_____	_____
		_____	_____
Safety Manager	_____	_____	_____
		_____	_____
Technical Manager	_____	_____	_____
		_____	_____
Human Resources Manager	_____	_____	_____
		_____	_____
Environmental Manager	_____	_____	_____
		_____	_____
Division Manager	_____	_____	_____
		_____	_____
Marketing Manager	_____	_____	_____
		_____	_____
Public Affairs Manager	_____	_____	_____
		_____	_____

REVISION DATE _____

Figure 6–2

PUBLIC OFFICIALS MASTER LIST

EMERGENCY DIAL:		

CITY OF:	CITY #	PHONE #s
Mayor		
Civil Manager		
Police Chief		
Fire Chief		
Health Officer		
Civil Defense/EMA		

COUNTY OF:	COUNTY #	PHONE #s
County Administrator		
County Supervisor		
Sheriff		
Health Officer		
Fire Chief		

STATE OF:	STATE #	PHONE #s
Governor		
Chief of Staff		
Attorney General		
State Senator		
State Representative		
State Police		
Environmental		

FEDERAL:	FEDERAL #	PHONE #s
Congressman		
Con. Administrative Assistant		
Sen. Administrative		
EPA Reg. Director		
Disaster Officer		
Civil Defense/EMA		

For Additional Details, See Public Official's Individual Data Sheet

REVISION DATE _____

Figure 6–3

PUBLIC OFFICIAL INDIVIDUAL DATA

BRANCH OF GOVERNMENT:

OFFICIAL		PHONE #s:
NAME:	OFFICIAL TITLE:	OFFICE _____
		HOME _____
		EMERGENCY _____
		OTHER _____

BACKUP OFFICIAL		PHONE #s:
NAME:	OFFICIAL TITLE:	OFFICE _____
		HOME _____
		EMERGENCY _____
		OTHER _____

STAFF:	POSITION:	PHONE #s:

RESPONSIBLE FOR SERVICE:	PHONE #s:

RESOURCES	EQUIPMENT

Figure 6–4

PUBLIC AGENCY CONTACT REPORT

INCIDENT:		Date: _____ Time: _____

GOV'T AGENCY:	Time of Contact:	Key Questions:
CONTACT:		
		Response:
Phone:	Reply Deadline:	
Spokesperson:		
		Follow-up:

GOV'T AGENCY:	Time of Contact:	Key Questions:
CONTACT:		
		Response:
Phone:	Reply Deadline:	
Spokesperson:		
		Follow-up:

GOV'T AGENCY:	Time of Contact:	Key Questions:
CONTACT:		
		Response:
Phone:	Reply Deadline:	
Spokesperson:		
		Follow-up:

GOV'T AGENCY:	Time of Contact:	Key Questions:
CONTACT:		
		Response:
Phone:	Reply Deadline:	
Spokesperson:		
		Follow-up:

Revision Date: _____

Figure 6–5

PRINT MEDIA MASTER LIST

Revision Date: _____

PUBLICATION:
Mailing Address

PHONE #s:

OFFICE _____

EMERGENCY _____

Publication Type: _____ ☐Daily ☐Weekly ☐Other   OTHER _____

Managing Editor: _____

News Editor: _____

Key Reporters: _____

Circulation: _____   Coverage Area: _____

PUBLICATION:
Mailing Address

PHONE #s:

OFFICE _____

EMERGENCY _____

Publication Type: _____ ☐Daily ☐Weekly ☐Other   OTHER _____

Managing Editor: _____

News Editor: _____

Key Reporters: _____

Circulation: _____   Coverage Area: _____

PUBLICATION:
Mailing Address

PHONE #s:

OFFICE _____

EMERGENCY _____

Publication Type: _____ ☐Daily ☐Weekly ☐Other   OTHER _____

Managing Editor: _____

News Editor: _____

Key Reporters: _____

Circulation: _____   Coverage Area: _____

PUBLICATION:
Mailing Address

PHONE #s:

OFFICE _____

EMERGENCY _____

Publication Type: _____ ☐Daily ☐Weekly ☐Other   OTHER _____

Managing Editor: _____

News Editor: _____

Key Reporters: _____

Circulation: _____   Coverage Area: _____

Figure 6–6

RADIO MEDIA MASTER LIST

Revision Date: _____

STATON:
Mailing Address

Dial Position/Freq.:

PHONE #s:

OFFICE _____

EMERGENCY _____

Station Format: _____ ☐ AM ☐ FM   OTHER _____

News Broadcast Times: Local _____   Network _____

News Director: _____

Key Reporters: _____

Signal Strength: _____ (Watts)   Coverage Area: _____

STATON:
Mailing Address

Dial Position/Freq.:

PHONE #s:

OFFICE _____

EMERGENCY _____

Station Format: _____ ☐ AM ☐ FM   OTHER _____

News Broadcast Times: Local _____   Network _____

News Director: _____

Key Reporters: _____

Signal Strength: _____ (Watts)   Coverage Area: _____

STATON:
Mailing Address

Dial Position/Freq.:

PHONE #s:

OFFICE _____

EMERGENCY _____

Station Format: _____ ☐ AM ☐ FM   OTHER _____

News Broadcast Times: Local _____   Network _____

News Director: _____

Key Reporters: _____

Signal Strength: _____ (Watts)   Coverage Area: _____

STATON:
Mailing Address

Dial Position/Freq.:

PHONE #s:

OFFICE _____

EMERGENCY _____

Station Format: _____ ☐ AM ☐ FM   OTHER _____

News Broadcast Times: Local _____   Network _____

News Director: _____

Key Reporters: _____

Signal Strength: _____ (Watts)   Coverage Area: _____

Figure 6–7

TELEVISION MEDIA MASTER LIST

Revision Date: _____

STATON: Mailing Address	CHANNEL:	PHONE #s:

STATON:
Mailing Address

CHANNEL:

PHONE #s:

OFFICE _____

EMERGENCY _____

Station Format: _____ ☐ VHF ☐ UHF   OTHER _____

News Broadcast Times: Local _____   Network _____

Assignment Editor: _____

Key Reporters: _____

Live Coverage?: _____ ☐   Coverage Area: _____   Network? _____

STATON:
Mailing Address

CHANNEL:

PHONE #s:

OFFICE _____

EMERGENCY _____

Station Format: _____ ☐ VHF ☐ UHF   OTHER _____

News Broadcast Times: Local _____   Network _____

Assignment Editor: _____

Key Reporters: _____

Live Coverage?: _____ ☐   Coverage Area: _____   Network? _____

STATON:
Mailing Address

CHANNEL:

PHONE #s:

OFFICE _____

EMERGENCY _____

Station Format: _____ ☐ VHF ☐ UHF   OTHER _____

News Broadcast Times: Local _____   Network _____

Assignment Editor: _____

Key Reporters: _____

Live Coverage?: _____ ☐   Coverage Area: _____   Network? _____

STATON:
Mailing Address

CHANNEL:

PHONE #s:

OFFICE _____

EMERGENCY _____

Station Format: _____ ☐ VHF ☐ UHF   OTHER _____

News Broadcast Times: Local _____   Network _____

Assignment Editor: _____

Key Reporters: _____

Live Coverage?: _____ ☐   Coverage Area: _____   Network? _____

Figure 6–8

MEDIA CONTACT REPORT

INCIDENT:	Date: _____ Time: _____

MEDIA ORGANIZATION:	Time of Contact:	Key Questions:
REPORTER:		
		Response:
Phone:	Reply Deadline:	
Spokesperson:		
		Follow-up:

MEDIA ORGANIZATION:	Time of Contact:	Key Questions:
REPORTER:		
		Response:
Phone:	Reply Deadline:	
Spokesperson:		
		Follow-up:

MEDIA ORGANIZATION:	Time of Contact:	Key Questions:
REPORTER:		
		Response:
Phone:	Reply Deadline:	
Spokesperson:		
		Follow-up:

MEDIA ORGANIZATION:	Time of Contact:	Key Questions:
REPORTER:		
		Response:
Phone:	Reply Deadline:	
Spokesperson:		
		Follow-up:

Revision Date: _____

Figure 6–9

- Is the problem under control?

- Was anybody injured or killed?

- What caused the incident?

In preparing to answer such questions, remember that the reporter isn't your real audience. His or her pen, recorder, or camera are just the tools by which your message will be transmitted to your real audiences:

- Customers

- Neighbors

- Employees and their families

- Stockholders

- Special interest groups

- Legislators and regulators

The media is the conduit through which you'll be persuading these groups that you are doing everything possible to solve the problem. Think of the needs and wants of such groups and respond to them. Satisfy *their* concerns. Know what you're talking about, and you can communicate effectively if you apply the skills and principles as stated above.

The importance of proper communications cannot be overstated. Some factors that influence effective crisis communications are:

- *Outrage value:* The public responds to the outrage value it places on the information it receives regarding the event. Perception is reality! High outrage will elicit a large response.

- *Communication of data:* People do not listen with discrimination. Less attention is paid to data in a perceived high hazard/outrage situation. What you say may not be what they hear.

- *Level of awareness:* The level of outrage corresponds to the level of awareness. The higher the degree of awareness, the lower the level of outrage in most situations. The more aware people are, the less they will suspect things are being covered up.

- *Improving perception:* By sharing knowledge and being open you can change the perception of the public and media. Remember, perception is reality.

- *Educating:* The target audience must be reached. By educating your audience you can reduce the level of outrage. A low level of outrage assumes a low hazard value and elicits a much smaller response.

- *Independent sources:* Whenever and wherever possible use independent sources. This will confirm data and lessen the outrage level. Do not, however, make the independent sources appear as if they are acting as your spokesperson. These sources have to remain credible sources of information to the general public.

- *Reducing advocacy:* Do not mobilize outrage. Work hand-in-hand with community, activist groups, local government, and others to reduce the potential for confrontation.

- *Timing releases:* By carefully timing information releases you can maintain a greater degree of control over the situation. Explain the data to the community. Make the information relate to measurable and observable data.

Here are some things that the public wants to know concerning your crisis. In explaining these things to the public you should always attempt to correlate them to measurable and observable data.

- How safe is it?

- How do you know what you know?

- What are you going to do about it?

- What are your limitations?

- What can we do about it?

- What is this stuff?

- Why didn't you tell us sooner?

- How can we trust you?

- Don't you care?

In order to address the above concerns during a crisis situation, it is necessary to communicate with the public, media, and regulatory groups.

THE CRISIS COMMUNICATIONS PLAN: ELEMENTS AND GUIDELINES

Two considerations must be uppermost in your mind as you prepare for a crisis. One cannot be separated from the other without seriously jeopardizing the success of your crisis communication program.

You must immediately control the *incident*. Fast action must be taken to execute your emergency management plan fully and use all the resources necessary to control the incident. You also must *communicate* your actions immediately, constantly, and consistently to all appropriate audiences in clear, nontechnical language.

View these twin responsibilities as a balancing act of equal parts. A fully developed and rehearsed crisis communications plan must be an integral part of your Emergency Management Plan.

There are instances where companies have done a fine job of containing and correcting an incident, but they failed to communicate their actions. Failure to communicate creates the perception that the crisis is continuing out of control, or that the company is hiding something and is indifferent to public concern.

The crisis communication plan should be developed to supplement the Emergency Management Plan. It should address such issues as:

- Who gets called first?

- Who handles the media? Do you have on-site facilities with telephones for the media if they are covering an incident at the plant?

- Who are your spokespersons and their backups?

- How is the community informed of an incident?

- Does the community know what to do?

- Do your employees know what to do?

- What should employees tell their families or the media if they are questioned?

- Who will provide health risk and medical advice?

- Have logistics been worked out with medical and emergency response personnel?

Figures 6–10 through 6–15 provide examples of additional workpapers that can be used in the preparation and execution of the emergency management and crisis communications plans.

The effectiveness of a crisis communications plan depends not only on the plans and guidelines developed on paper, but also on the specific assignments made by name long before an emergency occurs and on the regular updating and testing of Emergency Plan Implementing Procedures (EPIPs). A communications plan's effectiveness also depends on the commitment of the company at the highest levels to the urgent task of providing prompt and publicly understandable information about events that may affect—or simply worry—the nearby community and the public at large.

Specific site plans and procedures for handling public information at the time of an emergency may vary; however, they should keep in mind the following general principles:

Any incident has a high probability of becoming a "crisis"—at least in the minds of the regulatory agencies, the press, politicians, and some of the public. This is often true even if the event is not technically reportable. Businesslike procedures that may suffice for any other activity will often not be adequate if the incident involves a release of hazardous material or any nuclear material.

It is too late to develop a crisis communications planned program only, after an incident occurs. How well the incident is handled will depend largely on the thought and work that have been put into a program in advance, on the competence of the personnel, on the procedures and policies that have been developed and tested, and on how well these procedures and policies are followed.

Note that public information about a significant accident should differ only in degree, not in kind, from information about reportable events that may occur fairly frequently. Even for small reportable events that would be of special interest, contact should be made with appropriate government officials (local, state, and federal), the press, the local community, and employees. Those audiences need to be kept informed, perhaps through a tiered telephone tree, until the event has passed.

During an emergency, utmost importance should be placed on the consistency of information reaching the public. Every effort should be made to have a single

RESPONSE CHECK LIST

Revision Date: _____

| INCIDENT: | EMERGENCY CALLED: |
| | Time: _____ By: _____ |

Date:	Time:	ACTION:	COMMENTS:	X
		NOTIFICATION:	Start Log of each event, call and take action	
		Mobilize Team		
		Notify Facility Management		
		Inform Employees		
		GET THE FACTS:	Gather Known Facts and log entries	
		What Happened		
		When, Where & How		
		Any Casualties	No Names	
		Raw Material or Finished Goods		
		Obvious Product Qualities		
		Quantity of Volume Involved		
		Spill or Emission Involved		
		Public Health or Environment Risk		
		Authorities on Scene		
		Quantity of Volume Involved		
		INFORM OTHERS:		
		Contact Public Affairs		
		Contact Senior Management		
		Notify Government & Legal Officials		
		Inform Immediate Neighbors		
		Organize Info. Updates		
		PREPARE FOR MEDIA:		
		Start Media Contact Record		
		Designate Spokesperson(s)		
		Arrange Access to Experts		
		Coordinate Media Contact with Gov't		
		Set Media Communication Lines		
		Arrange Food/Coffee		

Figure 6–10

RESPONSE CHECK LIST

Revision Date: _____

INCIDENT:	EMERGENCY CALLED:
	Time: _____ By: _____

Date:	Time:	ACTION: COMMENTS:	Human Res.	Facil. Res.	Comm. Team	Safe Haz/Eny	Tech. Team	Pub. Agency Team	Yen. Cont. Team	C.M. Team
		EMRO Notified								
		EMRO in Place								
		Initiate Response								
		Set Up ERF								
		Assessment Report								
		Progress Analysis								
		Compile Fact Sheet								
		Report to Senior Mgt.								
		Advise Public Affairs								
		Notify Public Officials								
		Inform Neighbors								
		Inform Customers								

Revision Date: _____

Figure 6–11

RESPONSE UPDATE

INCIDENT:	EMERGENCY CALLED:
	Date: _____ Time: _____

CALLER NAME:	AFFILIATION:	PHONE #s:
		OFFICE _____
RESPONDENT:		HOME _____
		EMERGENCY _____
		OTHER _____

INCIDENT DESCRIPTION: (Known Facts Only)
_____
_____
_____
_____
_____
_____

CURRENT SITUATION:
_____
_____
_____
_____
_____
_____

Injuries: _____ Yes _____ No If yes, list below   Property Damage: _____ Yes _____ No

NAME:	AFFILIATION:	NATURE OF INJURY:

Received By: Distribution:
_____

REVISION DATE _____

Figure 6–12

PERFORMANCE CHECK LIST

Revision Date:_____

INCIDENT:	EMERGENCY CALLED:
	Time:_____ By:_____

Date	Time Started	Time Finished	ACTION:	Lists O.K.? YES	NO	Last Update
			EMRO Notified Start Log			
			Facility Management Notified			
			EMRO Assembled			
			Set Up ERF			
			Designate Press Area			
			Establish Communication Lines			
			Issue Backgrounder to Media			
			Fact Assessment Report			
			Progress Analysis			
			Compile Fact Sheet Update			
			Report to Senior Management			
			Advise Public Officials			
			Inform Neighbors			
			Inform Customers			
			Respond to Follow-up Queries			
			Assessment Report			
			Program Analysis			
			Compile Fact Sheet Update			
			Report to Senior Management			
			Advise Public Affairs			
			Notify Public Officials			
			Inform Neighbors			
			Inform Customers			
			Respond to Follow-up Queries			

Comments:

Figure 6–13

CLEANUP, CONTRACTOR, CONSULTANT DATA

SERVICE:

COMPANY OR AGENCY & ADDRESS:

PERSONNEL –	TITLE –	HOME PHONE –

PHONE #s:

OFFICE _____

HOME _____

EMERGENCY _____

OTHER _____

BACKUP & ADDRESS:

PERSONNEL –	TITLE –	HOME PHONE –

PHONE #s:

OFFICE _____

HOME _____

EMERGENCY _____

OTHER _____

CAPABILITIES & ASSIGNMENTS:

AREAS OF EXPERTISE:

CRITICAL SUPPLIES & EQUIPMENT:

REVISION DATE _____

Figure 6–14

ACTIVITIES RECORD SHEET

DATE:

| EMERGENCY TITLE: _____ | NAME: _____ | PAGE ___ of ___ PAGES |

TIME:	SUMMARY OF ACTIVITIES

SIGNATURE: _____

Figure 6–15

company spokesman and to coordinate data and other information with federal, state, and local agencies. The principal communications requirement at the time of an emergency is a steady flow of accurate, reliable information, internally and externally. Wire services and networks abhor a vacuum, and they will fill it; if not with facts from the source then with conjecture, random background material, and comments from critics. Facts must be presented promptly, straightforwardly, and in a context of the total significance of the event.

Some special audiences must be given special priorities: local and state government officials, federal officials, neighboring communities, company employees and stockholders, and the local press. Local opinion leaders need to be approached on the company's initiative with full information and offers of special background briefings.

A decisive factor in the success of a crisis communications program may be the internal relationship between the company's operating and technical staff and its public information staff. An immediate and continuing free flow of information internally is essential to avoid misinformation and exaggeration. This requires fast, simple, and well-understood procedures for clearing information.

The senior public information representative should have immediate access to the senior operations officer to develop policy-level statements and guarantee internal information flow.

For many nonroutine events, especially those involving even minute quantities of hazardous material, the choice is often not whether they should be announced to the public, but whether the announcement should come from the company or a federal agency. Since the federal agencies have shown that they are likely to make a public announcement of even nonreportable events, experience has consistently shown that the reaction is preferable when the information originates with the company.

It is important to show evidence of openness and candor—avoid the appearance of whitewashing the event. Facts should be stressed over judgments or interpretations. The press and others should be invited to see for themselves the affected area and to question company officials as soon as possible. The use of remote television cameras and pool reporters and photographers could show openness even before a full media visit would be possible.

Also, you should assign responsibilities for the crisis communication team. The team should represent a cross section of supervisory and management people. They should meet regularly to review and rehearse the Emergency Management Plan, crisis communications plan, and EPIPs. Think of your crisis team as you would any other piece of critical equipment that must work perfectly in an emergency.

Typically, the team should have the following representatives:

- Spokesperson (facility management and/or corporate representative)

- Public relations

- Operations analyst

- Safety, environment, and health analyst

Other representatives as needed may include:

- Human resources

- Legal

- Security

- Marketing personnel

- Noncompany experts

A smaller company may have only a few of these types of employees. In these cases, personnel may fill multiple roles. A representative team should assist in constructing the crisis communications plans, integrating it with the Emergency Management Plan.

Develop worst-case scenarios for communications crises, as well. You cannot anticipate every potential problem. But a detailed assessment can identify situations that may contribute to a crisis. The most effective way to conduct the assessment is to select personnel who have a cross section of knowledge.

They should review all material available from hazard analyses and HAZOPs, and apply their collective knowledge to detect vulnerabilities. The best technical people should be selected to serve on the assessment team. As discussed in the Emergency Management Plan appendix on hazard analysis, the results of the hazard analysis should be reviewed herein as necessary.

In addition to the approach discussed in the hazard analysis, you should also include in your assessment the following:

- Use your planning team or some of its members and request help from operations, environmental, health, and safety experts to conduct the assessment.

- Inspect the facility thoroughly to assess potential vulnerabilities (worst-case scenarios).

- Clean up the facility's appearance.

- Assess all findings, set priorities, and make changes.

- Prioritize all worst-case scenarios and develop plans to handle them.

Also, you must identify and analyze key public representatives by preparing contact sheets. There are many important people who must receive information during a crisis, even though there may be no legal requirement. They can help you through a crisis. These audiences can be your allies and communication partners during a crisis. All of these public representatives may not be relevant to each facility.

Organizations and individuals outside the company who should be assigned to company employees for prompt contact after an incident in a planned order of priority, depending on its severity, should include:

- Governor and governor's press aide

- State police

- Local police

- Civil defense agency

- State emergency response commission

- Local newspapers and radio/TV stations

- Regional press (if warranted), including wire service offices

- Mayor of the local community and other local officials, as appropriate

- Local hospital (if necessary)

- U.S. Environmental Protection Agency (EPA)

- Major customers (large industries, etc.), if warranted

- Employees, board of directors, and the financial community (where warranted)

- Key customers

- Suppliers

- Trade groups

- Technical experts

- Stockholders, investors

After the initial notification of these officials, based on a standard format, they should then be kept up to date on additional information and the company's response until the event has ended and all information about it becomes known. If the event is a significant one, communication with these officials should be frequent, including personal briefings by company spokesmen to answer their questions and explain the context of the incident.

Finally, internal and external communications systems during a crisis are two extremely important factors. You need to take a hard look at phone and radio systems that may become seriously overloaded during an emergency. If the emergency affects the community, expect to receive hundreds of calls an hour from surrounding residents and media representatives. You need the systems and the people to accommodate these calls. You need lines dedicated to handling communication with authorities, families, neighbors, and media.

Internal phone and radio communications normally need to be bolstered during a crisis. Make sure the equipment is adequate and technically sound and test it during a drill. Team members assigned to handle media calls and escort reporters need clear instructions and procedures. Switchboard capacity should be evaluated, and operators should receive appropriate training. It is advisable to have arrangements with outside telephone and radio suppliers in case more equipment is needed on short notice.

GENERAL CRISIS INFORMATION PROCEDURES

The first public information obligation of a company after a release of hazardous materials is to inform without delay government authorities (federal, state, and local), the press, and other important groups (employees, local townspeople, large customers, and others as needed).

Procedures for the first notification of these groups should be specific and constant. The appropriate employees—perhaps using a tiered or telephone tree system—should telephone them immediately after the public information director or information duty officer is told (by an assigned source) of an event that the federal authorities consider reportable. The group must be notified of any other development that would be of concern to the local public, as well.

A standard incident report form, comparable to the storm information forms used by many utilities, should be helpful in getting consistent information quickly to company employees who will make external contacts.

After notifying authorities, set up a news center and supporting facilities. Provide a safe location that is reasonably comfortable; have facility information (plot maps, maps, models, etc.) electricity, and phones. Plan to have such things as coffee, soft drinks, and food delivered as soon as practicable.

Even though you can't predict where a crisis will occur, you can note areas that would give reporters and camera crews a good, safe vantage point wherever the emergency occurs.

In an emergency, explain and emphasize to the media any safety hazards that may exist. TV crews and still-camera photographers will want to get as close as possible to the scene and may try to do so without permission. Provide a representative to escort them as close to the scene as safety permits. Make it clear that if the escort decides that the area is no longer safe, the media must cooperate and immediately leave the area.

Besides the primary news center, you should also consider an alternate facility should evacuation be required. Other facilities that will help your emergency management and crisis communication efforts are the rumor control center and the employee injury/fatality center.

Located with the news center or nearby, the rumor control center should be used for answering inquiries and dispelling rumors from local populations, employees not involved in the incident, and news media speculation.

The employee injury/fatality center can be set up together with normal human resource department operations. It should be responsible for tracking the names of all injuries/fatalities and the conditions of those who are hospitalized. This should include consideration of any contract employees and/or contractors.

TYPES OF EVENTS FOR NOTIFICATION

Appropriate officials should be notified quickly of any significant incident, including:

1. Nonroutine release of hazardous material on-site

2. Release of nonroutine quantities of hazardous material off-site

3. A hazardous materials event off-site

4. Serious injuries to or death of any employee on-site from any cause

5. Abnormal exposure or contamination to employees or members of the public

6. Incidents causing any substantial damage, such as fires or explosions

7. Environmental effects, such as fish kills, oil spills, or chemical or toxic releases

8. Construction or maintenance interruptions (including those resulting from regulatory action)

9. Enforcement actions, such as fines or other sanctions

10. Nonscheduled shutdowns expected to last for more than 72 hours, regardless of cause

11. Shutdowns that exceed one day and result from failure of or damage to safety-related equipment

12. Theft, diversion, loss of licensed material, or sabotage

13. Security breaches

14. Hazardous material transportation incident

15. Any incident that requires assistance from any outside agency (such as the fire department, ambulance, police, etc.) for any cause

16. Operational or other changes made by the company to improve safety, reliability, training, or environmental impact

17. Any event or development not covered above that may result in political, media, community, or general public interest. It should be assumed that even many events that are technically not reportable will be announced by the federal regulators, if not by the company.

KEY PERSONNEL ASSIGNMENTS

Specific assignments must be made well before an incident to assure adequate internal communications. The following functions must be assigned, by name and title, for around-the-clock responsibility:

ON-SHIFT EMERGENCY MANAGER AND/OR INCIDENT SUPPORT DIRECTOR

A facility management representative with assigned responsibilities in the Emergency Management Plan such as the on-shift emergency manager or incident support director, must notify management and the assigned public information representative immediately of any reportable incident. He should be assigned responsibility, on a priority basis, for continuing to inform the public information representative about further developments until a news center is established or the incident is terminated.

PUBLIC AFFAIRS DIRECTOR

The public affairs director, a member of the EMRO, is responsible for formulating all information to be released by the company during an emergency situation and ensuring that approved information is promptly transmitted to company headquarters offices following its release at the news center. The public affairs director will be the ranking site representative designated to deal with the media. This person or the facility manager should serve as primary spokesperson for the company at news conferences.

NEWS CENTER COORDINATOR

The news center coordinator, a member of the EMRO, reports to the public affairs director and is responsible for activation and operation of the news center. The news center coordinator should be responsible for supervising most members of the news center support staff, and overseeing operations of the media facility and rumor control center. With information from the public affairs director, the news center coordinator keeps other employees assigned to the news center informed about the emergency situation. The news center coordinator acts as the assistance to the public affairs director, ensuring that the news center is properly staffed and equipped.

PUBLIC AFFAIRS MANAGER

The public affairs manager will generally be located at the company headquarters offices. The public affairs manager is not assigned to the EMRO. Upon notification from the public affairs manager (or his official designee), the public affairs manager should immediately begin working with key senior management on the company's official statement about the incident. The public affairs manager should be responsible for the quick development of official company statements and positions, and must keep the public affairs manager regularly informed about the official position of the company.

SENIOR MANAGEMENT REPRESENTATIVE

Appropriate members of senior management must also be assigned, on an around-the-clock basis, to be available to receive emergency information reports from the facility and to act on them immediately. They should notify other members of senior management and the board of directors, as appropriate; begin working with the public information manager on the initial response or official statement (beyond the first notification of the facts); and perhaps make some key notifications (such as the governor or state emergency services director).

One of the keys to crisis communications is to have a designated, trained spokesperson ready to go into action. You should establish a clear policy on who will talk to the media.

Spokespersons should be prepared to meet the following criteria:

- *Availability:* Spokespersons should be available until the crisis is resolved. There should be at least two designated alternates who can step in at any time.

- *Believability:* Credibility is a precious commodity and may be the most important attribute. Credible does not mean a smooth talker. Positive impressions are created by people who honestly project confidence and concern, who remain calm, and who are sincerely trying to do the right thing.

- *Knowledge:* It is assumed that most spokespersons on duty during a crisis are knowledgeable. A spokesperson's level of technical expertise should never get in the way of communications. You can supplement the spokesperson with assistants in the areas of operations, environment, health, safety, and other technical areas.

- *Clarity:* The ability to convey simple, concise messages in nontechnical language is essential. As indicated in Section 4.1 of the example Emergency Management Plan, one cannot overlook the importance of proper communication.

FORMULATING, TESTING, AND UPDATING

Once your emergency management plan and crisis communication plan supplement are written, hypothetical drills must be held to test every aspect. Clearly, organizations that rehearse their plans and train their teams are far more successful when the crisis is real. As in any rehearsal, the value directly parallels the degree of realism.

Consider involving outside agencies such as fire, police, and health officials. Some facilities even involve local media representatives in mock crises.

Have members of your crisis team, with help from other company resources, write a scenario for the exercise. In your audit, you will already have considered worst-case scenarios. Select one. To fully test the plan and its systems, the mock crisis should be a tough test of a key operation.

Emergency Plan Implementing Procedures (EPIPs)—including assignments by name, their contacts by name, telephone numbers, locations of assignment, etc.— should be formalized in an internal manual and reviewed regularly for changes and updated information.

The first phases of emergency communications—the tiered telephone contact— -may be exercised frequently, because of the government's strict definition of reportable events. Later phases designed for more serious accidents, including the summoning of ambulances and fire departments and establishment of an emergency news center, should be tested in a full-scale drill at least once a year.

Train a number of spokespersons. There is no substitute for practice, practice, practice. Make sure those who are designated to speak for the facility notify appropriate parties and handle subsequent inquiries from the media and the community.

APPENDIX A

Sample Emergency Management Plan Outline

PREAMBLE

SECTION 1: ADMINISTRATION

1.1 Purpose

1.2 Objectives

1.3 Incident Information Summary

1.4 Planning Factors

    1.4.1 Mission

1.5 Site Description

    1.5.1 [YOUR FACILITY] (fill in Name)

    1.5.2 Off-Site Land Use

SECTION 2: ORGANIZATION

SECTION 3: CONCEPT OF OPERATIONS

SECTION 4: COMMUNICATIONS

SECTION 6: EMERGENCY FACILITIES AND EQUIPMENT

SECTION 7: PUBLIC INFORMATION

SECTION 8: POST-INCIDENT OPERATIONS

SECTION 9: MAINTAINING EMERGENCY PREPAREDNESS

SECTION 10: EVALUATION

10.6 Commitment Tracking

APPENDICES:

Appendix A: Letters of Agreement

Appendix B: Emergency Management Plan and Emergency Plan Implementing Procedures Cross-Reference

Appendix C: List of Emergency Plan Implementing Procedures

Appendix D: List of Associated Emergency Management Plans

Appendix E: List of Acronyms, Recognized Abbreviations, and Definitions

Appendix F: Cleanup, Contractors, Consultants, and Other Resources

Appendix G: Technical Library

Appendix H: Hazard Analysis

Appendix I: [Your Facility] Evacuation Routes

Appendix J: Community Maps

Appendix K: Chemical Information Resources

Appendix L: EMAs, Police Departments, Fire Departments

Appendix M: Emergency Radio Channels

Appendix N: Local Radio and Television Stations

Appendix O: Hospitals

Appendix P: Equipment Resources

Appendix Q: Cross-Reference to Regulatory Requirements

Appendix R: [Your Facility] Emergency Management/Response Organization Key Position Descriptions

Appendix S: Forms

List of Emergency Plan Implementing Procedures

ADMINISTRATIVE

	Procedure	Rev. Date
Preparation, Revision, Approval and Control of the Emergency Management Plan and Emergency Plan Implementing Procedures	EPIP-110	_____
Maintenance and Inventory of Emergency Equipment and Supplies	EPIP-120	_____
Control of Emergency Use Vehicles	EPIP-130	_____

ORGANIZATION

	Procedure	**Rev. Date**
Duties of the Emergency Manager	EPIP-210	_____
Duties of the On-shift Emergency Manager	EPIP-220	_____
Duties of the Field Incident Commander	EPIP-230	_____
Duties of [YOUR FACILITY] EMRO During Emergencies	EPIP-240	_____
Activation of [YOUR FACILITY] EMRO	EPIP-250	_____
[YOUR COMPANY] Support	EPIP-260	_____
Off-site Support and Assistance	EPIP-270	_____
Duties of the Affected Unit Personnel During Emergencies	EPIP-280	_____

OPERATIONAL

Emergency Damage Control Operations	EPIP-310	_____
Emergency Search and Rescue Operations	EPIP-320	_____
Access Control During Emergencies	EPIP-330	_____
Transporting Contaminated Injured Personnel	EPIP-340	_____

	Procedure	Rev. Date
Bomb Incident Response	EPIP-350	_____
Environmental Releases	EPIP-360	_____
Leak Stoppage	EPIP-370	_____
Oil Spill Response	EPIP-380	_____
Emergency Notification	EPIP-410	_____
Emergency Communications	EPIP-420	_____
Assessment of Emergency Conditions and Emergency Classification	EPIP-510	_____
Evacuation	EPIP-520	_____
Sheltering	EPIP-530	_____
Protective Action Recommendation Guides	EPIP-540	_____
Personnel Assembly and Accountability	EPIP-550	_____
Unusual Operations Procedures	EPIP-560	_____
Worst Case Scenario Response	EPIP-570	_____
Activation of the Mobile Command Center and Personnel Duties	EPIP-610	_____
Activation of the Incident Support Center and Personnel Duties	EPIP-620	_____
Activation of the Emergency Operations Center (EOC) and Personnel Duties	EPIP-630	_____

	Procedure	Rev. Date
Activation of the News Center and Personnel Duties	EPIP-710	_____
Instructions for News Center Support Personnel	EPIP-720	_____
Release of Emergency-Related Information to the Public	EPIP-730	_____
Rumor Control Operations	EPIP-740	_____
Employee Information	EPIP-750	_____
Postincident Sampling	EPIP-810	_____
Reentry and Recovery Operations	EPIP-820	_____
Humanitarian Assistance	EPIP-830	_____
External Resources	EPIP-840	_____
Maintaining Emergency Preparedness	EPIP-910	_____
Emergency Preparedness Drills and Exercises	EPIP-920	_____
Emergency Preparedness Commitment Tracking System Operation	EPIP-1010	_____
Emergency Preparedness Audit Guide	EPIP-1020	_____

References

"When Every Second Counts... Crisis Communications Planning," Western Union IDP01000754.

Bean, M. (1987). "Tools for Environmental Professionals Involved in Risk Communication at Hazardous Waste Facilities Undergoing Siting, Permitting, or Remediation." Report No. 8730.8. Reston, Virginia: Air Pollution Control Association.

Covello, V.T. (1983). "The Perception of Technological Risks: A Literature Review." *Technological Forecasting and Social Change,* 23,1983, 285–297.

Covello, V.T. (1988). "Informing the Public About Health and Environmental Risks: Problems and Opportunities for Effective Risk Communication," in N. Lind (ed.), *Risk Communication: A Symposium.* Waterloo: University of Waterloo.

Covello, V. and F. Allen (1988). *Seven Cardinal Rules of Risk Communication.* Washington, D.C.: U.S. Environmental Protection Agency, Office of Policy Analysis.

Covello, V., D. von Winterfeldt, and P. Slovic (1987). "Communicating Risk Information to the Public," in J.C. Davies, V. Covello, and F. Allen, eds., *Risk Communication:* Washington, D.C.: The Conservation Foundation.

Covello, V. D. McCallum, and M. Pavlova, eds. (1988). *Effective Risk Communications: The Role and Responsibility of Government,* New York: Plenum.

Davies, J.C., V.T. Covello, and F.W. Allen, eds. (1987). *Risk Communications.* Washington D.C.: The Conservation Foundation.

Fessenden-Raden, J., J. Fitchen, and J. Heath (1987). "Risk Communication at the Local Level: A Complex Interactive Process." *Science, Technology and Human Values,* December, 1987.

Fischhoff, B. (1985). "Protocols for Environmental Reporting: What to Ask the Experts." *The Journalist,* Winter, 1985, 11–15.

Fischhoff, B., S. Lichtenstein, P. Slovic, S.L. Derbe, and R.L. Keeney, (1981). *Acceptable Risk.* Cambridge University Press: New York.

Fischhoff, B. (1985). "Managing Risk Perception." *Issues in Science and Technology,* 2, 1985, 83–96.

Fischhoff, B., P. Slovic, and S. Lichtenstein, (1979). "Weighing the Risks." *Environment,* 21, 1979.

Hance, B., C. Chess, and P. Sandman (1987). *Improving Dialogue with Communities: A Risk Communication Manual for Government.* Trenton, New Jersey, Office of Science and Research, New Jersey Department of Environmental Protection, December, 1987.

Johnson, B. and V. Covello, eds. (1987). *The Social and Cultural Construction of Risk: Essays on Risk Selection and Perception.* Boston: Reidel.

Kahneman, D., P. Slovic, and A. Tversky, eds. (1982). *Judgment Under Uncertainty: Heuristics and Biases.* New York: Cambridge University Press.

Kasperson, R. (1986). "Six Propositions on Public Participation and Their Relevance to Risk Communication." *Risk Analysis,* 1986, 6, 275–282.

Kasperson, R. and J. Kasperson (1983). "Determining the Acceptability of Risk: Ethical and Policy Issues," in J. Rogers and D. Bates, (eds.). Risk: A Symposium, Ottawa: The Royal Society of Canada, 1983.

Klaidman, S. (1985). "Health Risk Reporting." Washington, D.C.: Institute for Health Policy Analysis, Georgetown University.

Mazur, A. (1981). "Media Coverage and Public Opinion on Scientific Controversies." *Journal of Communication,* 106–115.

Nelkin, D. (1984). *Science in the Streets.* New York: Twentieth Century Fund.

President's Commission on the Accident at Three Mile Island (1979). *Report of the Public's Right to Information Task Force.* Washington, D.C.: U.S. Government Printing Office.

Ruckelshaus, W.D. (1983). "Science, Risk, and Public Policy." *Science,* 221: 1026–1028.

Ruckelshaus, W.D. (1984). "Risk in a Free Society," *Risk Analysis,* September 1984, 157–163.

Ruckelshaus, W.D. (1987). "Communicating About Risk," 3–9 in J.C. Davies, V.T. Covello, and F.W. Allen (eds.) *Risk Communication.* Washington, D.C.: The Conservation Foundation, 1987.

Press, F. (1987). "Science and Risk Communication." 11–17 in J.C. Davies, V.T. Covello, and F.W. Allen (eds.) *Risk Communication.* Washington D.C.: The Conservation Foundation, 1987.

Sandman, P.M. (1986). "Getting to Maybe: Some Communications Aspects of Hazardous Waste Facility Siting," *Seton Hall Legislative Journal,* Spring 1986.

Sandman, P.M. (1986). *Explaining Environmental Risk.* Washington, D.C.: U.S. Environmental Protection Agency, Office of Toxic Substances.

Sandman, P., D. Sachsman, M. Greenberg, and M. Gotchfeld, (1987). *Environmental Risk and the Press,* New Brunswick: Transaction Books.

Sandman, P., D. Sachsman, and M. Greenberg (1987). *Risk Communication for Environmental News Sources.* Industry/University Cooperative Center for Research in Hazardous and Toxic Substances: New Brunswick, New Jersey.

Sharlin, H. (1987). "EDB: A Case Study in the Communication of Health Risk," in B. Johnson and V. Covello, (eds.). *The Social and Cultural Construction of Risk: Essays on Risk Selection and Perception.* Boston: Reidel.

Slovic, P. (1987). "Perception of Risk." *Science* 236: 280–285.

Slovic, P. (1986). "Informing and Educating the Public About Risk." *Risk Analysis,* vol. 4: 403–415.

Slovic, P., B. Fischhoff, and S. Lichtenstein (1982). "Facts Versus Fears: Understanding Perceived Risk," in D. Kahneman, P. Slovic, A. Tversky, (eds.). *Judgment Under Uncertainty: Heuristics and Biases.* Cambridge University Press: Cambridge, 1982.

Slovic, P., and B. Fischhoff (1982). "How Safe is Safe Enough? Determinants of Perceived and Acceptable Risk." In L. Gould and C. Walker (eds.). *Too Hot to Handle,* New Haven: Yale University Press, 1982.

Thomas, L.M. (1987). "Why We Must Talk About Risk," 19–25 in J.C. Davies, V.T. Covello, and F.W. Allen (eds.) *Risk Communication.* Washington, D.C.: The Conservation Foundation, 1987.

Wilson, R. And E. Crouch (1987). "Risk Assessment and Comparisons: An Introduction." *Science,* Vol. 236 (17 April 1987): 267–270.

TECHNICAL GUIDES, DOCUMENTS, AND RESOURCE MATERIALS

Technical Guidance for Hazard Analysis Emergency Planning for Extremely Hazardous Substances; December 1987.

Handbook of Chemical Hazard Analysis Procedures. U.S. Environmental Protection Agency, Federal Emergency Management Agency, U.S. Department of Transportation.

Hazardous Materials Emergency Planning Guide (NRT-1). National Response Team, May 1988.

Criteria for Review of Hazardous Materials Emergency Plans. National Response Team, May 1988.

Operational Safety Program, Union Carbide Company.

Transportation of Hazardous Materials: State and Local Activities. Office of Technology Assessment, March 1986.

Truck Loading Rack Safety, Industrial Risk Insurers.

Hydrorefining Process Units: Loss causes and guidelines for loss prevention. Oil Insurance Association.

Major Transportation Carrier Disasters: Improving Response and Coordination. American Hospital Association.

Guidelines on Biological Impacts of Oil Pollution. International Petroleum Industry Environmental Conservation Association.

Management of Process Hazards: American Petroleum Institute Recommended Practice 750, January 1990.

Bomb and Physical Security Planning. U.S. Department of the Treasury, Bureau of Alcohol, Tobacco and Firearms, July 1987.

Chemical Emergencies: Guidance for the Management of Chemically Contaminated Patients in the Pre-Hospital Setting. Agency for Toxic Substances and Disease Registry.

Interservice Procedures for Instructional Systems Development. TRADOC Pamphlet 350–30.

Development of a Checklist for Evaluating Emergency Procedures Used in Nuclear Power Plants. NUREG/CR-1970 SAND81-7070.

Emergency Operating Procedures Writing Guidelines. INPO 82-017, July 1982.

Chemical Emergencies: Hospital Emergency Department Guidelines. U.S. Department of Health and Human Services.

Oil Spill Prevention - Marine Terminals. Management Guidelines, March 27, 1990, American Petroleum Institute.

Incident Command System, Fire Protection Publications, Oklahoma State University.

HAZ-MAT Response Team Leak and Spill Guide. Fire Protection Publications, Oklahoma State University.

Fire Protection Guide on Hazardous Materials, Seventh Edition. April 1981, National Fire Protection Association.

"Oil Spill Response Guide." *Pollution Technology Review No. 174,* Robert J. Meyers & Associates, Research Planning Institute, Inc., 1989.

Crisis Management: Planning for the Inevitable. Steven Fink, 1986.

Hazardous Chemical Safety. J.T. Backer Chemical Company, Prod. No. 3-4525.

Fire Service Supervision: Increasing Personal Effectiveness. National Fire Academy.

Fire Command. National Fire Protection Association.

Pre-Fire Planning. Lamar University.

Preparing for Incident Command. National Fire Academy.

The Incident Command System and Structural Firefighting. National Fire Academy.

Commanding the Initial Response. National Fire Academy.

Preparing for Incident Command. National Fire Academy.

Construction of Written Achievement Tests, Second Edition. The Detroit Edison Company, Employee Training Division, October 1972.

Overview of Emergency Planning. Emergency Planning Workshop, October 5, 6, 1987, Geary W. Sikich.

Emergency Planning and Preparedness: The Planning Function. Emergency Planning Workshop, October 5–6, 1987, Geary W. Sikich.

Evaluating Compliance. Emergency Planning Workshop, October 5–6, 1987; Presented at Financial Reporting of Environmental Exposures, Washington, D.C., December 5–6, 1988, Geary W. Sikich.

WHAT IF...., Corporate Responsibility and Shareholder Rights: The Impact of Environmental Legislation on Shareholders. March 1988. Presented at Financial Reporting of Environmental Exposures, Washington, D.C., December 5–6, 1988, Geary W. Sikich.

Environmental Laws Hold Hospitals Liable for Wastes. Hospital Materials Management, October 1988, Geary W. Sikich.

"Environmental Risks Can Be Made Acceptable Through Awareness and Careful Management." *Midwest Real Estate News,* January 1989, Geary W. Sikich.

Overview of Emergency Planning Under SARA Title III. Chicago Bar Association Continuing Legal Education Seminar, April 18, 1989, Geary W. Sikich.

A Strategic Approach to Reducing Vulnerability for Industries Covered Under CERCLA, RCRA, SARA, OSHA. Chicago Bar Association Continuing Legal Education Seminar, April 18, 1989, Geary W. Sikich.

Crisis Communications Planning. Emergency Planning Workshop, Hazwaste Expo Atlanta '89; May 1–4, 1989, Geary W. Sikich.

Regulatory Compliance. Hazwaste Expo Atlanta '89; May 1–4, 1989, Geary W. Sikich.

What You CAN Do: Ways to Assess and Mitigate Your Company's Environmental Risks. Home Center Industry Presidents' Council, National Hardware Show, Chicago, August 13, 1989, Geary W. Sikich.

"You Can Lose at Regulatory Roulette." *Safety and Health Magazine,* August 1989, Geary W. Sikich.

"Buyer Beware." *Perspective,* Laventhol & Horwath, Volume 15 Number 1/1989, Geary W. Sikich.

Overview of Emergency Planning. Hazwaste Expo Chicago '89. Emergency Planning Workshop, October 16, 1989, Geary W. Sikich.

Emergency Planning and Preparedness: The Planning Function. Hazwaste Expo Chicago '89. Emergency Planning Workshop, October 16, 1989, Geary W. Sikich.

Evaluating Compliance. Hazwaste Expo Chicago '89. Emergency Planning Workshop, October 16, 1989, Geary W. Sikich.

Crisis Communications Planning. Hazwaste Expo Chicago '89. October 16, 1989, Geary W. Sikich.

Regulatory Compliance. Hazwaste Expo Chicago '89. October 16–19, 1989, Geary W. Sikich.

Regulatory Compliance. Abbott Laboratories Corporate Environmental Conference; October 24–25, 1989, Geary W. Sikich.

Seminar on Emergency Planning: An Introduction to Emergency Planning; Emergency Plan Development Communicating Emergency Information; Evaluating Regulatory Compliance; Indiana Civil Defense Council; April 27, 1990, Geary W. Sikich.

"Industry Expectations Concerning Healthcare Response to OSHA 1910.120, Hazardous Waste Operations and Emergency Response. *Environmental Health Manager;* Spring Issue 1990, VOL. 4, No. 1. Geary W. Sikich and Nelson S. Slavik.

Reducing Vulnerability: Accountants and Environmental Regulations in the 90's. 1990 Midwest Accounting and Business Management Show, August 31, 1990, Geary W. Sikich .

"Reducing Environmental Vulnerability." *New Accountant,* March 1991, Geary W. Sikich.

"The Accountant's Role in Environmental Liability." *Insight,* Vol. 41, No. 1, June 1991, Geary W. Sikich.

What a CPA Needs to Know About Environmental, Health and Safety Regulations. Business Valuation Curriculum Series, Illinois CPA Foundation. Presented as a continuing education course, July 1991 and December 1991, Geary W. Sikich.

Current Environmental Issues. Illinois CPA Foundation Agribusiness Conference, September 20, 1991, Geary W. Sikich.

Emergency Planning: Managing Compliance with Overlapping Environmental, Health, and Safety Regulations. Institute of Business Law Seminar, Chicago, October 16, 1991, Geary W. Sikich.

Community Emergency Response Exercises. Chemical Manufacturers Association, 1986.

A Conceptual Approach to State and Local Exercises. Civil Preparedness Circular, 84–2; Federal Emergency Management Agency, 1984.

Scenario Development Manual: Exercise Development. Federal Emergency Management Agency, 1985.

Exercise Design Course: Guide to Emergency Management Exercises. Federal Emergency Management Agency, January 1989.

Exercise Design Course. Exercise Design Course. Exercise Scenarios. SM-170.3, Federal Emergency Management Agency, January 1989.

Hazardous Materials Exercise Evaluation Methodology (HM-EEM) and Manual. Federal Emergency Management Agency, October 1989.

Exercising Emergency Plans Under Title III; SM–305.4; Federal Emergency Management Agency, September 1990.

Developing a Hazardous Materials Exercise Program: A Handbook for State and Local Officials. National Response Team, September 1990.

On Scene Coordinator/Regional Response Team, Oil, and Hazardous Substances Ddischarge Simulation, Planning Manual. U.S. Department of Transportation, United States Coast Guard.

Guide to Exercises in Chemical Emergency Preparedness Programs. U.S. Environmental Protection Agency, May 1988.

Radiological Series (Train the Trainer) for Radiological Instructors III in Emergency Management Institute, National Emergency Training Center 1985–1986 Course Catalog; Federal Emergency Management Agency, 1985.

Exercise Design Course; Federal Emergency Management Agency, 1984.

Index